American Women During World War II

Claudia Hagen

Printed in the United States of America

Copyright 2015 by Claudia Hagen

ISBN: 13: 978-1516844128
ISBN: 10: 1516844122

Front and back covers designed by Marty Bicek, Bicek Photography - Modesto, California - 2015

2

Dedicated to the amazing, courageous moms, grandmas, and great-grandmas who kept America running smoothly during World War II and unknowingly left a legacy for their daughters, granddaughters, and generations still to come.

Table of Contents

Dedication 3

Introduction 6

1. 'A Day Which Will Live in Infamy' 10

2. Trauma and Triage: Pearl Harbor 22

3. Preparations Begin 29

4. WAC, WAVES, WASP, SPARS 40

5. Army and Navy Nurse Corps 65

6. The Battling Belles of Bataan 84

7. Long Held Secrets 106

8. Rosie, Wendy, Sally 120

9. The Eight-Hour Orphans 152

10. WWII Women in Science 159

11. The Manhattan Project Women 173

12. The Women's Land Army 196

13. The Red Cross & Donut Dollies 207

14. First Lady Eleanor Roosevelt 227

15. Boosting Wartime Spirits-
Radio & Music 246

16. Boosting Wartime Spirits - Film 273

17. Boosting Wartime Spirits-
Entertainment 295

18. Women War Correspondents 313

Table of Contents

(continued)

19. Home Front Soldiers-
    Without-Uniforms   337

20. Bonds, Mail, and Stars   379

21. We Regret to Inform You...   392

22. It's Over!   403

23. We Did It!   416

Afterword   425

Acknowledgements   428

Bibliography   430

Introduction

Hundreds of books have been written describing the horrific combat stories, in the air and on the ground, of World War II (WWII), the most brutal war in human history. Many books were autobiographical or written by historians, each detailing the struggles, triumphs, death, and destruction witnessed by millions of our great-grandfathers, grandfathers, fathers, husbands, brothers, sons, and the boys next door. A total of sixteen million Americans served in the United States Armed Forces during WWII.

Few books have been written describing the efforts of the American women during that time. Sixteen million men off to war left more than sixteen million mothers, wives, girlfriends, and children on the home front to keep America running smoothly.

From one of President Franklin D. Roosevelt's Fireside Chats, delivered on April 28, 1942 came the encouragement, the direction and the definition of the now familiar phrase, "home front:"

Not all of us can have the privilege of fighting our enemies in distant parts of the world.

Not all of us can have the privilege of working in a munitions factory or a shipyard, or on the farms or in oil fields or mines, producing the weapons or the raw materials that are needed by our armed forces.

But there is one front and one battle where everyone in the United States - every man, woman, and child - is in action, and will be privileged to remain in action throughout this war.

That front is right here at home, in our daily lives, in our daily tasks. Here at home everyone will have the privilege of making what-ever self-denial is necessary, not only to supply our fighting men, but to keep the economic structure of our country fortified and secure during the war and after the war.

This will require, of course, the abandon-ment not only of luxuries but of many other creature comforts.

Just as combat changed the lives of American men, the home front circumstances of war shaped a new way of thinking and living for American women. The women of that era were raised to believe their life goals were to finish high school, get married, have children, and maintain a happy home. Higher goals might have included college to prepare for a teaching position or a career as a nurse. WWII changed all that for American women. In *The Greatest Generation,* Tom Brokaw wrote:

...women were essential to and leaders in the greatest national mobilization of resources

and spirit the country had ever known...they raised the place of their gender to new heights; they changed forever the perception and the reality of women in all disciplines of American life.

Three hundred-fifty thousand women chose to wear a military uniform at that time and serve as nurses or in non-combat roles. They flight tested new aircraft and ferried the planes across the United States to different airbases. The planes were then flown by Army Air Corps pilots to the European or Pacific theaters. Women also served as couriers, drivers, telephone/telegraph operators, cryptographers, entertainers, and more.

Unknown to Americans during this time, several women scientists were also working secretly with their male counterparts to produce plutonium for the atomic bomb(s) that would eventually end the war, devastate Japan, and change the world forever.

Another six million women worked in war related jobs across the United States building ships and aircraft, working in munitions plants, factories, laboratories, research and development of new medicines, products, machinery... the list goes on and on. Factory jobs paid wages women had never dreamed of. For those wages, the women worked long hours - nine to twelve hour days, six days a week - doing physically demanding work they had never done before.

Introduction

Not included in the above figures were the hundreds of thousands of women on the home front raising their children, managing their family farms, or backyard Victory Gardens, working in their town's grocery stores, department stores, butcher shops, pumping gas, fixing machinery, taking management positions, or as bank tellers, teachers, or non-military hospital nurses.

Many fields of employment had never been accessible to women until the rush of those sixteen million American men going off to war, leaving their jobs behind. American women stepped up to the proverbial home front plate, pushed up their sleeves and got to work to hold our nation together. It has been said that America's secret weapon in winning the war was its women who voluntarily mobilized and met every challenge they faced.

American Women During World War II takes a generalized look at what the women were doing and what was happening on the home front. What did the women do to hold our nation together while the men were fighting in countries many had never heard of? What battles did the women face on a daily basis to keep our nation running smoothly?

World War II not only changed American society forever, but also the world. The most drastic changes began on our own home front.

The war gave birth to the women's revolution and the atomic age, both explosive in their own right, both changed the world forever.

Chapter 1

"A Day Which Will Live in Infamy"

Long after World War I ended, Americans maintained their great sense of pride and patriotism. Even through the Great Depression, they remained true to their country and its values. Thousands were out of work, hungry, and feeling hopeless about not being able to feed their families. Women were discouraged from seeking work outside the home because it would take the jobs away from men. Slowly the economy began to improve as government programs created jobs including building dams, roads, and constructing government buildings across the country.

As millions of Americans were still recovering from the Great Depression, war broke out in Europe and Asia. The politicians and their constituents were against getting involved in another war; however, the United States did provide war supplies to their allies. Providing supplies created factory and shipyard jobs as well as work in munitions plants. Farm food production increased due to the increased need for wheat exports to the allied European sectors.

The Germans and Japanese had world domination dreams, each with their own agendas.

The United States and Japan were in diplomatic negotiations with each other at the time; the goal was to maintain peace in the Pacific between the two nations while war was escalating in Europe. Negotiations failed.

On Sunday, December 7, 1941 the Imperial Japanese Navy positioned six of their aircraft carriers near the Hawaiian islands (a U.S. held territory at that time). At precisely 0748 hours (7:48 A.M.), 353 Japanese fighters, bombers, and torpedo planes attacked the U.S. Military Pacific Fleet in Pearl Harbor. The vicious surprise attack was carried out in two waves of aircraft and lasted ninety long minutes.

The beautiful, bright sunny morning was

Rescue boat looking for survivors in the water.

suddenly overcome with heavy black smoke billowing from the crippled ships. Confusion and chaos sent sailors scrambling to safety as smoke and flames blinded them. Attempts to extinguish the horrific fires where in vain as the explosions from the bombs and torpedoes sent huge chunks of metal flying through the air. Ruptured fuel tanks spewed burning fuel everywhere. Some men jumped into the harbor waters to avoid being burned alive on their mangled ships. Floating patches of burning fuel overcame them and flying debris injured them

severely. Hundreds were killed aboard their ships, trapped below decks, as the ship slowly sank.

The aftermath: eight U.S. battle-ships, three cruisers, three destroyers, an anti-aircraft training ship, one mine-layer ship, all damaged or sunk. One hundred eighty-eight aircraft destroyed. Americans killed 2,403; wounded, 1,178.

The Japanese plan was to first destroy the Pacific Fleet thereby crippling our military. Without U.S. interference, the Japanese would begin military conquests in Southeast Asia headed for their quest of world domination. The Japanese also wanted to thrust a severe blow to American morale in hopes of weakening our desire to wage war against them.

Many Americans had no idea where Pearl Harbor was situated in the vast Pacific Ocean, but they quickly educated themselves. They also learned where Japan was situated, as well as other important Pacific Island territories held by the United States.

Although Americans were in profound shock over the attack, the Japanese learned in a matter of hours that their hopes of weakening this Country's morale backfired. Any thoughts of antiwar sentiment evaporated as news reports of the attack spread like a dark, stormy cloud across the nation. Americans were mad as hell!

President Franklin Roosevelt stood before a Joint Session of Congress in Washington, D.C. on Monday, December 8, 1941 at 12:30 P.M. to deliver his response to the attack on Pearl Harbor. Now commonly referred to as the "Infamy  Speech," President Roosevelt issued a formal request to Congress to declare war against Japan. His entire speech follows:

> *Mr. Vice President, Mr. Speaker, members of the Senate and the House of Representatives. Yesterday, December 7th, 1941 - a date which will live in infamy - the United States of America was suddenly and deliberately attacked by naval and air forces of the Empire of Japan.*
>
> *The United States was at peace with that nation, and, at the solicitation of Japan, was still in conversation with its Government and its Emperor looking toward the maintenance of*

13

peace in the Pacific. Indeed, one hour after Japanese air squadrons had commenced bombing in the American island of Oahu, the Japanese Ambassador to the United States and his colleague delivered to our Secretary of State a formal reply to a recent American message. And while this reply stated that it seemed useless to continue the existing diplomatic negotiations, it contained no threat or hint of war or of armed attack.

It will be recorded that the distance of Hawaii from Japan makes it obvious that the attack was deliberately planned many days or even weeks ago. During the intervening time the Japanese Government has deliberately sought to deceive the United States by false statements and expressions of hope for continued peace.

The attack yesterday on the Hawaiian Islands has caused severe damage to American naval and military forces. I regret to tell you that very many American lives have been lost. In addition American ships have been reported torpedoed on the high seas between San Francisco and Honolulu.

Yesterday the Japanese Government also launched an attack against Malaya.

Last night Japanese forces attacked Hong Kong.

Last night Japanese forces attacked Guam.

Last night Japanese forces attacked the

Philippine Islands.

Last night the Japanese attacked Wake Island.

And this morning the Japanese attacked Midway Island.

Japan has, therefore, undertaken a surprise offensive extending throughout the Pacific area. The facts of yesterday and today speak for themselves. The people of the United States have already formed their opinions and well understand the implications to the very life and safety of our nation.

As Commander-in-Chief of the Army and Navy, I have directed that all measures be taken for our defense. But always will our whole nation remember the character of the onslaught against us. No matter how long it may take us to overcome this premeditated invasion, the American people in their righteous might will win through to absolute victory.

I believe that I interpret the will of the Congress and of the people when I assert that we will not only defend ourselves to the utter- most but will make it very certain that this form of treachery shall never again endanger us.

Hostilities exist. There is no blinking at the fact that our people, our territory and our interests are in grave danger.

With confidence in our armed forces - with the un-bounding determination of our people -

we will gain the inevitable triumph - so help us God.

I ask that the Congress declare that since the unprovoked and dastardly attack by Japan on Sunday, December 7th, 1941, a state of war has existed between the United States and the Japanese Empire.

Immediate applause erupted throughout the Chamber following the speech, a tremendous feeling of unity and cooperation among the members was apparent. The speech lasted only seven minutes and has been regarded as one of the most famous American political speeches of the 20th Century. The speech was broadcast live over radio with over 80% of Americans tuned in, the largest audience of radio listeners in U.S. radio history. The feeling of unity and cooperation noted in the Congressional Chamber spread like wildfire across the country.

After the speech, it took just thirty-three minutes for Congress to pass the formal Declaration of War against Japan. With that, the United States was officially involved in World War II.

Shortly thereafter, world famous aviator Charles Lindbergh, announced to Americans via radio:

Now (war) has come and we must meet it as united Americans regardless of our attitude in the past toward the policy our Government has followed...our country has been attacked by force of arms, and by force of arms we must retaliate. We must now turn every effort to building the greatest and most efficient Army, Navy and Air Force in the world.

Within hours, recruiting stations across America began seeing long lines form outside their doors. Within days the stations were overwhelmed with men of all ages eager to enlist. Although working twenty-four hours a day to process the volunteers, the lines continued to form and remained long. Many young boys felt the need to support their country and lied about their age and parental consent.

Three days later, on December 11, 1941, Germany and Italy declared war upon the United States which required even more troops, not only to fight in the Pacific, but also in Europe and Africa. Many Americans wanted to see the eventual destruction of Japan in retaliation for the Pearl Harbor attack and did not understand the reasoning for fighting in other countries they had never heard of.

Even so, the U.S. Armed Forces had thousands of eager volunteers ready, willing and (mostly) able to fight for their country, no matter where they were sent. Sixteen million Americans signed up and served during WWII. Of those, the Army had 8,300,000 enlisted, the Navy had 4,204,662, the

Marines had 599,693, and the Coast Guard had 172,952.

American women serving non-combat military positions included: Army 140,000, Navy 100,000, Marines 23,000, Coast Guard 13,000, Air Force 1,000, Army and Navy Nurse Corps 74,000.

Most of these sixteen million Americans did not enlist for the high pay or benefits. New recruits or "buck privates" received fifty dollars a month if they were single or married. If married with one child, they would receive eighty dollars a month and an additional twenty dollars a month for each additional child. If single but with persons dependent upon them for their main source of support, their monthly pay ranged from fifty to sixty-eight dollars. If the recruit advanced in rank, a pay raise was given. Those serving within the United States received the above amounts while those serving abroad were given an increase of twenty percent of their base pay.

Married soldiers with children or single with dependents (such as elderly or disabled parents, or younger siblings) had twenty-two dollars deducted from their paychecks each month and sent directly to the wives or dependents by the government. Many soldiers chose to have their entire monthly checks sent home.

Other pay incentives included "longevity pay" - for every three years spent in service, the base pay was increased five percent. Paratroopers received an additional fifty dollars a month above their base pay. Those receiving any type of medal while serving received an additional two dollars a month. Besides the officers, Army Air Corps pilots received the highest wages. As long as they were flying frequent or regular flights, their pay was an additional fifty percent of base pay plus the pay increase for foreign service and any awards they might receive while in combat.

Christmas in 1941 was confusing, chaotic, full of fear and distress across our great land. War had been declared just seventeen days earlier and many Americans were still in a state of shock. Families were turned upside down as their men and boys rushed to enlist leaving the women and children behind. Christmas plans were overshadowed by war preparations. German and Japanese made toys did not appear under Christmas trees that year which left thousands of disappointed children who thought those were the best toys to have.

Three days before Christmas, British Prime Minister Winston Churchill and his entourage arrived at the White House for a visit with President Roosevelt. These Allies met to begin planning and mapping out military and political strategies to end the war and end it quickly. The Prime Minister wanted help with fighting the Germans while President Roosevelt was focused on the Pacific and Japan. News journalists referred to Washington, D.C. as the wartime capital of the world while the two great men met daily to develop their plans of attack.

On Christmas Eve the two men took a break. Together they stepped out on the White House balcony before a crowd of 20,000 gathered on the snowy lawn below, while thousands more listened on their radios at home. President Roosevelt concluded his message by saying:

Our strongest weapon in this war is that conviction of the dignity and brotherhood of man which Christmas Day signifies - more than any other day or any other symbol.

Prime Minister Churchill wanted to assure the American people that although there was war raging around the world, we could still pause and reflect on the spirit of Christmas:

This is a strange Christmas Eve. Almost the whole world is locked in deadly struggle, and with the most terrible weapons which science can devise, the nations advance upon each other.

Let the children have their night of fun and laughter. Let the gifts of Father Christmas delight their play. Let us grown-ups share to the full in their unstinted pleasures before we turn again to the stern task and formidable years that lie before us, resolved that, by our sacrifice and daring, these same children shall not be robbed of their inheritance or denied their right to live in a free and decent world.

After the speeches the two world leaders ceremoniously lit the National Christmas Tree before the cheering crowd. The next morning they both attended a Christmas service at a nearby church. One of the hymns sung during the service was a familiar favorite, *"O Little Town of Bethlehem."* As Christmas church bells rang across the nation, a lyric from the hymn *"...the hopes and fears of all the years are met in thee tonight,"* rang true.

Life in America was about to change forever.

Chapter 2

Trauma and Triage: Pearl Harbor

On December 7, 1941 there were a total of 119 military nurses serving at the Army and Naval hospitals near Pearl Harbor: 29 Navy Nurse Corps and 82 Army Nurse Corps. When the bombing began at 0748 hours (7:48 A.M.), the nurses not already on duty rushed to their respective hospitals and prepared for casualties. Sadly, they did not have long to wait. Within ten minutes of the initial attack, the first casualties began to arrive.

A receiving area was quickly established in the former nurses' quarters where the injured were unloaded from ambulances, wagons, trucks, civilian cars - anything with wheels. The hallways quickly became crowded with badly burned and bleeding men waiting to be triaged. Many suffered gunshot and shrapnel wounds, mangled and amputated arms and legs, and horrific burns resulting in charred body parts. The stench of fresh blood, charred flesh mixed with smoke, black oil, and gasoline was overwhelming. The screams and cries of the injured and frightened young men were enough to make even the most stoic of nurses cry.

Nurses gave morphine injections to many of the severely wounded and marked a large red M on their forehead to alert other nurses and physicians the patient had been medicated.

Officers and corpsmen, as well as two surgeons from destroyed ships, rushed to the hospitals to help. One hundred fourteen Red Cross nurses also rushed from the civilian hospitals to lend a hand. A (military) surgeon, who was recovering from major surgery, got out of bed and went to the operating room where he worked for three straight days until he became too exhausted to continue. Several wives of enlisted men who had nursing backgrounds but were not currently working, also rushed to help.

Japanese planes were relentless as they continued to drop bombs on the massive ships or spray them with machine gun fire. Huge explosions shook the area, followed by fires that dotted the harbor. Thick, black smoke billowed high into the air, drifting in every direction like a heavy blanket of death.

When the USS *Arizona* was struck, the tremendous explosion violently shook the ground like a massive earthquake. Frightened nurses inside the Naval Hospital thought the hospital had been hit and scurried around the wards checking their terrified patients. As the thick smoke slowly moved toward the hospitals, the nurses began closing all the windows to prevent the acrid cloud from filling the rooms.

First aid stations were quickly set up in nearby locations. Minor wounds and injuries were treated, bandaged, and the men went back to duty wherever they were needed. The hospital ship *Solace* was not damaged in the attack nor was the ship USS *Argonne*. Crews from both ships dropped rescue boats into the water and pulled wounded and burned men from the water while the Japanese continued to fire upon, torpedo and bomb the surrounding ships. Many of the men pulled aboard the rescue boats were covered with thick black oil and were on fire. They were immediately taken to the hospital ship for treatment then if needed, transferred to the base hospitals. Nurses and corpsmen on board the hospital ship treated one hundred thirty-one casualties admitted to the ship; eighty were given primary first aid; however, twenty-eight died from trauma and/or severe burns.

By 1030 hours (10:30 A.M.) supplies and equipment from the *Argonne* were used to set up a field hospital on the dock next to the ship. One hundred fifty cots lined the length of the dock and were quickly filled with wounded pulled from the water by *Argonne* crew members. The field hospital also served as a triage point where nurses assessed the most critical patients and sent them on to the Naval Hospital. Eventually, this field hospital was moved to the nearby Officers Club which was less exposed to enemy fire in case the Japanese returned.

Two other ships in the area, the USS *Nevada* and the USS *Pennsylvania*, were also able to treat the wounded. Nurses and corpsmen assigned to these ships treated the injured for shrapnel wounds and burns, and confirmed the dead.

Within the first three hours of the attack, 546 casualties and 313 dead were received at the military hospitals. By the end of the day 960 casualties had been admitted to the hospital which had a bed capacity of 500. Ambulatory (walking) wounded were sent to vacant buildings nearby where a field hospital was established and tended to by nurses and corpsmen. Five large tents, field hospital style, were also set up behind the hospital for non-ambulatory patients. The most critical and the post-operative patients remained in the main hospital.

Luckily, bandaging material, surgical instruments and gloves, suture material, syringes, morphine, and antibiotic supplies were sufficient to handle the mass of casualties. A Mobile Base Hospital was being constructed by the Navy prior to the attack. The supplies and equipment for it had arrived three weeks earlier and had been stored awaiting the completion of the mobile unit. The supplies were quickly made available and utilized. The only medical need in short supply was plasma and tannic acid; sixty percent of the casualties were burns of every degree and plasma was needed for fluid replacement while tannic acid was used for cleaning and debridement of the burned areas.

The nurses and other medical personnel worked steadily for three straight days and nights triaging and caring for the 1,178 wounded. Many could not be saved, while even more did not make it to the hospitals. A total of 2,403 enlisted men were killed. A makeshift morgue was set up in the hospital basement. The grim process of identifying the remains and preparation of the bodies for burial was undertaken by corpsmen with direction from the hospital pathologist. Many were burned or dismembered beyond recognition and were buried as "unknown."

For the first three days and nights of controlled chaos, many of the nurses went without eating in favor of an hour or two of sleep. A cot or a grass mat in a restroom or locker room was an adequate bed. One nurse who fell asleep with a lit cigarette in her hand, subsequently set her cot on fire. She had worked 24 hours straight without a break for food or sleep.

Through all of the chaos, the nurses wearing uniforms and shoes covered with blood, sweat and tears took charge and held things together because it was their duty to do so. Many were frightened and worried about their families on the mainland, but too busy to give it more than a passing thought. The younger nurses had never seen so much suffering and death nor had they experienced such shock and fear of what was to come.

Air raid sirens sounded off and on, day and night causing the nurses to scramble for cover, often just crawling under their patient's bed or cot. All the windows were covered with black tar paper, or blankets at night. No lights were allowed on within the hospital so nurses carried flashlights covered with blue paper. This gave their patients a bit of a cyanotic color that frustrated the nurses; a bluish color to the skin indicates lack of oxygen, among other problems.

By the third day, patients were triaged and sorted again for placement according to their injuries: orthopedic patients to the orthopedic ward, surgical patients to the surgical ward, and burn patients to the medical ward. Some patients were still awaiting surgery while others died during the night most often from massive burns over large areas of the body.

No military job is complete without paperwork. As things became more organized, the task of establishing a chart for each patient became a priority. Many of the critically injured were not identified or identifiable. Dog tags had been lost somewhere along the way. Those that were able to talk were asked their name, rank and serial number. The nurse would then list the extent of the injuries suffered, the treatment plan undertaken so far, and to follow. It was a tedious task for the exhausted nurses.

As the wounded slowly began to heal, preparations were made to begin sending them back to the mainland for specialized care and/or convalescence. The first to go were the walking wounded and the amputees. On Christmas Eve, December 24, 1941 the men set sail for the mainland. The war was over for them. Their nurses remained in Hawaii caring for the more seriously injured in an attempt to stabilize them enough for the long journey home via ship. For the seriously burned victims, they would spend years undergoing plastic surgeries and recovery in stateside military hospitals.

President Roosevelt later honored the Pearl Harbor nurses with a Presidential Citation which read:

You are the bravest of the brave with a devotion to duty and to mankind that will be forever unmatched.

Chapter 3

Preparations Begin

When President Roosevelt declared war on Japan December 8, 1941, and Germany and Italy on December 11, 1941, an immediate political, psychological and economic shift spread rapidly across America. The United States was not prepared to enter war. Although production of military arms for our British and French Allies had been underway earlier, our own Armed Forces were sadly lacking in defense equipment and munitions. The naval fleet was in shambles at Pearl Harbor.

Less than a month after the Pearl Harbor attack, President Roosevelt addressed Congress and reached across America via radio by saying, in part:

> *Powerful enemies must be out-fought and out-produced. It is not enough to turn out just a few more planes, a few more tanks, a few more guns, a few more ships than can be turned out by our enemies.*
>
> *We must out-produce them overwhelmingly, so that there can be no question of our ability to provide a crushing superiority of equipment in any theater of the world war.*

On January 16, 1942, FDR announced Executive Order 9024 establishing the War Production Board and later, the Office of War Mobilization. These two governmental war agencies were tasked with supervising war production - primarily converting civilian industries to war production or, in other terms, peacetime industry to wartime industry. The WPB established guidelines and priorities for the distribution of materials and services, prohibited nonessential production, and rationed commodities such as gasoline, heating oil, metals, rubber, paper, and plastics. It also insured that each factory had the materials needed to produce the most war goods or products in the shortest amount of time.

Once in place, the President set unprecedented goals for these particular factories: 60,000 aircraft in 1942, with an increase to 125,000 in 1943; 120,000 tanks and 55,000 antiaircraft guns within the same time frame.

The production goals profoundly changed American industry as it was known prior to Pearl Harbor. The automobile industry, which was beginning to prosper following the Great Depression, produced three million cars in 1941. Only 139 cars were produced during the war years. Instead of cars, Chrysler produced fuselages, General Motors produced airplane engines, guns, trucks, and tanks. The powerful Rolls-Royce engines used by the British Air Force were built by Packard. In Michigan, the Ford Motor Company built the B-24 Liberator, a much needed long-range bomber. The company prided itself by assembling the 1,550,000 parts needed to build one bomber, with one plane coming off the assembly line every sixty-three minutes.

Other factories and manufacturing companies quickly filled war department needs: those formerly making silk ribbons produced parachutes; typewriter companies converted to machine guns; an upholstery maker manufacturing upholstery nails switched to making cartridge clips for rifles; a merry-go-round factory was making gun mounts; a kitchen stove company made lifeboats; a pinball-machine maker was producing armor-piercing shells; brass and copper companies made more than 50 million cartridge cases, mortar shells, and more than a billion small caliber bullets.

Government subsidies were granted under the jurisdiction of the WPB giving smaller industries an economic boost as long as those industries produced products considered essential to victory. The Coca Cola company increased production and shipped Coca Cola to troops in Europe and the Pacific. They spent large amounts of their subsidies on advertising their product portraying men in uniform. Many of the posters showed the uniformed men with locals in faraway lands enjoying a coke. In 1944 Coca Cola became known as "The Global High Sign" as if to say, "Hello, we are friends." Coca Cola also created ads strongly acknowledging the company's support

of the war effort, our troops, and the need for Americans to purchase war bonds.

Another well-known company flourishing during this time was Wrigley's Chewing Gum. The company sent all of their products (Spearmint, Doublemint and Juicy Fruit gums), to troops at home and abroad. They also supplied any American factory producing war related products with generous amounts of their products. Ads were posted in the factories recommending five sticks of gum a day for every war worker (the same number of sticks in one pack!). The posters announced, "Factory tests show how chewing gum helps men feel better, work better." Since the gum was not readily available to anyone else, ad campaigns were initiated to keep their products on the minds of consumers. Posters showed the different packs of flavors with "Remember This Wrapper" in bold letters. Chewing gum became a hot item on the black market during the war years.

Chewing gum was considered an essential war product for soldiers' relief of tension, dry mouth, and throats when undertaking long marches and other duties. The G.I.s also used gum for quick repairs in remote places to patch tires, gas tanks, life rafts and airplane parts.

The Hershey Chocolate Corporation was contracted to provide the army with a chocolate

"survival ration bar" that would be a part of the soldiers' K-ration kits as well as emergency ration kits and prisoner-of-war packages sent by the Red Cross. The bars were nothing like the sweet chocolate we enjoy today. Instead, the bars were four ounces of bitter, hard to bite into, chocolate made with cocoa fat, oat flour, dry powdered skim milk, vanilla crystals, a bit of Vitamin B1, a tiny bit of sugar and artificial coloring. The bars were for survival not dessert, and the bitterness was meant to discourage the troops from eating them as a treat.

Because of the huge government contracted orders, the factory had to increase production and run three shifts a day, seven days a week - the first time in Hershey's history. Hundreds of extra workers were hired to fill all three shifts. By the end of the war, Hershey's had produced over 420 million bars of this type.

With the massive increase in war production taking place across the U.S. came the massive need for workers. Many workers had been unemployed for years following the Depression and eagerly stepped into the employment lines in hopes of landing a coveted, high-paying defense job. Twenty-four million men and women were quickly hired, with or without experience, into defense positions. Eight million women, including African Americans and Latinos, also found jobs for the first time, in non-defense positions.

Pay scales ranged from 64 cents an hour for unskilled, inexperienced workers to $7 an hour for skilled, experienced workers, whether the position was a factory worker or bank teller. The higher paying jobs went to experienced construction workers or college graduates, usually younger men that could not pass the military physicals for one reason or another. The majority of women had never worked outside of the home and were eager to work any type of job to support their family while husbands or fathers were fighting abroad. The women were always at the lower end of the pay scale no matter what position they filled.

Propaganda posters were popping up everywhere encouraging women to join the work force in support of the war effort. One poster announced: "If you've used an electric mixer in

There's work to be done and a war to be won. . . *NOW!*

SEE YOUR U. S. EMPLOYMENT SERVICE

your kitchen, you can learn to run a drill press!"
Women, young and older, operated machinery,
large cranes used to move heavy tanks, artillery,
drill presses, welders, riveters, and more. Rosie
The Riveter became a well-known fictional
character symbolizing the millions of women
working in the aircraft factories, shipyards, and
munitions plants. Women who joined the war
production labor force were referred to as
"production soldiers"- likely a psychological ploy
by the government to increase patriotism and
encourage women to enter the workforce.

Schools and colleges experienced a sharp drop
in enrollment just after war was declared as
students rushed to enlist. It did not take long for
the educational systems across America to
restructure and accelerate their curricula to meet
the needs and demands the war presented. When
the factory workers realized they would make
more money with a college, technical or vocational
education, the colleges scrambled to meet the
sudden increase in demand for enrollment.

Four year colleges began offering accelerated programs allowing students to graduate in three years. Year-round school became the norm by changing the two semester systems to a three term system: two terms of sixteen weeks each and one term of eight weeks during the summer. Summer session classes might focus on the war and post-war problems or offer courses in typing, steno-graphy, photography, motor mechanics, first aid, or art for advertising - all classes that would prepare students for usefulness in the war effort.

Colleges gave admittance preference to Armed Forces personnel and civilians planning to enlist. Over one hundred-thirty-one colleges across the nation partnered with the military in providing the education needed for the recruits to graduate with a bachelor's degree then enter the service as an ensign or second lieutenant. The V-12 Navy College Training Program as well as the Army Specialized Training Program were examples of that partnering. Specific classes in these programs taught economics, statistics, calculus, drafting, machine design, electrical engineering, aero-nautical science, and cartography. Advanced programs pushed recruits to additional education in medical, dental, and theological fields.

Women with a desire for a career were encouraged to enter nursing school or a liberal arts college to become a teacher. When WWII was declared these two professions became highly coveted and in great demand. Existing nursing schools had sharp increases in admissions requests. As many of the hospital nurses left their positions to join the military nurse corps, a large void occurred on the home front. The government stepped in to encourage the nursing schools to increase admissions and fast track students through to graduation. Priority was given to students interested in military nursing. Over

become a Nurse
YOUR COUNTRY NEEDS YOU

one million dollars was allocated to help the schools train and hire additional nursing instructors, assist students with tuition, and establish refresher courses for non-practicing nurses. An advertising campaign strongly encouraged trained nurses to return to their professions; many had married, had children and chose not to return to hospital duties.

For years the liberal arts colleges (also referred to as teachers colleges) had been educating women with a focus on literature, language, music, art, history, etc. Now the colleges had to restructure their curricula for women that were needed to take over the many roles previously held by men. Psychology classes trained students to care for adults and children in times of stress. Social science classes taught upper level mathematics, economics, and statistics. Home Economics focused on nutrition in wartime, as well as gardening, and canning techniques.

Vocational schools enrolled women as never before who were eager to learn how to use tools in manly mechanical jobs and intricate piece work. Because secretarial work was in high demand women learned typing skills, stenography, writing and preparing reports, bookkeeping, and map reading. With all of these new educational opportunities women became more confident in the variety of new roles they would assume during the war.

Within a matter of months, the United States was fully engaged in war preparations. The greatest production escalation in the nation's history was underway. New job opportunities for both men and women improved the home front economy and lifted the spirits of Americans away from the gloom of the Depression years. Mobilizing the economic output was a major factor in supporting combat operations.

And, for the first time in history, American women were being recognized as trailblazers in areas never before open to them.

Christmas 1941 was dismal for many Americans as well as the traditional celebration welcoming in the New Year of 1942. In New

York, the famed Times Square ball drop ushers in the New Year with a sixty-second countdown as the glittering ball drops one hundred forty-one feet and stops at the stroke of midnight to the cheers of thousands of revelers. Due to the wartime lighting restrictions and blackouts, the ball drop was cancelled. Instead, a moment of silence was observed followed by the sound of chimes ringing loudly from sound trucks.

The traditional West Coast New Year's Day Rose Bowl football game was moved to North Carolina for fear of ongoing threats to the Pacific coastal regions.

Across the nation the New Year was ushered in without much fanfare as families continued to prepare for war.

Chapter 4

WAC, WAVES, SPARS, MCWR, and WASP

Women's Auxiliary Army Corps - WAAC, later WAC

When war was declared, thousands of women wanted to contribute and support the war efforts in a variety of ways other than nursing. The initial response by men and the government was one of resistance and reluctance. But, as the war quickly raged on with increased demands for troops, the vociferous women volunteers became viewed as a valuable source of labor, freeing more manpower for combat.

First Lady Eleanor Roosevelt, and a variety of women's groups, were instrumental in garnering support from General George Marshall by introducing the Women's Auxiliary Army Corps, (WAAC) in May, 1942. Many women did not like the acronym because it sounded like "wacky." The only change made later was to drop the "Auxiliary" and the unit became the Women's Army Corps (WAC).

Women recruits had to be U.S. citizens between the ages of twenty-one and forty-five, no dependents, at least five feet tall, and weigh one hundred pounds or more. When requirements were met, the women recruits entered basic training, learned military ways, then moved on to specialized training in a variety of fields including meteorology, mechanical, electrical, transportation, signal corps, radio, medical (non-nursing positions), chemical laboratories, munitions, quartermaster corps, and more.

The majority of recruits were initially moved to secretarial positions, "female jobs," but the rising need for personnel in "non-female" jobs became so overwhelming the men soon began assigning women to them. By filling the positions, more men were freed to the front lines which allowed the women to work at positions they had been trained for.

A short list of some of the jobs WACs held included:

Meteorologists, weather observers, forecasters
Cryptographers
Map designers
Telephone, telegraph and radio operators; radio
    operations and repairs
Control tower operators
Photographers
Aerial photograph analysts
Ordinance analysts, munitions loaders,
    gunpowder loaders
Motorpool drivers
Parachute packers

Quartermasters - control of stock and supplies across the U.S.

Processing of recruits - issuing uniforms and weapons, personnel paperwork

Laboratory workers - glass blowers making test tubes, laboratory testing

The Manhattan project - top secret work at Oak Ridge, Tennessee, Hanford, Washington, or Los Alamos, New Mexico producing plutonium and designing the atomic bombs (to be discussed in chapter 11)

Once the men slowly became accustomed to the hard working women in uniform, the furor of opposing them in the workplace slowly ceased. General Douglas MacArthur called the WACs "My best soldiers." He stated, "They worked harder, complained less and were better disciplined than men." General Dwight D. Eisenhower said, "Their contributions in efficiency, skill, spirit, and determination are immeasurable."

When feisty little **Mary Hallaren** arrived at a nearby recruiting station in 1942, the recruiter chuckled at her diminutive five foot frame. He asked what a little five foot woman could do in the Army. She looked up at him and replied, "You don't have to be

COL Mary A. Hallaren
(1907-2005)

six feet tall to have a brain that works!" Within a year Mary became a Captain commanding the first women's battalion to go overseas. The WAC personnel were attached to the 8th and 9th Army Air Corps. In 1945, she commanded all WAC personnel in the European Theater as a Lieutenant Colonel. In 1947, she became the director of the entire WAC as a full Colonel.

When the Women's Armed Services Integration Act became law in 1948, women gained permanent status in the armed services. Mary became the first woman to serve as an official Army officer with the rank of Colonel.

Nearly 150,000 women proudly served their country as WAC during WWII.

Women Accepted for Volunteer Emergency Service - WAVES

Two months after the WAC formed, First Lady Eleanor Roosevelt once again worked her magic with Congress to authorize the formation of a women's reserve group for the Navy - the Women Accepted for Volunteer Emergency Service (WAVES). The unusual acceptance of women into the naval armed forces was considered an "emergency" due to the war. Once the war ended, the women would no longer serve as a group. The Women's Armed Services Integration Act of 1948 changed that line of thinking and women have long since pursued Naval careers to this day.

The difference between the WAC and the WAVES was that the WAC was an auxiliary organization serving **with** the Army, not **in** the Army. The WAVES served as a **part** of the Navy and held the same rank and pay rates as the men serving. They were also subject to the same military discipline.

When these women enlisted, they attended an intensive twelve week training course with eight hours a day of difficult classroom studies. Although the need for secretarial and clerical positions was high, the demand for aviation, medical, communications, intelligence, science, and technology related fields was higher. A variety of training programs in those fields were available and quickly filled.

Requirements for aviation related positions, especially control tower operators, included: twenty-five to thirty years old, 20/20 vision, normal auditory (hearing) acuity, clear speaking ability, and quick reactions in stressful situations.

Cryptology classes were provided for those interested in the cryptologic field (writing and/or solving codes). A three-month cryptology course was available at Smith College in Massachusetts. Graduates with the highest scores were immediately sent to Washington, D.C. where they were sworn to secrecy about their duties and put to work. Discussing their duties outside of work would be considered an act of treason in wartime.

The WAVES maintained the Naval administrative duties at home while the men served on ships around the world. WAVES did not serve aboard combat ships or combat aircraft but were assigned duties in U.S. held territories.

Within the first year over 27,000 women were serving as WAVES led by the first director, **Lieutenant Commander Mildred McAfee.** McAfee took a leave of absence from her position as President of Wellesley College to serve in 1942. She was instrumental in establishing rules, regulations, and training programs as well as campaigning for the right of equal pay and benefits for her troops. At the peak of WWII, she served over 80,000 WAVES. By the end of the war over 100,000 women had served under her. In 1945, Mildred McAfee was the first woman to receive the Navy Distinguished Service Medal.

Semper Paratus Always Ready - SPARS

In November 1942, President Roosevelt signed legislation into law creating opportunities for women to serve in the Coast Guard as reservists. Just as the other branches of service utilizing women were created, the Coast Guard needed to free its men from stateside service duties to fight overseas.

Dorothy Stratton took a leave of absence from her teaching position at Purdue University in 1942 and entered the WAVES as a senior lieutenant. Soon after, she transferred to the Coast Guard and was appointed Director of the Women's Reserve. Stratton instituted many  programs that encouraged women to pursue interests never available to them before the war. She was also a strong proponent of higher education for women in areas other than home economics, teaching, and nursing, which were the main college courses available to women at that time. Dorothy was promoted to Commander within a year and to Captain in 1944.

The official name of the newly formed group was the United States Coast Guard Women's Reserve. Dorothy quickly developed the SPARS acronym using the following logic: The Coast Guard motto was <u>S</u>emper <u>P</u>aratus meaning "<u>A</u>lways <u>R</u>eady"- she also noted the name could refer to the four freedoms of <u>S</u>peech, <u>P</u>ress, <u>A</u>ssembly, and <u>R</u>eligion. Stratton also pointed out that a spar is a nautical term for a ship's support beam. Therefore, the group of women would become the support beams for the Coast Guard.

The SPARS requirements for acceptance were more specific than the other service branches. Age requirements were about the same, but the ideal recruit had to be extremely physically fit, athletic, a good swimmer and have some sort of nautical knowledge and/or experience. Advanced education (college) was strongly encouraged for advancement. Graduation from the rigorous basic training earned the recruit a blue braid signifying the rank of ensign and a member of the Coast Guard Reserve.

The response to recruiting efforts, like the other service branches, was overwhelming. Naval, Marine and Coast Guard recruits initially trained together then went on to specialized training directed at the branch of service they had chosen. Many of the Naval recruits actually transferred to the Coast Guard after their basic training for a variety of reasons.

At first the SPARS were relegated to clerical and administrative duties but due to the need to send more men into active wartime duties, the women were trained to take a variety of positions.

One small group scoring high academic achievements was selected to undergo specialized and classified communication training. They were to operate the top secret LORAN monitoring stations. LORAN stands for Long Range Aid to Navigation which was a top secret electronic system developed in WWII enabling navigators of aircraft and ships to fix (locate) their positions. This was especially useful in vessel dim outs, blackouts, or under poor weather conditions.

The first LORAN station in the world to be totally operated by women was located in Chatham, Massachusetts. The SPARS were on duty 24 hours a day monitoring and recording radio signals then calculating the locations of aircraft and ships. At the Chatham base their duties were to monitor Atlantic shipping and submarine traffic.

Other SPARS positions included divers, photographers, supply officers, pharmacist's mates, radio communication operators, port security, logistics, and public relations assistants. Public relations personnel were responsible for recruiting across the U.S.

At the end of the war, more than 13,000 women had been recruited and served as SPARS. Their beloved Captain Stratton left SPARS after the war and became the first director of personnel at the International Monetary Fund for several years. She then accepted the position as National Executive Director of the Girl Scouts of America, and retired in 1960. Dorothy Stratton died in 2006 at the age of 107.

Marine Corps Women's Reserve - MCWR

The Army, Navy and Coast Guard's successful recruitment of women during 1942 released thousands of military men to serve overseas and in combat positions. The Marines also needed manpower and a reluctant Corps Commandant,

General Thomas Holcomb, finally agreed to begin recruiting women in February, 1943. Although the other service branches had acronyms identifying themselves, General Holcomb resisted suggestions such as BAMs - Beautiful American Marines, Sub-Marines, Femarines, Glamarines…and simply chose Marine Corps Women Reservists or MCWR. In an article published by *Life* magazine in 1944, when questioned about the choice, his reply was terse: "They are Marines. They don't have a nick-name and they don't need one. They get their basic training in a Marine atmosphere at a Marine post. They inherit the traditions of Marines. They are Marines."

Mrs. Ruth Cheney Streeter, 47, had been class president at Byrn Mawr college before marrying a prominent lawyer and businessman. She had never held a paying job, but she was the mother of four grown children and active in her local community's health and  welfare work. She was also a commercially rated pilot and owned her own plane. In 1941, she joined the Civil Air Patrol and wanted to patrol the Eastern coastline to watch for enemy submarines. The CAP relegated her to duties that did not include flying, much to her dismay. When the WAVES formed, she inquired about a piloting position but was told the only position available to her would be as a ground instructor. She politely declined.

A month after declining the ground instructor position, Mrs. Streeter was selected from an impressive field of twelve women to head the newly established MCWR. Commissioned as a Major, her job was to facilitate recruiting efforts, training and administrative duties. Major Streeter had been skeptical about men selecting women prior to her appointment so one of the first changes she put into place was assigning women to the recruitment duties. She also worked closely with the directors of the other three service branches to obtain tips and insights into the difficulties they had experienced when they first started.

Eligibility requirements for service in the MCWR were similar to the other service branches with a few exceptions. Women recruits had to be U.S. citizens, not married to a Marine, single or married with no children/dependents under the age of eighteen, height not less than five feet, weight not less than ninety-five pounds, good vision and teeth. Age limits were from twenty to thirty-five, with at least two years of high school. Officer candidates were required to be from twenty to forty-nine years of age with at least two years of college or a college degree, as well as two years of work experience.

Recruitment was very hectic but successful. By June 1944, over 18,000 women had enlisted in

MCWR. Some were so desperately needed to fill a variety of positions, they were immediately sworn in and sent directly to work in procurement offices or to administrative positions. Military training would have to come later. At the end of the war, records showed over 225 different specialties were accomplished by 23,000 MCWR. Most were similar to the other service branches including truck drivers, gunnery instructors, cooks, bakers, laundry operators, post exchange managers, and agriculturists. They were also trained for mobilization preparedness and emergencies.

When General Holcomb was presented with the figures and saw the results of the MCWR at wars end, he released this simple statement: "Like most Marines, when the matter first came up, I didn't believe women could serve any useful purpose in the Marine Corps...Since then, I've changed my mind."

Women Airforce Service Pilots - WASP

The last women's military group to form was the Women Airforce Service Pilots - WASP. Although it seemed to take this group a bit longer to form, there were actually two separate programs operating independently prior to their formal merging in August, 1943. The two pioneering programs of civilian female pilots were the Women's Flying Training Detachment (WFTD), and the Women's Auxiliary Ferrying Squadron

(WAFS), organized in September 1942. Two famous women pilots, Jacqueline (Jackie) Cochran and Nancy Harkness Love, were instrumental in organizing the programs and remain synonymous with women's aviation today.

Jackie Cochran fell in love with aviation after a friend took her for an airplane ride in the early 1930s. She began taking flight lessons and was flying solo within three weeks of her first lesson.  Within two years she had accumulated the necessary hours to obtain her commercial pilot's license as well as her need for speed. She was the first woman to compete in the MacRobertson Air Race in 1934, the only woman to compete in the Bendix race in 1937, as well as setting a new woman's national speed record and a new trans-continental speed and altitude record. Jackie became known as the "Speed Queen." Along with her friend, Amelia Earhart, the two promoted women flying wherever they went.

Before Pearl Harbor and the declaration of war, Jackie joined the "Wings for Britain" flying American built aircraft to the U.S. allies in Britain. She was the first woman to fly a bomber across the Atlantic and worked for several months recruiting qualified women pilots in the U.S. to join the British Air Transport Auxiliary.

Seeing the success of the British Air Transport Auxiliary's use of women pilots, Jackie wrote to First Lady Eleanor Roosevelt in September, 1940 with an idea and proposal for a women's flying division in the Army Air Corps. She pointed out that qualified women pilots were capable of flying domestic, noncombat jobs thus freeing men pilots for oversees duties.

Chief of the Army Air Corps at that time was Lieutenant General Henry "Hap" Arnold who was well aware of the women flying in Britain. Jackie lobbied Lt. General Arnold, with help from Eleanor Roosevelt, to expand the flying opportunities in the U.S. for women pilots. She continued to focus on the fact that women pilots at home would free men pilots for oversees duty.

In September 1942, Lieutenant General Arnold authorized the formation of the Women's Auxiliary Ferrying Squadron (WAFS) with **Nancy Harkness Love** as the director. This group would only ferry aircraft from the factories to the airbases across the U.S. Jackie insisted that women could do much more than  just ferry aircraft and demanded that Arnold form another group. Under relentless pressure from Jackie and Eleanor Roosevelt, he finally consented. The Women's Flying Training Detachment (WFTD) was formed with Jackie as the director. The WAFS and the WFTD merged in August, 1943. The Women Airforce Service Pilots (WASP) was thereby formed with Jackie as Director and Nancy as head of the ferrying division.

With the merger came decisions on how to proceed with the two groups training. The Nancy Love group had to be trained in the ways of the military and expand their flying skills from cross country flights to such challenges as towing targets for live anti-aircraft artillery practice, simulated strafing missions, test piloting new and newly overhauled aircraft, and transporting military cargo and troops.

The Jackie Cochran group would be qualified pilots new to either program. They would not be trained for any type of gunnery or combat duties. They would only learn a small amount of formation flying and aerobatics as well as flight maneuvers necessary to recover from a variety of critical aerial situations.

After its formation, 25,000 women applied to become WASP. Acceptance was based on the following requirements: U.S. citizen between the ages of twenty-one and thirty-five, a minimum of a high school diploma, a commercial pilot's license with a minimum of five hundred hours of flight time of which fifty hours having been flown in the past year, a two hundred horsepower rating (flight time in a higher powered aircraft), and two letters of recommendation. Only 1,830 were accepted, of which only 1,074 passed the rigorous four month flight training.

Completion earned them their wings and bragging rights to have become the first American women to fly military aircraft. The women did not hold any type of military rank; they were strictly civilian service personnel. They received no health or other benefits, no insurance, and for a time were not even provided uniforms; most wore their own flight suits when on duty. WASP were paid an average of $250 per month plus $6 per day when on duty while male pilots received $380 per month.

Pilot **Nancy Love** and her co-pilot **Betty Gillies** were the first women to be certified to fly

the B-17 bombers as well as the P-51, C-54 transport and the B-25 bombers. Lieutenant General Arnold did not think any young woman could handle wrestling a mighty B-17 Flying Fortress in bad weather, but time and again the women proved him wrong. They not only flew B-17s, but B-18s, B-24s, B-25s, B-26s, and B-29s (all bombers), but also flew large cargo planes, the pursuit planes, P-38s, P-39s, P-40s, and the awesome P-51 fighter and bomber escort planes.

Florene Miller Watson finished flight school and completed her first solo flight by the age of nineteen. She went on to receive her instructor's rating then became a flight instructor at the War Training Program in Texas. Florene celebrated her twenty-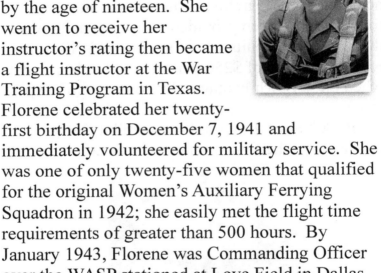
first birthday on December 7, 1941 and immediately volunteered for military service. She was one of only twenty-five women that qualified for the original Women's Auxiliary Ferrying Squadron in 1942; she easily met the flight time requirements of greater than 500 hours. By January 1943, Florene was Commanding Officer over the WASP stationed at Love Field in Dallas, Texas. She served as a test pilot for a variety of aircraft as well as testing newly developed radar equipment in 1944.

After the war, Florene remained active in the aviation community with memberships in the Ninety-Nines, Women's Military Aviators, the WASP WWII, and many more. She received various awards and honors for her exceptional contributions to aviation as well as being featured in the 1993 television documentary *Women of Courage* where she explained the important role of women pilots during WWII as WASP. Her most coveted awards include the Air Force Association's Lifetime Achievement Award, its highest honor, renaming the Reagan County, Texas airport (where she grew up) in her honor, and being inducted into the International Women in Aviation's prestigious Pioneer Hall of Fame.

Florene Miller Watson died February 4, 2014, at the age of 94.

Between September 1942 and December 1944, 12,650 aircraft, consisting of seventy-eight different models, were delivered by WASP. As a whole, the WASP logged over sixty million flight miles and became nicknamed **"Fly Girls."**

Thirty-eight WASP were killed in accidents while serving during the war. Eleven were killed while in training and twenty-seven while on active duty. Unfortunately, since they were not considered military, the fallen WASP were sent home at the families' expense - no military funeral, no military honors, not even an American flag to drape their coffins.

Prejudice against the WASP continued in many areas including the maintenance of their aircraft. Several of the fatal crashes that occurred during training were attributed to poor maintenance by male mechanics as well as blatant sabotage. Inspection of a fuel tank following a minor crash involving a WASP found the tank full of sugar.

Black women pilots were refused acceptance into the WASP as well as the other branches of service. Rejection letters sent to them stated they were not eligible due to their race. These women aviators faced discrimination just as the white women aviators did, but they also faced racial discrimination. That did not stop several black women with dreams of pursing an aviation career just as it did not stop the white women. These woman are relatively unknown, as their stories have fallen through history's prejudicial cracks. A small sample of three African-American women who made a difference include:

Willa Brown Chappell who became the first African-American woman to earn a private pilot's license in 1938. In 1939, Willa, along with Cornelius Coffey and Enoch Waters, helped form the National Airmen's Association of America with the main goal of getting black aviation cadets into the U.S. military. The program was to train civilian pilots for use during national emergencies. She continually lobbied the government for integration of black pilots into the segregated Army Air Corps and into the federal program of Civilian Pilot Training. When Congress finally allowed the participation of blacks in the flight training program, Willa's flight school in Chicago was chosen to participate. With WWII demanding more fighter pilots and the government's agreement to establish the Tuskegee Institute, Willa's school was called upon to provide black trainees for the Tuskegee Airmen experiment.

Janet Harmon Bragg worked as a registered nurse for several years. Following her passion to fly she enrolled in the segregated black aviation school managed by Willa Chappell and Cornelius Coffey. Janet was the only woman in a class with twenty-four black men who earned her private pilot's license. She helped the school purchase its first airplane by contributing $600 of her own money, then helped build the school's private airfield in Robbins, Illinois. In 1943, Janet submitted her application to join the WASP as well as the Army Nurse Corps - her applications for both were denied because she was black. Her rejection letter was signed by Jacqueline Cochran, head of WASP. Despite the rejection and undaunted in her pursuit to fly she made her way to Tuskegee and completed the Civilian Pilot Training Program. Along with forty-one other black nurses, she worked at the Tuskegee air base hospital and happily flew when she could.

Mildred Hemmons Carter was just eighteen years old when she earned her pilot's license becoming the first black woman in the state of Alabama to do so. To pursue her love of flying, she left home for Tuskegee to become a member of the first graduating class of Tuskegee Institute's Flight School. Mildred was the first civilian to be hired by the all Negro military installation at the Tuskegee Army Air Field and convinced the base's chief flight instructor to give her more flying lessons. The flight instructor was Alfred "Chief" Anderson. One bright sunny afternoon the Chief and Mildred were out flying their Piper Cub planes. Upon landing, the Chief noticed an unusual gathering of (white) people as he taxied his plane on the tarmac. Mildred landed her plane just a few minutes later; her landing also witnessed by the gathering. That gathering was First Lady Eleanor Roosevelt and her entourage! Eleanor graciously greeted Mildred shook her hand and excitedly asked, "How's flying?"

Mildred was not assigned flying duties on the base but she was a leader in many other jobs. She used a bulldozer to clear trees and brush for a new runway then oversaw the construction to completion. Many referred to her and remember her as the "Lady Red Tail" (the Tuskegee Airmen painted the tails of their fighter planes red. The pilots were then referred to and became historically known as the "Red Tails"). Mildred later married pilot Herbert Carter, who was one of the original Red Tail Tuskegee Airmen.

The Tuskegee Air Women made history along side the Tuskegee Airmen as they supported each

other in fighting for integration and fulfilling their need to be a part of patriotic duties for the war effort. These women were assigned duties as weather observers and forecasters, cryptographers, radio operators, repairmen, sheet metal workers, parachute riggers, link trainer instructors, bombsight maintenance specialists, aerial photograph analysts, and control tower operators at the Tuskegee base. Many of the Tuskegee Air Women taught the Airmen more about flying than their flight instructors - lessons in weather, radio usage, airplane maintenance, repairs, and more. The men and women worked together as a team; they both had aviation vision and service to their country foremost in their minds as they worked hard to prove themselves to the segregated-mindfulness of America. The Tuskegee Air Women's determination and passion for aviation - to follow their dreams of flight - opened the hangar doors to the wild blue yonder for ALL women, black or white, with a desire to fly.

Although the WASP was disbanded in 1944, many of the women continued to fly. Some became airmail pilots, some barnstormers, others became flight instructors at their home town airports. Many joined the Ninety-Nines, the International Organization of Women pilots, which promoted the advancement of women in aviation through scholarships, instruction, and mutual support of women's passion for flight. Pilot Betty Gillies had been the President of the Ninety-Nines from 1939 to 1941 and had logged over 1,400 hours of flying time before she had been selected to become a WASP.

Jackie Cochran, the Speed Queen, continued her quest to establish "firsts" in aviation for women. She became the first woman to break the sound barrier at 652.337 mph; the first woman to land and take off from an aircraft carrier; the first woman to make an instrument only landing; the first woman to fly a jet aircraft across the Atlantic, and many more amazing accomplishments.

Jackie died in 1980 at the age of seventy-four with her records of speed and distance still unbroken by any pilot living or dead, man or woman. Cochran has been recognized as the most outstanding woman pilot in the world. Even in death she remains a true inspiration to women everywhere.

At the end of the war, statistics showed 350,000 women had served in the United States Armed Forces. No matter which branch the women served they were met with difficulties and problems never before encountered. Women had not been allowed in these positions prior to the war; they had to set policies and parameters in which to operate, blindly and on their own. They were also subject to ridicule from men for taking their jobs, questionable looks and stares from folks passing them on the street, even scorn from their own families. These were perhaps the biggest distractions from the duties they took very seriously.

Factory jobs in war related industries paid much more than positions in the Armed Forces. Women working in war industry factories were always discouraged from enlisting in any one of the established service branches. This took away from production capabilities. Armed Forces recruiters were often caught between a rock-and-a-hard spot when a potential recruit coming from a factory job presented herself. The recruiter needed recruits, but the war factories also needed workers. The candidate was then required to obtain a written notice from her employer stating she was released "with prejudice" or "without prejudice" to enter a service branch. If she was released with prejudice she was required to wait a period of sixty to ninety days in order to "think about it." Workers released without prejudice were usually not performing to the high factory standards and no great loss to them. Those workers may or may not have been accepted into a branch of service.

Despite the choice between the higher paying factory jobs or enlisting, the women that chose to go into the service branches were truly dedicated in their desire to serve their country.

(Author's note: Many books and memoirs about WAC, WAVES, SPAR, MCWR, and WASP discussed above are available for readers' further in depth discovery. Please refer to the bibliography at the end of this book for a sampling of what is available.)

Chapter 5

Army and Navy Nurse Corps

In early December 1941, there were less than 1,000 Army Nurses and 800 Navy nurses serving forty military hospitals and 176 dispensaries across the United States. Nurses also served in the hospitals within U.S. held territories such as Hawaii, Guam and the Philippines. Navy nurses cared for enlisted sailors, Marines, Coast Guardsmen, and their dependents. Army nurses cared for soldiers, Air Corpsmen and their dependents. With the Declaration of War it became clear that nurses were needed just as badly as soldiers. As mentioned earlier, American women in the military services were stationed in non-combat areas; however, military nurses served in or near combat zones or aboard military ships.

Of all the women's jobs serving their country in wartime, nurses had the most dangerous job of all. Nursing in wartime required courage and skill to meet challenges never experienced before. It must also be noted and credited that soldiers enlisted or were drafted, but all nurses volunteered.

Within six months after the attack on Pearl Harbor nearly 12,000 nurses joined the Army Nurse Corps and 11,000 nurses joined the Navy

Nurse Corps. This left the civilian hospitals across America tremendously understaffed. Congress quickly passed bills establishing accelerated nursing school programs that gave precedence to women interested in military nursing. Aggressive publicity and recruiting posters blanketed the U.S. encouraging young women to consider a nursing career as well as targeting retired nurses to return to hospitals, clinics, dispensaries, and office nurse duties.

As briefly mentioned earlier, a flurry of governmental enticements followed the publicity and recruiting in hopes of increasing nursing school admissions. In 1943, the U.S. Public Health Service established the Cadet Nurse Corps which recruited nursing students to work in military and civilian hospitals while they finished their studies. Free tuition, living costs, uniforms and a $15 per month stipend were offered to those accepted into the program. In return, the graduates were obligated to join either the Army or Navy Nurse Corp or work in the critical care nursing area of a civilian hospital until the end of the war plus six months. Requirements for the Cadet program included those who were age seventeen to thirty-five, high school graduate or college student (preferably in a nursing school), in good health, and mentally alert.

The American Red Cross also began recruiting efforts to train volunteers as Nurse's Aides. Upon completion of training, the Aides would work under the direction of Registered Nurses in the civilian hospital settings. Refresher courses were also offered, free of charge, to retired nurses as encouragement to return to civilian hospital duties.

Once nurses had graduated and received their Registered Nurse degree, it was their decision whether they wanted to enter into the military nurse corps or a civilian hospital. Nurses choosing military service entered as a commissioned officer after meeting the following requirements: U.S. citizen, age twenty-one to forty years old (Army) or twenty-eight to forty years old (Navy). Navy nurses were also required to be able to swim 440 yards within ten minutes, swim one mile, and tow or push a victim for 220 yards in the water. All military nurse recruits had to be specifically trained for wartime combat nursing as well as any specialty area they might be interested in. Once accepted, immediate training began.

Nurse anesthetists were in high demand and short supply. The Army developed a six month specialty training course which taught the R.N. how to administer anesthesia, oxygen therapy and to recognize, prevent, and treat shock.

Psychiatric nurses serving the military hospitals across the United States were also in high demand. They would also be in short supply when soldiers returned from war duties suffering severe cases of shell shock and/or battle fatigue (now known as Post Traumatic Stress Disorder). The Army established a twelve week program for nurses to teach them the signs of shell shock and battle fatigue along with the specific treatments and medications for the newly diagnosed psychiatric patients.

Nurses with a desire to specialize in **surgical/ operating room nursing** underwent specialized training specific to wartime needs. They learned how to set up and take down a field hospital, operating room requirements, instrument handling, and sterilization techniques, field sanitation, defense against air, chemical, and mechanical attacks. The nurses also learned map reading skills, Army regulation procedures and physical endurance. Training lasted a mere four to six weeks before teams of nurses were sent to combat zones or military hospitals - wherever the need was greatest.

Combat nursing was something none of the new R.N.s had ever experienced. Although nursing duties are basically the same anywhere, combat nursing was rarely a chapter in nursing textbooks. It took a special type of nurse to work in non-hospital situations. Military officials looked for nurses with strong stomaches, were physically fit, able to take the initiative, make quick decisions in difficult situations, and invent solutions to problems never before experienced or confronted by. Combat nurses worked twelve to fifteen hours a day and night near the front lines or in the field hospitals. It was heart wrenching for them to see such young men, some younger than eighteen years old, with such devastating wounds or to hold their hands as they died.

Since WWII was a global war, U.S. troops were sent far and wide. Casualties had to be returned to the U.S. from Europe, Africa, the Pacific, China, Burma, and other locations utilizing cargo planes for transport. The C-47, C-46, and C-54s became flying hospitals as well as cargo transporters. The military soon realized that nurses were a necessity aboard the aircraft to care for the wounded as they were transported. The **flight nurse** became a new specialty.

Nurses interested in a flight nurse position were required to have served six months in a military hospital and to have completed the Flight Nursing School which was a six to nine week course. The nurses learned to start IVs, administer oxygen, administer sedation, recognize and treat shock and hemorrhage, and handle medical emergencies in flight (prior to that time, only doctors were allowed to start IVs, start oxygen, administer IV sedation, diagnose and treat shock and hemorrhage).

Flight nurses also learned aeromedical physiology, field survival techniques, map reading, camouflage, ditching, and crash procedures as well as how to parachute from an airplane. Many of the flight nurse recruits had never flown in an airplane let alone parachute from one! Nurses had to participate in daily physical conditioning and practice simulated attack and crash scenarios.

The Army and Navy flight nurse training schools graduated 1,079 women who were promptly assigned to overseas duties. The first WWII flight nurses became pioneers in the intensive care of patients aboard aircraft. January 17, 1943 was the first aerial evacuation, in nursing history, of an Army nurse caring for five wounded patients on a flight from India to Washington, D.C.

Because cargo planes were also used to transport supplies and cargo as well as wounded soldiers, the Red Cross sign, which indicated a non-combat flight, could not be painted on the sides of the plane. The aircraft, therefore, was vulnerable to enemy fire. Later in the war, as more aircraft became available, some of the planes were designated as "medical only" transports with the bright Red Cross clearly painted on both sides.

Although there were only a little over one thousand flight nurses, their work was in high demand, hectic and highly praised. They were instrumental in urging scientists to develop better oxygen equipment for pilots, crew, and passengers flying at high altitudes. The nurses also reported the effects of flying on their wounded patients, which in turn, prompted the need for pressurized cabins in aircraft.

The large C-47 transport planes could carry up to eighteen litters of wounded who would be cared for by one or two nurses and a medical technician or corpsman during the flight. Litter patients received priority transport while walking wounded

Inside a transport plane carrying stacked
litters of wounded with flight nurse and
medical technician attending to their needs.

took space available or waited for flights
designated for them. Flight nurses carried an
evac (evacuation) kit full of supplies and
equipment that might be needed for every flight.
The kits included blood plasma, sterile saline for
reconstitution of the plasma, oxygen, morphine,
first aid medications, bandaging supplies, tape,
portable heaters, and more.

There were thirty-one air transport squadrons,
with 500 flight nurses worldwide, evacuating
1,176,000 patients by air to higher level of care
medical facilities; only forty-six patients died
en-route. In 1943 alone, the cargo planes stationed
in the Mediterranean evacuated 61,000 wounded
soldiers - all were attended by flight nurses.

Unfortunately, seventeen flight nurses were
killed while on duty in plane crashes during WWII.

General Dwight D. Eisenhower, Commander of the European Theater Operations, was very impressed with the air evacuation of the wounded and the reduction of the fatality rate of battle casualties and announced, "We evacuated almost everyone from our forward hospitals by air, and it has unquestionably saved hundreds of lives, thousands of lives."

There were four types of hospital settings in combat nursing: field, evacuation, station and general hospitals. The Army developed "chain of evacuation" procedures that began with triage at the field hospitals.

A tent city field hospital somewhere in the European theater.

Field hospitals were large, mobile tent cities close to the front lines or combat areas that usually followed the infantry. If an abandoned or bombed out building, church or school could be utilized, the field hospital was quickly set up there for business. The wounded arrived from nearby combat areas by litter (stretcher) bearers or ambulance. Doctors and nurses quickly (triaged) assessed their wounds and determined where and when the patient was to be sent. Many required immediate surgery, others were quickly stabilized

A group of field hospital nurses
awaiting next delivery of wounded.

Wounded being unloaded for
care at field hospital.

and sent on to the evacuation hospital.

Field hospitals were equipped to care for 75 to 150 patients at a time with eighteen nurses assigned to their care. The nurses also assisted with the surgeries. It was not unusual to have as many as eighty surgeries a day, depending on the severity of fighting nearby.

In nearly all cases, there was no running water or electricity. Field hospitals were clearly marked with the big Red Cross indicating medical services but stray bullets or bombs were a constant threat due to the hospital's close proximity to combat and air strike areas.

Evacuation from field hospitals was via ambulance, train, ship, or airplane. At each hospital setting, specific nurses were assigned evac duties. They would receive a report on each patient from the field hospital nurse including the assessment for further care needed.

Trains could usually accommodate larger numbers of patients - both litter and ambulatory. One train car might have thirty-two beds for litter patients with one nurse assigned to each car; ambulatory patients could occupy several cars and have just one nurse watching over them.

Evacuation by airplane could be accomplished with patients loaded and airborne within ten minutes. One nurse and one medical corpsman were usually assigned to each aircraft.

From the field hospital, most of the wounded, depending on their condition and immediate needs, were sent to an evacuation hospital.

Evacuation hospitals were also mobile but further from the fighting and a bit more secure. Evac hospitals were able to handle larger numbers of wounded (some could care for up to 750

Evacuation hospital somewhere in France.

patients at once) and those in need of surgery not done at the field hospital. Fifty-three nurses were assigned to each evac hospital. Casualties were treated and either sent back to the states for more intensive care and therapy, sent on to a station hospital, or returned to duty after a short recovery.

When the concentration and POW camps were liberated across Germany, it was the evac hospital teams that moved in quickly and began treating the survivors. When the huge camp at Buchenwald was liberated, the Army's 120th Evacuation Hospital moved into the nearby city of Weimar. The staff of 273 doctors, nurses, medics, ambulance drivers, and enlisted men treated over 3,000 captives and prisoners of war suffering from starvation, dehydration, typhus, dysentery, tuberculosis, infections, and infestations of lice.

Station hospitals were in semi-permanent locations further from the front lines and usually in friendly territory. They may have been located in abandoned buildings, or even a once utilized hospital in the area. Most had running water and sometimes power. Although the water was usually

Train station where ambulances delivered wounded
soldiers from the station hospitals. First stop on
their way back to the U.S. for further care.

contaminated, the nurses boiled large buckets full
constantly for use in washing and sterilizing
instruments and hygiene needs.

Casualties arrived via military ambulances or
aircraft transports from the evac hospitals to
receive further surgery, specialized treatments,
wound care and more. When patients were ready
for long distance travel back to the states, they
were transported via convoys of ambulances to
nearby train stations then on to airports or ships
bound for the U.S.

Station hospitals, stateside, were scattered
across the United States and provided continued
care of the wounded from around the world. They
also treated local community civilians and military
dependents suffering from minor infections,
injuries, minor surgical procedures, and childbirth.

General (military) hospitals were located furthest from the front lines and combat zones in more permanent locations as well as stateside; these facilities served military wounded and sick. Because these hospitals had the necessary equipment, they provided more specialized care to the patients. The major cases treated at general hospitals included orthopedic care, plastic surgery for repair of amputations and facial disfigurements, wounds and burns, thoracic care for chest wounds, and neurological care for head and spine trauma, as well as evaluation for shell shock.

Convalescent centers (now known as rehabilitation hospitals) were not considered combat nursing facilities. Many were located within the United States beginning in late 1943. Servicemen and women were transferred to these centers to receive long-term care for their injuries and illnesses. Placement was made with some consideration of the servicemen's proximity to their families, if possible. It quickly became apparent that psychiatric nurses were desperately needed in these facilities to assess and treat the servicemen suffering from shell shock and battle fatigue.

Shortly after Pearl Harbor, the government, expecting a large flow of casualties returning home for care, authorized the construction of military hospitals across the U.S. To hasten efforts, the military converted large abandoned buildings and warehouses to fit and fill the needs as a hospital.

The conversions did not always meet the cleanliness and sanitation needs for a hospital since most abandoned buildings were infested with vermin and insects that did not want to be disturbed. Nurses often spent more time killing rats than caring for their patients.

Medical personnel credited three drugs with saving thousands of lives during the war: sulfa, penicillin and atabrine. **Sulfa** powder, an antibiotic used to control bacterial infections, was issued to every soldier in his first aid pouch which was carried on the waist belt. Soldiers were instructed to sprinkle the powder on any open wound and cover with a bandage. The sulfa powder helped prevent the start of infection until the wounded soldier could be treated properly at a field hospital.

Penicillin, also an antibiotic, was not as readily available as sulfa at the beginning of the war. The pharmaceutical companies were pushed by the government to produce the massive quantities needed for the war effort; they were able to develop new techniques that improved quality and increased production which ultimately saved thousands of soldiers lives.

Atabrine, a synthetic quinine, was used to treat malaria which plagued thousands of soldiers fighting in the South Pacific islands and other jungle-like areas. The soldiers did not like taking the large yellow pills because they were very bitter, caused headaches, nausea, vomiting, and turned the skin a deep yellow color. The alternative, suffering from malaria, was just as unpleasant. DDT was used to kill mosquitos that caused malaria, as well as infestations of lice. If supplies were available, the nurses would spray the DDT directly on the soldiers and around the camps. The Atabrine tablets proved a much better treatment, as DDT later proved extremely hazardous to health and the environment.

Morphine was also extensively used by medics in the field and nurses in the hospitals, for relief of pain. The syrette, used by medics, was a tiny self- contained device about an inch long 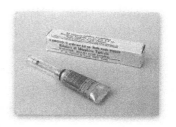 with a needle and tiny pouch containing the morphine. The medic would break the seal and pierce the wounded soldier in a fleshy, exposed area of the body (upper arm, thigh or stomach) and squeeze the liquid morphine through the needle into the soldier. In an effort to avoid an overdose, the medic pinned the syrette to the soldier's collar as a way of letting the field hospital nurses know the wounded soldier had been medicated. The morphine, combined with extreme fatigue, quickly rendered the wounded soldier unconscious.

Nurses and physicians in the field and evac hospitals began noticing strange signs and symptoms experienced by incoming wounded with the morphine syrette attached to their collars. The dose in the tiny syrette was 30 milligrams of morphine (quite a large dose by today's standards). Morphine causes respiratory depression and other dangerous side effects. The question posed by the nurses and physicians in the field was, "Were the wounded dying from their wounds or from morphine overdoses caused by respiratory arrest?"

Finally in 1943, after extensive studies on the effects of morphine dosing of the combat wounded, the Chief Surgeon of the North African Theater of Operations established new guidelines for administration. All nurses and medical personnel were quickly educated: no more than 15 mg., or half of the syrette dose, was to be administered at one time. Injections were not to be given to patients in shock or with wounds to the chest. Smaller amounts (less than 15 mg.) were given to patients being transported by air. Other guidelines for morphine administration were later established and utilized throughout the Army's vast number of medical units.

Blood and **blood plasma** also saved thousands of lives in the field hospitals, the evac hospitals and the station hospitals. Whole blood is not easily stored in wartime conditions and quickly deteriorates in a few days. Blood plasma is the liquid portion of whole blood which provides the volume necessary to carry the red and white blood

cells and platelets. Volume keeps the blood
pressure stable, especially when a patient is losing
large amounts of blood from a wound(s). When
the plasma is separated from the blood cells, it has
a much longer shelf life. It can also be dried and

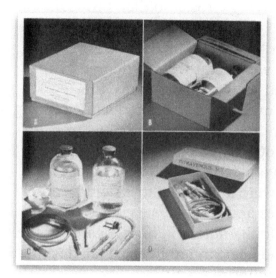

A packaged kit
of dried
plasma, sterile
saline and intra-
venous access
equipment for
administration
of plasma.

shipped to the front lines for reconstitution and
administration. Nurses reconstitute the plasma
with sterile saline and administer via intravenous
infusion as rapidly as possible. By the end of the
war, the American Red Cross had collected over 13
million units (a unit is about one pint) of blood and
converted nearly all of it to plasma.

At the end of the war, the statistics for the
medical accomplishments were amazing. More
than 60,000 Army nurses served stateside, overseas
and as flight nurses. More than 14,000 Navy

nurses served stateside, overseas on hospital ships and as flight nurses. Combined, Army and Navy nurses received nearly 2,000 medals, citations, commendations and service awards including the Distinguished Service Medal, Silver Star, Distinguished Flying Cross, Soldier's Medal, Bronze Star, Air Medal, Legion of Merit, Army Commendation Medal and the Purple Heart; sixteen medals were awarded posthumously to nurses who died as a result of enemy fire. Unfortunately, over 200 nurses died while serving during the war.

Nurses and other medical personnel treated over 670,000 wounded. Over 96% of those wounded who were able to get to a field hospital staffed by nurses and doctors, survived. General Eisenhower held the nurses in high regard for the tireless work they performed in less than desirable conditions by stating,

> *Any words by me would be inadequate to pay proper tribute to the American nurses and to the work that they are doing here and elsewhere. From Bataan to Normandy, the contributions of American women serving as nurses in our Army have spoken for themselves. One needs only to talk with the wounded or witness our nurses at work in the field and*

*in hospitals to realize that they are
taking their places alongside the
greatest women in the history of
our country. Nothing stops them
in their determination to see that our
troops receive the best attention
humanely possible.*

Chapter 6

The Battling Belles of Bataan
Bataan and Corregidor, Philippines

While the Japanese were attacking Pearl Harbor, they simultaneously attacked the Philippines, Guam, Wake Island, and Midway Island. Because these targets are on the Asian side of the International Date Line, history records the attacks as occurring on December 8, 1941.

Military medics, doctors, eighty-eight Army nurses, and twelve Navy nurses were assigned duty at Sternberg General Hospital in Manila, Philippines; other nurses were assigned to several smaller hospitals in outlying areas. At that time, Sternberg was utilized as a military hospital but also served the locals. Military personnel considered the Philippines a plumb assignment - a tropical paradise with golf, swimming, polo, and other off-duty activities.

At 0819 hours (8:19 A.M.), Japanese bombs were dropped over large areas of the Philippines. All military airbases were attacked, which destroyed all but one plane. The attack left thousands dead or wounded and quickly overwhelmed all the hospitals. The majority of injuries consisted of extensive trauma from amputations, burns, and shrapnel wounds. Medical teams worked day and night performing surgeries, administering blood, plasma, dressing wounds, and relieving pain with morphine. Bombing was relentless as it spread into civilian suburbs thereby increasing the number of wounded seeking treatment at the hospitals.

When Japanese soldiers began invading the island, General MacArthur ordered all U.S. military personnel to retreat to the Bataan Peninsula and Corregidor. Under cover of darkness the last week in December, Army nurses began loading as many wounded military patients, in groups of twenty, as they could aboard a makeshift hospital ship and fled to Bataan. The perilous journey across the bay encountered heavy Japanese fire while the small ship's captain zigzagged the vessel to avoid being hit. Other nurses escaped on open flatbed trucks as artillery fire flew overhead. By New Year's Eve all eighty-eight Army nurses had been evacuated from Manila. The nurses were the first American military nurses sent directly onto the battlefield while on duty.

Twelve Navy nurses remained in Manila to care for the seriously wounded who would not have survived the move. All of the Navy nurses were immediately captured by the Japanese when they took control of Manila. The captives were then taken to the Santo Tomas Internment Camp and became the first American military nurses to be held as prisoners-of-war.

The Peninsula of Bataan extends out from the mainland into the South China Sea and forms Manila Bay. Bataan is covered by dense tropical forest, deep ravines and the foothills of two extinct volcanoes. It is inhabited by millions of malarial carrying mosquitoes breeding in many swampy areas, various snakes, large rats, billions of ants, and other strange insects all living in a sweltering, humid jungle.

As the nurses arrived in Bataan, dazed and exhausted, imagine their thoughts as they gazed at a large clearing in the midst of the jungle. One nurse surveyed the site and asked incredulously, "This is a hospital?" It was quite literally a "field hospital" in the truest sense of the term. The nurses got right to work and established Hospital #1 and Hospital #2. Twenty-nine bamboo and grass sheds were home to Hospital #1 which served as the surgical center. A fifty-kilowatt generator powered by a diesel motor pumped water and provided electricity.

Hospital #2 was simply row upon row of cots in the open air of the dense jungle where the wounded were to recover. These were the first open air hospital wards utilized in U.S. history since the Civil War. The nurses cared for up to 1,000 patients at a time in the open air wards. Over four months, more than 6,000 patients were treated at Bataan by the eighty-eight American nurses along with a handful of Filipino nurses.

The Japanese soon learned that the peninsula was harboring a makeshift hospital and proceeded to bomb and strafe it as often as they could. Bullets and shrapnel whizzed by the medical staff on a daily basis. One nurse was hit and wounded by flying shrapnel but patched herself up and continued to work. Frightened patients that could move quickly often ducked under their flimsy cots which did little to protect them from bombs or burning shrapnel.

The nurses and their military superiors quickly realized that starchy white long dress uniforms and white shoes were not practical in the 104 degree jungle heat or as they crawled along the damp jungle floor to care for their patients lying on low level cots or mats. They were issued two pairs of standard Army olive drab coveralls and a pair of boots - in men's sizes! Scissors, thread and safety pins fixed the size problems. These nurses became the first military women to wear "fatigues" (field uniforms) while on duty.

Nurses and their patients battled jungle diseases as fiercely as they battled the Japanese. Malaria overcame almost everyone. Dengue fever, dysentery, worms, skin fungus, and lice infestations were common. Flies were everywhere contaminating whatever they landed on. Food and water were contaminated with parasites. Medical supplies dwindled and food rations were cut twice.

In early April, it was reported that Japanese soldiers were advancing just miles from the jungle hospital compound. On April 8, 1942 the new commander of the U.S. Army in the Philippines ordered all the military nurses to immediately evacuate to the island of Corregidor; they were to stop what they were doing at that very moment, gather their belongings and report to the boats for transport. The nurses were furious and vocal - in good conscience they could not abandon the thousands of sick, wounded and helpless in the midst of the jungle. Because military orders were to be followed without question the nurses reluctantly obeyed and reported to the boats. Many of them were heartsick about leaving their patients and carried the guilt for years to come.

(Author's note: When the Japanese captured the hospital site, the wounded and sick American and Filipino soldiers were taken as prisoners-of-war. Approximately 8,800 soldiers were force-marched sixty miles through the rugged, steamy jungle to Japanese POW camps. Soldiers caught trying to escape or who succumbed from lack of food, water, exhaustion, dysentery or infected wounds were tortured, shot, beheaded, eviscerated or simply left beside the jungle path to die. The number of deaths varies by report; however, most agree that over 2,500 Filipino and 650 American soldiers died along the way. Many were able to escape into the jungle while others died when they reached the

*camps. History records this as the **Bataan Death March**.)*

Corregidor is a tiny island of rock at the tip of the Bataan Peninsula. In 1922, the U.S. Army Corps of Engineers built the secret Malinta Tunnel deep within the rock as a bomb proof storage and personnel bunker; it took ten years to complete the massive underground fortress. Ammunition, food and medical supplies were stored throughout the complex labyrinth of tunnels as well as a fully equipped thousand-bed hospital wing. The tunnel was self-sufficient with its own water and power supply. It was also the last stand for the Americans against the Japanese taking the Philippines. For some time the Japanese were unaware of the tunnel but were aware that Filipino and American soldiers still protected the island.

The eighty-eight nurses were anxious about being evacuated from the jungle site and bitter over leaving their patients. They did not say a word to each other as they made their way toward their new assignment. The boats they were in shook and rocked in the rough water as they crossed to Corregidor watching all the while for mines floating in the water, dodging sniper fire, and explosions.

Upon arrival inside the tunnel, the nurses were relieved to see they would have a roof over their heads, fresh water, and lights, no ants, snakes or iguanas crawling in their beds. And food! Nursing

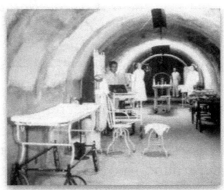

One of the hospital wings in the
Malinta tunnel.

duties were quickly assigned as the wounded were transported into the tunnels. Surgery was performed in a clean area and patients had a real bed, not a cot or grass mat. Several of the nurses were still trying to recover from malaria and dysentery, but with fresh water, food and medicine they regained their strength enough to begin working again.

Meanwhile, the war raged on outside the tunnel as the Japanese continued to fight for the complete takeover of the Philippines. Bombs shook the tunnels stirring clouds of dust with nowhere to go. When a gasoline dump was hit by artillery fire, smoke entered some of the tunnel air vents causing respiratory difficulties for many already compromised.

During the last week of April the military command received word that two PBY (Patrol Bomber) seaplanes would attempt to slip past the

Japanese and deliver supplies to the beleaguered Americans on Corregidor. Military dependents and several of MacArthur's staff were to be taken aboard the returning aircraft. Twenty nurses were also selected to go based on the following criteria: older nurses in their forties and early fifties showing signs of duress with the war circumstances, several who were seriously ill with malaria or tropical diseases, several who were wounded at Bataan and suffering wound infections. Under cover of darkness and close to midnight, the two PBYs lifted effortlessly off the water and flew their passengers to safety.

A few days later a U.S. submarine was to approach the island and take another group to safety. A couple of elderly military colonels, six Naval officers, and thirteen more nurses were chosen to go, leaving fifty-five of the original eighty-eight. One of the nurses had lost nearly seventy pounds and was showing signs of beriberi and malnutrition.

The beleaguered group climbed aboard a converted yacht and motored out into the dark sea. They were to rendezvous with the submarine at a point four miles out from the island. They waited anxiously, ever fearful of being discovered by the Japanese. Silently, a massive dark form lifted out of the water - it was the submarine. A series of blinking lights signaled the yacht captain to approach the vessel and transfer the passengers.

Once aboard and secure, the submarine slipped underwater and took another group to safety.

There were now fifty-five American military nurses and twenty-six Filipino nurses tending over a thousand patients in the tunnel. Capture by the Japanese was inevitable. Although the nurses had never been educated on capture protocol, they began establishing guidelines for themselves:

1. Wear your khaki uniforms at all times and carry your gas mask.
2. Wear your Red Cross armbands on your sleeves at all times.
3. Do not wander in the tunnels alone for any reason.

The Red Cross was the universal symbol for noncombatants under the Geneva Convention; however, Japan did not sign, nor follow the guidelines and consequently tortured and killed thousands of POWs and civilians.

On May 6, 1942 United States General Wainwright surrendered Corregidor to Japanese General Homma. Japanese soldiers began filtering into the tunnel ordering the Americans to line up at attention. The Filipino nurses were frightened and quivering while the American nurses, also frightened, stood at attention, stern faced. The

Japanese soldiers seemed confused when they saw the American women in military uniforms and sporting the Red Cross armband; they weren't sure what to do with them.

One of the Japanese soldiers spoke perfect English and ordered ten of the nurses to step outside the main entrance to the tunnel for a photo. The nurses did not trust the soldier and feared he was going to shoot them. He assured them he just wanted a photo of them in front of the tunnel for his superiors. The photo would then be sent to General MacArthur to assure him the nurses were alive and being well cared for after the Japanese overtook the tunnel (many civilians and military personnel felt General MacArthur was hiding from his Pacific theater duties during this time. He had fled the Philippines earlier and stationed himself in Australia).

Seven thousand American and five thousand Filipino soldiers were taken prisoner by the Japanese from Corregidor. The nurses, doctors and corpsmen were ordered to stay in the tunnel hospital areas and treat the wounded. As soon as the wounded were able to walk, they were removed from the hospital by Japanese soldiers and taken to perform hard manual labor in various locations on the island. The wounded soldiers were given no food or water and due to their injuries, were tortured and died when they were unable to do the work.

On July 2, 1942 the Japanese notified the hospital staff to prepare for new arrangements. All sick and wounded men and all male medical staff were being transported by freighter to Manila that afternoon. The next day, all the nurses would be transported to Manila also by freighter. Once again, the nurses were being taken away from their patients. Because they did not trust their Japanese captors, they quietly followed orders and climbed aboard the ship.

Santo Tomas University before the Japanese captured it for use as an internment camp.

The Santo Tomas University was a beautiful sixty-acre Dominican academy in the center of Manila surrounded by a twelve-foot

The University after becoming an internment camp. Note the shanties which housed the POWs in this area.

concrete and stone wall. When the bombing of Manila began, six thousand students and three-hundred faculty members fled the campus. When the Japanese took Manila, barbed wire was strung along the containment walls and the Santo Tomas Internment Camp began receiving prisoners of war. The Santo Tomas Internment Camp housed thousands of foreign civilians who had been living and working in Manila or outlying areas prior to the takeover. Many of the 4,000 detainees were professionals, business men and women, shop and store owners, as well as their dependents including hundreds of children under eighteen years of age.

The fifty-five nurses from Corregidor were taken to Santo Tomas July 3, 1942. The Camp was under the jurisdiction and control of the Japanese Bureau of External Affairs while the military POW camps were under the control of the brutal Japanese Imperial Army.

The nurses quickly integrated into camp life but continued to be upset about losing their patients and wondered where they had been taken. Over time, they established a make shift medical facility to treat their fellow prisoners. Food was rationed but the internees could buy fresh fruit, vegetables, and bread from Filipino residents on the outside. They planted a vegetable garden in an unused corner of the compound and shared the harvests with those not able to purchase from the outsiders.

As conditions became too overcrowded, the Japanese singled out 800 men, including one of the doctors, and the eleven Navy nurses initially captured. The doctor had been in Manila for a conference when the fighting began and was captured by the Japanese when the city was overtaken. This group was transported to the Los Banos Internment Camp. The Japanese captors ordered the doctor and nurses to establish a makeshift hospital and treat the 2,000 military prisoners being held there. Conditions at this internment camp were fierce and barbaric. The detainees, most wounded and ill transfers from Corregidor, were routinely beaten and tortured by the Japanese. The eleven nurses did what they could to treat their patients only to see them brutally beaten for minor infractions, many succumbing, and dying as a result. There were no medical supplies, very little food and water - all of which was contaminated. The nurses became known as the "sacred eleven" for the work they accomplished under such extreme conditions in the camp.

Monsoons dumped heavy rain on the camps creating in-humane conditions, increased diseases, and death among the detainees. The stench was overwhelming in the hot humid environment with poor sanitation and corpses piled high in a corner of the Santo Tomas compound awaiting burial. The Japanese expected the young teenage male POWs to dig large deep holes for mass burial of the dead. Many of the boys were sick with dysentery, measles, or jungle rot, and had very little strength. The Japanese whipped and beat the boys until the nurses intervened with threats of their own.

Despite the horrific conditions, the nurses did the best they could with what was available. There were no more medical supplies or medicines so they experimented with remedies to alleviate the suffering. They made a cough syrup from onion juice and sugar for those suffering from whooping cough; a tea from guava leaves for dysentery, and an elixir from mango leaves for elevated blood pressure and diabetes (this failed). A sticky paste was made from rubber tree sap and oil as an alternative to adhesive tape for securing makeshift bandages that were often torn pieces of clothing instead of sterile gauze. Coca-Cola and beer bottles found in student garbage left behind were made into drinking glasses. Straws were made from reeds and mosquito netting was made from material found in banana fiber. Hemp was used for sutures.

In 1944, the Japanese Imperial Army took control over the Santo Tomas Camp. Living conditions went from bad to unbelievably cruel. Food rations were cut frequently. Access to outside food assistance was cut off. Rare Red Cross relief packages for POWs were plundered of any food stuffs before being given to the prisoners. Contaminated water, when it was even available, had to be boiled. The nurses boiled weeds, flowers and roots for flavored hot water disguised as soup.

An early curfew was established that prevented prisoners from congregating in the evenings. The nurses also suffered along with their fellow prisoners. Many were sick with dysentery, tuber-culosis and jungle infections from the damp humid conditions.

By January 1945, food rations had been cut to 700 calories a day which barely sustained life. Lack of nutrition caused up to five deaths per day from starvation; malnutrition caused beriberi, scurvy, and further weakened immune systems. Measles, chickenpox, whooping cough, diphtheria, and tuberculosis were at epidemic proportions. Everyone had dysentery from the contaminated water and lack of sanitation. Jungle rot (a bacterial infection in tropical climates), afflicted the majority of detainees, especially the elderly. One of the nurses was critically ill with hepatitis after suffering earlier from malaria. All of the nurses lost nearly 30% of their body weight; one nurse lost 80 pounds. They were all sick, weary, fearful, and doubting they would ever be rescued.

Finally on the morning of February 3, 1945, after 36 months in captivity, American tanks from the 44th Tank Battalion rolled through the barricaded gates at Santo Tomas. One of the soldiers popped up from his tank and shouted, "Hello folks!" The POWs went crazy with gratitude and began joyfully singing "God Bless America" as loud as their frail bodies and parched throats could muster. Soldiers gave all of their K-rations to the starving survivors. Several American soldiers had been wounded in the takeover and six had been killed. The nurses went right to work treating the wounded with the supplies the soldiers carried with them. The next day more soldiers, equipment and food supplies arrived as well as more wounded. American soldiers were injured from continued fighting and sporadic gunfire. The Japanese were not going to give up easily.

The Battling Belles of Bataan aboard a transport truck after being rescued from Japanese POW camps in the Philippines.

When the Japanese realized the Americans were quickly advancing toward Manila, they had planned to execute all the prisoners, nurses, and children at Santo Tomas the morning of February 3rd. Luckily, the Americans got there first.

Six days later, on February 9, one hundred Army nurses arrived from the states to relieve their colleagues. Imagine what they thought at the sight of the starving, sickly nurses. The Battling Belles of Bataan had fought their last battle and were finally going home!

A daring raid, under cover of darkness, on the Los Banos camp by U.S. Army Airborne troops and Filipino guerrilla forces liberated the Navy nurses and over 2,000 prisoners on February 22,

1945. The disabled, wounded, women and children were quickly directed to the Amtrac vehicles (amphibious warfare vehicles) for evacuation. Those able to walk, hiked the short distance to the beach and final freedom from their Japanese captors. The American troops then set fire to the camps as Japanese gunfire was heard close by.

The nurses POW survival record of 100% is unmatched to this day.

When the nurses finally arrived back in the States, they were met with celebrations, ceremonies, parades, gifts, press interviews, and awards. Many were still extremely ill but were buoyed by the enthusiasm surrounding them. The military promoted each of the nurses up a rank, awarded them a Bronze Star, and a Presidential Unit Citation for extraordinary heroism in action. The two wounded nurses also received the Purple Heart.

The nurses, as a whole, were recognized as the first large group of American women in combat as well as the largest group of American women taken captive and imprisoned by an enemy.

The government used their story as a recruiting tool to enlist more women in the nurse corps and strongly encouraged the nurses to speak to groups across the nation to promote military nursing. Several of the nurses remained acutely ill for some time as a result of the diseases from malnutrition and starvation as well as the residual problems from malaria, hepatitis and various tropical diseases. They lost their teeth, hair and suffered skin problems as a result of beriberi. Chronic gastrointestinal problems and post traumatic stress symptoms followed them until their early deaths.

The government, for which each of these nurses gave of themselves, never followed up on their resultant health problems or care: recurrent skin problems and infections, loss of teeth, infertility, cancer, heart disease, post traumatic stress difficulties, or the causes of their early deaths. Many of the nurses were denied VA benefits.

As the government's demands on their time for recruiting efforts, and with the end of war in sight, these nurses were all but forgotten. Some continued to work in military hospitals, some married and left the military, most of them quietly slipped from the eyes of the public and history.

All of these nurses were true American heroes, in every sense of the word, and should never be forgotten.

A bronze plaque was placed in their honor on the Bataan Peninsula that states:

TO THE ANGELS - *In honor of the valiant American military women who gave so much of themselves in the early days of World War II. They provided care and comfort to the gallant defenders of Bataan and Corregidor. They lived on a starvation diet, shared the bombing, strafing, sniping, sickness, and disease while working endless hours of heartbreaking duty. These nurses always had a smile, a tender touch and a kind word for their patients. They truly earned the name - THE ANGELS OF BATAAN AND CORREGIDOR.*

The Angels of Bataan and Corregidor

Navy Nurse Corps POWs

Bernatitus, Ann
Cobb, Laura - Chief nurse
Chapman, Mary
Evans, Bertha
Gorzelanski, Helen
Harrington, Mary Rose
Nash, Margaret
O'Haver, Goldia
Paige, Eldene
Pitcher, Susie
Still, Dorothy
Todd, Edwina

Army Nurse Corps POWs

Aasen, Mina
Allen, Earleen
Anschicks, Louise
Arnold, Phyllis
Barre, Agnes

Bickford, Clara Mae
Black, Earlyn
Blaine, Ethel
Bradley, Ruby
Brantley, Hattie
Breese, Minnie
Burris, Myra
Cassiani, Helen
Chambers, Beatrice
Corns, Edith
Dalton, Mildred
Davison, Maude
Dollason, Kathyrn
Durrett, Sallie
Dworsky, Bertha
Easterling, Dorcas
Eckman, Magdalena
Fails, Eula
Foreman, Adele
Gardner, Helen
Garen, Eleanor
Gates, Marcia
Greenwalt, Beulah
Hahn, Alice
Hennessey, Helen
Henshaw, Gwendolyn
Henson, Verna
Hogan, Rosemary
Jenkins, Geneva
Kehoe, Doris
Kennedy, Imogene

Kimball, Blanche
Lee, Eleanor
Lewey, Frankie
Ludlow, Dorothy
McDonald, Inez
McHale, Letha
Madden, Winifred
Mealor, Gladys
Menzie, Mary
Meyer, Adolpha
Mueller, Clara
Nash, Frances
Nesbit, Josephine
Oberst, Mary
O'Neill, Eleanor
Palmer, Rita
Putnam, Beulah
Reppak, Mary
Rieper, Rose
Scholl, Dorothy
Shacklette, Edith
Stoltz, Ruth
Thor, Ethel
Ullom, Madeline
Whitlow, Evelyn
Williams, Anna
Wimberly, Edith
Wurts, Anne
Young, Eunice
Zwicker, Alice

Army Nurses evacuated from Corregidor 1942

Acorn, Catherine
Daley, Dorothea
Fellmuth, Floramund
Gastinger, Leona
Gallagher, Susan
Gillahan, Nancy
Hallman, Grace
Hatchitt, Eunice
Hook, Willa
Jenkins, Ressa
Lee, Harriet
Lohr, Mary
MacDonald, Florence
McKay, Hortense
Moultrie, Mary
Peterson, Mollie
Redmond, Juanita
Stevens, Mabe
Straub, Ruth
Summers, Helen
Veley, Beth
Wilson, Lucy

Chapter 7

Long-Held Secrets

Although WWII ended nearly seventy years ago, many stories have just recently become public. This may be due to the fact men and women of that era have now begun telling their families of their wartime experiences. Many, on their death beds, have revealed startling facts about their wartime activities and missions. At the time, they were ordered by their superiors not to reveal specific details for fear of further casualties among fellow military personnel and/or civilians. Two of those long held secrets have recently come to light with further first hand recollections of those involved:

The newly formed 807th Medical Air Evacuation Transport Squadron based in Catania, Sicily flew frequent missions to southern Italy. The C-53D Skytrooper transport planes, lovingly referred to as Gooney Birds, carried soldiers and equipment to different locations. When the mission was to return sick and wounded to hospitals in Sicily or North Africa, American flight nurses and medics flew with the transports.

The 807th had safely flown 1,651 patients to a variety of hospitals around the Mediterranean in October, 1943. The early days of November brought poor flying conditions which grounded all evac flights, creating a back-log of patients needing transport from Bari and Grottaglie. The base commander assigned thirteen flight nurses and thirteen medics to the transport plane's pilot, co-pilot, radio operator, and crew chief with orders to fly to Bari and begin transporting the awaiting patients. The commander had never assigned that many medical personnel to one flight, but he rationalized that the need of the sick and wounded soldiers outweighed the risks.

On the morning of November 8, 1943 the medical team and airplane crew climbed aboard their Gooney Bird and lifted off into the cloudless,

blue sky headed for Bari. Suddenly, and without previous reports of bad weather approaching, visibility was severely hampered when storm clouds quickly gathered and enveloped the plane. The pilot ascended above the clouds and noted the wings were icing, so he dropped back down into the clouds. The storm became more and more violent as strong winds pushed the aircraft way off course. The compass became unreliable, the radio was not functioning, and the flight crew became disoriented.

In an attempt to determine their location, the pilot, once again, descended. He spotted an abandoned airfield and advised the crew he would attempt an emergency landing. As he made his approach to the airfield, shots rang out from below striking the aircraft's tail. The pilot quickly changed his mind about that particular landing site and pushed the plane to climb out of the area as fast as it would go; the airfield was obviously held by the Germans.

Within moments the Gooney Bird was being pursued by a German fighter plane. The transport plane was not equipped with any fire power nor was it marked with the Red Cross insignia indicating non-combat, medical team. The situation became critical as the German plane advanced rapidly toward the Gooney Bird. It was up to the pilot to take evasive action with flight maneuvers in an attempt to get the plane down safely.

With the German fighter plane now lost in the clouds, the pilot spotted a long patch of ground next to a lake and alerted his passengers to prepare for a crash landing. The nurses and medics tightened their seat belts and assumed the crash position. As the plane touched the soft ground the landing gear immediately sank in the mud. This caused the plane to come to a violent stop which in turn caused equipment and the flight crew chief to be catapulted through the cargo area. The crew chief sustained a serious injury to his knee. Several medics sustained moderate injuries when they were struck by flying material. The nurses quickly unbuckled themselves, gathered their evac bags and began to assist the injured out of and away from the plane. They had no idea where they were but assumed they were in enemy territory based on the earlier gun fire and pursuit.

The area was surrounded by thick forest and tall mountains. Without warning, a large band of men with menacing looks and carrying rifles came out of the forest. When they saw the large gathering of uniformed nurses, one of the men stepped forward and asked if the group was British. The copilot announced they were Americans. The tension from the group was immediately reduced as their leader began speaking to the Americans in broken English. The storm's high winds had tossed the plane into Albania which the Germans had been invading since September.

As the nurses huddled together with the medics, the crew explained their circumstances: they were on a mission to transport wounded American soldiers to hospitals, encountered a vicious storm, were blown off course, fired upon, and chased by

Germans. The plane was destroyed and the team needed help.

Thus began an agonizing journey for the nurses, injured medics, and flight crew through snow covered mountains and villages of desperately poor and starving inhabitants. The nurses had a calming affect on the villagers and frequently rendered medical aid to them. In turn, the villagers hid them from the Germans at night and shared what little food they had.

The nurses, medics and flight crew were ill prepared for winter weather or a six hundred mile hike over rugged mountain passes. Their shoes quickly fell apart and their clothing did little to keep them warm. Sympathetic villagers gave them blankets and a warm fire to sleep next to at night. Food was scarce for everyone, but they shared what little they had with the American strangers.

As the nurses trudged along in the worst of conditions, they continued to think and act like nurses - never giving up, taking care of one another, and looking out for the health and well-being of their teammates. Even though they were exhausted, hungry, cold to the bone, most suffering dysentery, infected wounds, and lice, they plodded on.

One night, while sheltering in a small village, it was attacked by German soldiers. Three of the nurses were separated from the group as the others managed to escape and continue on their journey.

In the meantime, the U.S. Army began search efforts for the missing plane and crew. With little information or any field reports of wreckage, the search seemed futile and doomed. Telegrams were sent to the families of those on board notifying them their family member was declared "missing."

In late November, word regarding the missing American nurses, medic team and crew from native partisans reached British agents operating in Albania. The information they received was that local guides were leading the large group through the mountains to the coast. They were moving slowly in poor weather with sick and injured members and trying to evade the Germans. Once they reached the coast they would need assistance returning to Italy. The British agents began to formulate a plan.

November passed into December as the group continued on. They traipsed through blizzards and freezing rain often taking shelter in caves when villages could not be reached. An airlift rescue had been arranged by a British agent with details sent to the Albanian guides. The rescue attempt failed, thwarted by German troops in the area firing upon the aircraft as it attempted to land. The dis-heartened group pushed on toward the coast.

Finally, on January 9, 1945 the haggard and weary group rejoiced at the site and smell of the Adriatic sea. Aided by the continued efforts of the British agents and guided by their patriotic Albanian sympathizers, the bedraggled group

Rescued American
nurses showing their
worn shoes after the
600 mile trek
through Albania.

climbed aboard the armed rescue boat and headed
toward their original destination - Bari. After
recovering in the Bari hospital, most of the group
returned to their home base in Catania.

Ten of the thirteen American nurses recovering in Bari,
Italy after their two month ordeal escaping from German
occupied Albania.

The other three nurses did not reach safety until
the middle of March, over four months after their

112

plane crashed. Thanks to the Albanian villagers and help from the British agents, the nurses were smuggled out of the country dressed as peasant women with forged documents.

All of the nurses, medics and flight crew were under very strict Army orders not to divulge any of their ordeal to the press, family or friends. They were also discouraged from talking about it among themselves. The reason for the Army's strict orders was to protect the Albanian guides and villagers from the Germans. The Army released press details that the group had been rescued but gave very little specific information. Unfortunately, information eventually found its way to the Germans with terrible consequences. Several villagers who had been instrumental in assisting the Americans were imprisoned, tortured and executed for aiding the enemy.

After their recovery, some of the nurses took leave and went home to their families for a short visit and rest. Many of the nurses returned to nursing duties at home or abroad. A couple of the women returned to the U.S. and became nursing instructors.

Americans Traversing Albania 1943-1944

Flight Crew

Pilot, Charles Thrasher
Co-pilot, James Baggs
Crew chief, Willis Shumway
Radioman, Richard Lebo

Army Flight Nurses

Gertrude Dawson
Agnes Jensen
Pauleen Kanable
Ann Kopsco
Wilma Lytle
Ann Maness
Ann Markowitz
Frances Nelson
Helen Porter
Eugenie Rutkowski
Elna Schwant
Lillian Tacina
Lois Watson

Medics

Lawrence Abbott
Charles Adams
Paul Allen
Robert Cranson

Medics (continued)

James Cruise
Raymond Ebers
William Eldridge
Gilbert Hornsby
Harold Hayes
Gordon MacKinnon
Robert Owen
John Wolf
Charles Zebec

Lieutenant Reba Whittle
was an Army Nurse Corps
flight nurse with the 813th
Medical Air Evacuation
Squadron serving in Europe.
In September, 1944, she was
aboard a C-47 aircraft flying
from England to St. Trond,
Belgium delivering supplies

and picking up casualties when her plane veered
slightly off course and was shot down just outside
of Aachen, Germany. One of the pilots was killed,
the other badly injured as well as her medical
technician. The Lieutenant suffered severe head
and facial trauma, a concussion, lacerations to her
face, and back injuries. The three survivors were
able to crawl from the burning wreckage and were
quickly captured by German soldiers. They were

taken to a nearby village and given first aid then transported to a German hospital. While the German doctor treated Lieutenant Whittle, he told her the soldiers were unsure of what to do with a female officer prisoner. Reba informed the doctor she was a nurse and her plane had been en route to pick up casualties in Belgium.

After being treated at the hospital, the Germans transferred the three prisoners to the main Luftwaffe interrogation center in Oberursel. It was here that the Lieutenant was separated from her two crewmen *(Author's research is unclear if she ever saw them again)*. She was then sent to another hospital to further recover from her injuries. In October, she was transferred again to a military hospital run by British medical staff for Allied POWs, then another transfer a few weeks later to a POW hospital in Meiningen. The Germans were still at a loss as to what to do with the injured American female Army officer.

Although she had severe, incapacitating headaches as a result of the concussion received in the crash and slowly healing facial trauma, she was put to work. Her captors now knew she was a nurse so her assigned POW duties were to care for the hospitalized burn patients and amputees, who were also POWs.

Several weeks later, she was noticed by inspection members of the International Committee of the Red Cross as a female officer, American military POW. The State Department was notified and negotiations began for her release; she and her crew had been listed as "missing in action" since their aircraft failed to return to base in September. After nearly four months in captivity, she was released to the German Red Cross on January 25, 1945, along with 109 other injured American prisoners of war, and transported by train to Switzerland. With the combined efforts of the German Red Cross and the International Red Cross, the wounded POWs were then flown to the United States.

Lieutenant Whittle's story was kept quiet by the Army for many, many years for unknown reasons. There were no media celebrations upon her return to the United States. In February, 1945, she was quietly awarded the Purple Heart and the Air Medal for injuries she received from the crash, "for meritorious achievement while participating in aerial flights…in unarmed and unarmored aircraft." She was also promoted to First Lieutenant.

She returned to nursing duties in the States on May 11, 1945; however, one week later she underwent further medical assessment of her medical difficulties. As a result of the findings (recurrent severe and incapacitating headaches), her flying status was suspended. In her short career as a flight nurse from January to September, 1944 Reba had flown forty missions and logged over five-hundred flight hours.

Although she lost her flight nurse designation, Reba continued to work as a bedside nurse at the Hamilton Field hospital in California until her discharge from service January 13, 1946.

With her ongoing health problems as a result of the plane crash, she sought compensation from the Veterans Administration for military medical treatment and retirement. Her requests and appeals were constantly denied. In 1954, she was finally awarded a small disability settlement in the amount of $3,780 from the date of her application instead of backdated to her discharge date in 1946 or back to the cause of the disability, the plane crash in 1944. The Board ruled her disabilities were not "combat incurred." More paperwork, appeals and review garnered her an additional $999. If she had received what was rightfully due her for injuries suffered while on military duty with discharge due to those injuries, she should have received a total of $13,760. Reba continued fighting for what was rightfully hers and continued to be denied. She was also denied POW retirement benefits. In 1960, disgusted, tired of fighting, and in failing health, she made no further efforts on her own behalf.

Reba Whittle died from cancer January 26, 1981 at the age of sixty-one.

In 1983, when the Department of the Army honored the Army and Navy nurses captured and imprisoned by the Japanese and publicly declared that the Department of Defense and the Veterans

Administration knew of no other American military women to have been taken prisoner during WWII, Reba's surviving husband, Colonel Stanley Tobiason, wrote a very terse letter to the Department of the Army reminding them of her many years of denied requests for recognition as a documented POW in Germany. The Colonel also reminded the Army they had awarded his wife a Purple Heart and the Air Medal for the very service they had consistently denied her rightful compensation for.

As a result of Colonel Tobiason's intervention, history now recognizes Lieutenant Reba Whittle as the only American military female POW in the European Theater during WWII. That recognition was finally given September 2, 1983 two years after her death.

Chapter 8

Rosie, Wendy, and Sally

During the Great Depression, jobs were difficult to find for everyone. Women were discouraged from entering the workforce in order to leave the jobs for men, the family "breadwinners." World War II changed that as well as the definition of who the family breadwinner would be. With the vast numbers of men leaving their jobs for military duties, the government's need for factory, munitions, ship, and aircraft assembly workers became acute. America turned to its women to fill the need.

Right away, men across America did not like the idea of their wives and daughters going to work outside the home, especially in predominantly held male positions. At that time, young women graduating from high school, with eyes on college, were encouraged to major in nursing or liberal arts for a teaching career. However, not many female high school graduates had the financial resources to attend college. Those with a strong desire for a college education accepted low paying service jobs, scrimping and saving every penny to achieve their college goals and dreams.

Married women, with and without children to support, also had to take service jobs to provide for their families especially if their husbands had enlisted and left home for war duties. Cleaning women were paid $2 a week and waitress jobs paid $14 a week. Naturally, when word got out that shipyard workers were being paid $37 a week, single and married women alike left their service jobs and rushed to apply for the government jobs. In the beginning, money was the primary motivation, not necessarily patriotism.

Women felt torn between what their men wanted, the opportunities opening for them, and what they felt they could do for their country in time of war. The government began a media blitz across America with ads, posters, articles in magazines, newspapers and radio - all appealing to the patriotic participation of women in the war effort.

Every woman not doing vital work is needed NOW

The men still balked. The government was desperate, even considered drafting women to industrial jobs. Instead, they continued the media blitz and public relations through the campaign titled "Get-Women-To-Work." Henry L. Stimson, Secretary of War in 1943, was quoted in multiple media sources:

The War Department must fully utilize, immediately and effectively, the largest and potentially the finest single source of labor available today - the vast reserve of woman power.

"I've found the job where I fit best!"

FIND YOUR WAR JOB
In Industry – Agriculture – Business

Thousands of posters began appearing across the country from the "Get-Women-To-Work" campaign. Captions stated, "If you've used an electric mixer in your kitchen, you can learn to run a drill press; The more women at work, the sooner we win! Women in the war, we can't win without them; More airplanes are needed, women can help! Together, we can do it." Obviously, the message was clear to American women, "We need you, you can do it."

A magazine article in the July, 1943 issue of *The Nation* chastised American men for continuing to put pressure on housewives to work outside the home in war production jobs. The article pointed out that perhaps the underlying, subconscious problem was the men's refusal to share in the home responsibilities of cooking, cleaning, and tending the children. The article asked, "If a woman can learn to run a drill press, why can't a man learn to run a washing machine?" Needless to say, the article certainly created controversy, but it also encouraged women to boldly venture forth.

The doors were wide open for women to join the workforce as they began responding to the government's media calls. By the end of December 1941, thirteen million women were already at work; by the end of 1943, fifteen million, and by the end of 1944, twenty million. Of those twenty million women, six million were working in war production factories.

Many factory jobs did not require a high school diploma; however, some jobs required applicants to successfully pass a Civil Service exam. Once hired, the women began a vigorous two to six week training course in which they were taught how to read blueprints, the names of tools, the different machines, and how to use or operate them. Next, the women were instructed in the specific jobs they were hired for - precision drilling, riveting, arc welding, piece work, etc. If a new hire could not grasp the concept of their assigned job, was not physically capable of handling the machinery or tools, or did sloppy work, she was sent to a different job or another factory. Rarely was anyone terminated.

Women in war production factories caused a major change in the fashion industry. Dresses were not appropriate or safe for women crawling around inside aircraft, ships, or tank skeletons. Many companies had stylish

Boeing aircraft factory workers modeling their work pantsuits and head scarves next to a B-17.

uniforms and pantsuits designed for their women workers while others simply required the women to were slacks. Not many clothing stores carried heavy duty women's slacks at that time. Resourceful women bought men's coveralls and tailored them to fit their needs.

Women were also required to cover their hair because long hair and heavy machinery presented a safety concern. Bandanas or scarfs were used to meet the company requirements. In some factories, a variety of colored head coverings denoted job duties or specific shift workers and were usually supplied by the factory.

Some factories required the women to have their own tools and tool boxes. Metal tools were scarce during the war, but the war production factories all seemed to have a substantial supply. The new employees could purchase the tools required with payments deducted from their paychecks in an agreed upon amount over an agreed upon period of time.

Rosie the Riveter

The female American patriot during World War II was a fictional character who symbolized women working in the war production factories. A loyal, efficient, patriotic, compliant, and attractive woman, Rosie the Riveter, was exactly what the government envisioned for their recruitment purposes.

Different sources tell different stories about Rosie's "birth." Most agree the term came from a very popular 1942 song written by Redd Evans and John Jacob Loeb titled, *"Rosie the Riveter."* Their inspiration is said to have been a young woman, Rosalind "Rosie" Palmer Walter, working as a riveter in a nearby aircraft plant. The name was catchy and appropriate for the song title that flooded American radio waves during the war.

The May 29, 1943 issue of the *Saturday Evening Post* featured a Norman Rockwell cover depicting Rosie the Riveter. It was the first visual image of Rosie seen by the magazine's three million readers who also enjoyed the ever-popular song.

Mary Doyle Keefe was a nineteen year old telephone operator who lived in the same Vermont town as Rockwell. He asked her to pose for photographs and payed her $5 for each of the two sittings. The photographs would be used by Rockwell as a basis for the painting he had in mind. Although Mary was a petite redhead, Rockwell wanted "Rosie" to have large arms, hands, and shoulders to depict strength. Mary had never riveted anything, but a heavy rivet gun was placed across her lap to carry out the theme.

After the painting was published by the magazine, Norman Rockwell and the magazine loaned the image to the U.S. Treasury Department for use in war bond drives. Several other images graced a variety of magazine and poster recruitment efforts but Rockwell's was the first. The original painting is now located at the Crystal

Bridges Museum of American Art in Bentonville, Arkansas. Mary Doyle Keefe died April 22, 2015 at the age of 92.

Perhaps the most recognized image of Rosie is  a poster commissioned in 1942 by J. Howard Miller to boost the morale of Westinghouse employees in some of its Midwest factories. The poster was only seen by Westinghouse employees for a two week period in February, 1943 then it was retired to a warehouse.

In the early 1980s, the poster was rediscovered, shared with the public, and quickly became a national icon for women and the feminist movement. Many refer to the figure in the poster as Rosie the Riveter, but that was never Miller's intent. He titled the poster "We Can Do It." Today, the poster continues to be an iconic symbol of women's rights and struggles in the workforce.

During the first three years of the war, the largest, single need in war production factories was for riveters. The top three aircraft companies were Boeing, Douglas, and North American. The Boeing plant produced the heavy bombers, B-17s and B-29s; Douglas produced the transport planes

(C-47s) and medium sized bombers; North American produced trainers, medium bombers (B-25s) and fighters (P-51s). All aircraft were held together by rivets placed by riveters. Ships, tanks and many other military vehicles also utilized rivets.

A **rivet** is a short cylindrical metal pin or bolt with a forged head (like a mush-room cap) on one end and straight on the other end. Rivets are designed to  hold two metal plates together and come in a variety of sizes to suit the objects being joined together. Aircraft rivets were usually made of aluminum or aluminum alloys since weight is an issue. Rivets used for tanks or other heavy equipment were usually made of steel. Whatever they are used for, it takes hundreds of thousands of rivets to assemble the finished product.

Most of the rivets came from the Ford plant in Willow Run, Michigan which produced over seven million rivets each day in more than five-hundred standard sizes. They were then packaged and shipped daily to the various factories that utilized them.

Women from all walks of life applied for riveting jobs at the aircraft plants. Teachers worked during their summer vacations for the extra money, housewives and farm girls worked to supplement their families income, while others worked for the experience, college savings, or spending money for fun activities. Pay averaged $31.50 per week for women and $54.65 for men doing the same job.

Once the women completed their training they were assigned a partner, given their tools, and a bucket of rivets sized for the job they would be working on. One woman was the **riveter** while the

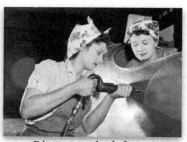

Riveter on the left, bucker on the right.

other was the **bucker**. Working opposite from each other, with the metal plates between them, the riveter would shoot the rivets through the drilled hole with the heavy rivet gun while the bucker held a steel bar (the bucking bar) on the opposite side.

When the air powered rivet gun slams the rivet into the bucking bar, the bar acts as a barrier to deform the end of the rivet into a mushroom shaped head. Then the rivet completely fills the drilled hole resulting in an extremely tight fit. If the

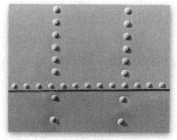

Completed panel of rivets on a B-17 bomber.

bucker did not hold the bar tight enough against the hole, the rivet would not flatten properly.

After each rivet was placed, the bucker would signal the riveter if it was good or needed to be removed and redone. Partners developed their own rhythm and were able to place hundreds of rivets in an hour.

In June, 1943, Rose Bonavita and her partner Jennie Florio, set a production record by drilling nine hundred holes and driving thirty-three hundred rivets while working on a Grumman TBF Avenger torpedo bomber during one, six-hour night shift. Their record was never broken during war production. President Roosevelt sent them a personal commendation letter.

The rivet guns were very noisy and hard to hang on to due to the vibration when riveting. "It took some getting used to," a former Rosie remembered. "My whole body shook and my teeth chattered with that thing! If the gun got away from you, it would fly all over the place and everyone had to duck for cover until somebody could shut it off."

Both riveting and bucking took terrific arm strength. When the women first began work, they joked among themselves about feeling that their arms would fall off. It didn't take long for them to gain well-toned bicep muscles! Some women were embarrassed about their large well muscled arms so they wore long-sleeved shirts or blouses to cover them.

Working the bucking bar required muscle, while riveting required skill. Partners would switch places often for a change of pace or to relieve sore arm and back muscles.

In some factories, at the end of each shift, inspectors would exam each piece that had been worked during that shift. If a bad rivet was found, it was circled in red indicating it had to be removed and replaced. One or two teams on the next shift would scout the inspected work looking for the red circles then remove and replace the bad rivets.

Riveters built up other muscles besides their biceps. Climbing up and down ladders, over and through aircraft, ship or tank pieces, hanging upside down to reach small, hard to get sections, squatting, kneeling or sitting on the cold metal frames...all required strong leg muscles, backs, and knees. At the end of one of her first shifts, one Rosie stated, "My feet and legs hurt so bad I thought for sure they were just bloody stumps. I had never been so tired in my life after just eight hours of work. I didn't think I could walk the quarter-of-a-mile to the bus stop, but the thought of a nice hot bath spurred me on."

Another Rosie working in an aircraft factory had this to say about her first few days of work, "I stubbed my toes, cracked my shins, and knocked my head three times on the metal sills above me. I broke all my fingernails, couldn't even see them for the black grime around them. I bit my tongue so bad when my teeth were chattering I got blood all over my blouse. My clean bright blue uniform was filthy in just eight hours with a tear in the knee, blood and grease across my blouse, dust and dirt all over me. I know I was quite a mess but I sure was proud of the work I did!"

Many women could not physically maintain the workload and quit or requested a different assignment. Rather than losing an employee, a less physical job was easily found. Instead of riveting, piece work could be done, electrical wiring strung, instruments installed...hundreds of positions were available.

At the Radioplane munitions factory in Burbank, California Rosies assembled aircraft drones which were used as targets for aircraft gunnery practice. Norma Jean Dougherty was a young married nineteen year old hired as an assembler in 1944. When her husband was sent overseas, she went to work at the nearby factory earning $20 a week. She was very attractive and well liked by her co-workers, even winning a $50 war bond after being chosen "Queen" at the annual company picnic.

Captain Ronald Reagan (yes, **that** Ronald Reagan, our future President!) of the Army's First Motion Picture Unit sent a photographer on assignment to the nearby Burbank factory. The FMPU was a unit made-up of film industry professionals tasked with producing training and recruitment films, as well as training combat cameramen and photographers. Photographer Private David Conover arrived at the factory with orders to photograph "pretty girls doing their jobs to help the war effort." Photographs were needed for an article to appear in *Yank* magazine.

As he moved down the various assembly lines, he spotted a young girl with curly, ash blonde hair and a delightful smile. He snapped a few pictures of her and moved on. The rest is history, as they

Norma Jean aka Marilyn Monroe

say in the Hollywood biz. Norma Jean Dougherty was discovered from those photographs.
We remember her today as Marilyn Monroe.

WOWs on a munitions line.

Munitions plant workers were also called Rosies even though they did not rivet. Some of the munitions line workers referred to themselves as **WOWs - Women Ordinance**

The Rosie WOWs produced all sizes and types of ammunition, bombs, rockets, hand grenades, tear gas canisters, and blank cartridges. Other manufacturing plants produced detonators, fuses and the powders needed for the different munitions.

Working with chemicals, acids, and other hazardous substances involved risk and the ever present danger of fire and/or explosions. For example, TNT was mixed in huge, hot vats then poured into bomb casings. The ingredients were highly toxic to workers when exposed to high levels. Most workers were not aware of the toxicity and suffered ill health effects later in life, never realizing or correlating the cause. Several women were killed and many were seriously injured as a result of explosions in different munitions plants.

The majority of munitions plants were built on vast open land away from populated areas and away from the West Coast. Tens of thousands of workers rushed to each plant seeking jobs which paid seventy to eighty cents an hour. Many workers shared rides and commuted to the plants from sixty to one hundred miles away, each way. Like the other war industries, munitions plants ran 24/7 to keep up with demand.

Rosies across America built 300,000 airplanes, 86,000 tanks, 49,000 jeeps, 91,000 military

vehicles, millions of small weapons and 44 **b**illion
rounds of ammunition for the war effort.

Wendy the Welder

Rosie the Riveter had a cousin. Her name was
Wendy the Welder. While Rosie riveted planes,
tanks and vehicles, her cousin welded steel plates
into troop carrying ships, supply ships,
submarines, and aircraft carriers.

Most of the shipyards on the West Coast were
built by Henry Kaiser including four in the San
Francisco Bay area and three along the Columbia
and Willamette Rivers in Oregon.

Ships were needed for the war effort just as fast
as aircraft but riveting ships together took time and
added tons of weight. Kaiser came up with the
idea of fabricating ships assembly-line style.
Welders pieced together the gigantic sections of
deck and hull then transported them to the next
area where more welding finished the pieces.
Utilizing this technique, the shipyards were
building Liberty ships in 1943 at a rate of three
per day.

Liberty ships were cheap and quick to build, but
they were also quite ugly! President Franklin
Roosevelt referred to them as "a dreadful looking
object." Dreadfully ugly or not, the Liberty ships

The Liberty ship John W. Brown

were the workhorses of WWII, hauling cargo and troops across the seas where needed. A total of 2,710 Liberty ships were built during the war and became a symbol of U.S. wartime industrial output. The ships could carry 10,000 tons of cargo which might include 440 light tanks or 2,840 jeeps.

Victory ships were built later at the same facilities. The difference between a Liberty ship and a Victory ship was based on redesign and upgrades. Victory ships had more powerful, faster engines, could carry more cargo, and were also fitted with guns.

Unnamed Victory ship

To accomplish this amazing shipbuilding feat 28,000 Wendys were hired and taught the art of welding. Some welding classes were taught in high schools near the shipyards or centers on shipyard grounds. After four weeks of instruction in vertical, horizontal, overhead, and angled techniques, the graduates (men and women) were quickly recruited and began work, often without graduating from high school.

(Author's note: Men working in war production factories were excluded from the draft. Schools such as the above mentioned were often overwhelmed with young men who, for various reasons, did not want to see combat duties but still felt a duty to their country.)

Wendy's had many of the same issues in the workplace their cousin Rosie faced including discrimination, lower wages, and harassment by their male counterparts. Clothing was also a problem. Heavy denim work pants, leather jackets, steel-toed boots, and leather gloves were not items found in any women's apparel shops. In the men's departments, even the smallest of sizes were still too big and had to be altered for a comfortable, safe fit. The men's smallest sized steel-toed boots purchased by women were stuffed with rags or newspapers for a tighter fit.

Wendy didn't graduate from welding school and immediately begin welding assignments. Instead, she worked chipping away badly welded seams, cleaning up after other welders, lugging heavy equipment and supplies - all to acquaint her with what the job entailed. Like her cousin, Wendy climbed into tight spaces to work, often so small that her male co-workers would not fit. To get the job done, it was not uncommon to climb down four stories to the bottom of the ship on a narrow steel ladder dragging heavy welding equipment behind.

Once deemed ready for actual welding work, the Wendys quickly learned the necessity for heavy denim coveralls, long sleeve leather jackets, heavy clunky leather gloves, a leather cap instead of a cotton scarf, the oversized steel-toed boots, the goggles, and heavy metal hoods. Welding sparks burned through light cotton fabrics and were painful when they landed on exposed skin. Sparks singed exposed hair that was not covered or pulled back from the face. Hands were especially susceptible to spark burns if the clunky leather gloves were not worn.

It took some getting used to, but the Wendys worked hard and took pride in their work. One Wendy smiled as she recalled her welding work; she said it reminded her of crocheting and embroidery - as she moved the welding rod in tiny, circular motions she made nice smooth half-crescent welds similar to needlecraft stitches.

Two Wendy Welders at work on a Liberty ship.

Welding was difficult and dangerous work. Horizontal welding was fairly easy as well as spot welding; vertical welding was a bit more challenging, but overhead welding took its toll. Arm strength was truly tested with long periods of overhead work. A perfect "welded dog" was a finished section that was looked upon with great pride and accomplishment.

The most common injuries were first and second degree burns on exposed skin from the sparks. Not wearing goggles or the protective hood could severely damage eyes, even cause permanent blindness. "Arc eye" was the name for a flash burn to the eye in which the ultraviolet light from the welding caused inflammation of the cornea that can burn through to the retina. The goggles and helmets have dark UV filtering plates to prevent exposure to the ultraviolet welding light.

Welding fumes and gases contained heavy metals which, when inhaled for long periods of time, could cause neurological problems and affect the lungs, liver, kidneys, and central nervous system. Welding in tiny, close quarters was not monitored well during that time and many Wendys suffered the consequences years later. Just as with the WOWs, the Wendys never connected or correlated their welding history exposures to their poor health later in life.

Starting pay for a Wendy was $1.20 per hour with a shift differential up to $2.00 per hour for graveyard shift. Men welders made substantially more per hour, including overtime.

America's Wendys built 2,710 Liberty ships, 531 Victory ships, 952 destroyers, 151 aircraft carriers, 126 submarines, 81 cruisers, 64,000 landing craft, and 9 battleships for the war effort.

Sally the Secretary - The Government Girls

Before the war, governmental jobs in Washington, D.C. were primarily held by men. Officials scrambled to fill positions vacated by the men who volunteered or were drafted for war duties. Thousands and thousands of women flocked to Washington D.C. to fill those administrative and secretarial positions. During the war, many new positions were created with the main objectives being to receive vital information, analyze it, then pass it along into the right hands thereby keeping the war machines running smoothly.

Most of the women hired were college educated and needed very little training. Wages ranged from $1,440 to $2,000 per year (about $27-38 per week), plus overtime. Housing was a big problem with the influx of so many women. Dormitories, boarding houses, rented rooms in private homes, and hotels were crowded with women workers. Dresses or slacks were appropriate apparel and no particular tools were needed.

The manufacture of typewriters ceased when factories switched to war production products that created a metal shortage. Secretaries assigned a typewriter took loving care of it knowing it could not be replaced in case of a major breakdown. Ribbons were changed when absolutely necessary and keys were cleaned daily to prevent ink build up and jams.

Sallys typed payroll rosters for the military, requisitions for everything from A to Z, military supplies for use at home and on the war fronts, heavy equipment, and ordinance requests. Although typing and filing was a tedious some-times boring job, the women were happy to have lucrative employment, good pay and felt that the wartime needs of the country gave them a noble purpose. They called themselves **"Government Girls."**

Many of the women quickly moved from secretarial positions to classified areas working with the FBI and the OSS (Office of Strategic Services, which later became the CIA, Central

Rows and rows of "Government
Girls" working at the FBI
Fingerprint Factory.

Intelligence Agency). The FBI oversaw the
Fingerprint Factory which employed over 21,000
workers categorizing and managing over 70
million fingerprint cards. All work was done by
direct magnified visualization - long before
computers as we know them today. All military
personnel, all federal workers, all workers in war
production plants, new immigrants, and criminals
were fingerprinted with each individual's card sent
to Washington, D.C.

The FBI also utilized Government Girls to
process information received regarding draft
dodgers, investigation of new immigrants, and
conduct background checks on federal workers in
highly classified areas. Top secret and highly
classified work often involved paperwork from
U.S. intelligence agents at home and abroad.
Reports were analyzed and forwarded to the proper
officials.

Cryptographers wrote and deciphered coded messages for the FBI and the OSS. Analysts and cryptographers were sworn to secrecy about their duties. If anyone asked what they did as Government Girls, they were to respond by saying they were "file clerks - no one is interested in file clerks."

The Computing Division.
Long rows of
human computers.

In 1942, thousands of women across America were secretly recruited by the military to become "computers" for the Army. These were not computers as we know them today, but human computers. This group of Government Girls had strong educational backgrounds in mathematics and analysis, many recruited directly from colleges across the country. They worked six days a week, often double or triple shifts, doing ballistics research and calculations. It was their job to create ballistics tables for every weapon in the U.S. arsenal. Their tools were pen, pencil, paper, and the clunky, electrically powered, mechanical calculating machines. The weapons trajectories they calculated were then passed on to the soldiers on the ground and the bombardiers in the air. It was a high stress, high pressure job that paid $2,000 per year, not counting overtime.

Many of the Government Girls who had worked on ballistics calculations were sent to top secret facilities at Hanford, Washington; Oak Ridge, Tennessee; and Los Alamos, New Mexico - the Manhattan Project's primary locations. Their precise calculations were needed for the design of the atomic bomb, although they had no idea the bomb was the end result. They worked closely and secretly with the Project scientists calculating such critical information as the tracking of the blast wave of a conventional explosion through the fissile material at the core of the bomb, then tracking the shock wave of the fission detonation back out. The work was extremely difficult as it had never been done before and was not easily understood, even by some of the project scientists. The concept of an atomic bomb and its power was difficult to grasp (more on the Manhattan Project in chapter 11).

Government Girls working for the OSS processed information covertly provided by agents who had gathered information about strategic locations and activities of the enemies. The agents also aided resistance groups overseas while monitoring enemy activity. Their reports were usually submitted in code and had to be deciphered by cryptographers then passed along to the appropriate agency.

OSS agents were spies for the U.S. and/or its allies. Four thousand women were used at home and abroad to gather information about the activities of the enemies. Hundreds of women were undercover agents, or "creeps," working in aircraft plants, shipyards, munitions plants and all Manhattan Project sites listening, watching, and reporting any indications of counterspies.

Perhaps the most famous WWII female spy was

Virginia Hall, a thirty-eight year old American college graduate - code-named Diane. Under many aliases and disguises, Virginia's cover was as a press correspondent for the *New York Post*. Her most successful disguise was an elderly, haggard, peasant woman tending cattle and goats. In this disguise, she wandered the countryside mapping drop zones for supplies and troops, found safe houses, and helped train resistance forces to wage guerrilla warfare against the Germans. The Germans considered her the most dangerous of all allied spies and placed a bounty on her, dead or alive. She did all of this with an artificial leg (a wooden peg leg) which did not slow her down! Virginia was the only civilian woman in WWII to have been awarded the Distinguished Service Cross for her work in France and Spain.

Two other operatives crucial to the OSS were **Genevieve Feinstein** and **Elizabeth McIntosh**. Genevieve was a cryptanalyst and specialized in the decryption and reading of Japanese diplomatic messages. She discovered a breakthrough in decryption that enabled the Army Intelligence Service to build an analog machine that broke the Japanese code and later broke Russian KGB messages. Elizabeth was assigned to Morale Operations. She produced false news reports, postcards, documents, and radio messages designed to spread disinformation and undermine Japanese morale. She was America's version of Tokyo Rose.

Josephine Baker, also known as the Black Pearl, was a very beautiful singer, dancer, and actress. She was the first African-American to become a world famous entertainer. Living in France during the war, she gathered information about German activities while attending or performing at parties then passed the information on to the French Resistance. She smuggled her information and military secrets by writing them on her sheet music with invisible ink.

Three OSS agents more commonly known today were **Julia McWilliams Child** the famous gourmet cook; **Marlene Dietrich**, and **Hedy Lamarr** the actresses.

Julia Child wanted to join the WACs or the WAVES to help in the war efforts; however, her 6'2" height disqualified her from both. The OSS hired her to work in research and development. There she literally cooked up and developed a shark repellant to be applied to underwater explosives (mines) used by the U.S. Navy to sink German U-boats. Sharks were bumping against the devices causing the explosives to detonate which then alerted the U-boats of their presence, thus warning them to alter their course.

Marlene Dietrich was a vampy German-American actress and singer who volunteered her services to the OSS after renouncing her German citizenship with the rise of the Nazis; she rejected Hitler's multiple requests for her return to Germany. Marlene was one of the first celebrities to sell war bonds across the U.S. as well as perform for allied troops throughout Europe. She spoke fluent German and recorded broadcasts designed to demoralize German soldiers. Marlene received the Medal of Freedom for her war work.

Hedy Lamarr was a strikingly beautiful Austrian-American actress and inventor. During WWII she and a partner found that radio-controlled torpedoes could easily be jammed by broadcasting interference at the frequency of the control signal which would then cause the torpedo to go off course. This frequency-hopping or high frequency switching became the basis for our modern day spread-spectrum communication technology (think Bluetooth, Wi-Fi networks, cordless and wireless telephones).

Alice Marble was a World Champion tennis player from 1936 to 1940. When she retired from tennis she worked as an Associate Editor for DC Comics creating the *"Wonder Women of History"* stories about prominent women in history told in comics form. During WWII her pilot husband was killed in action over Germany. A short time later, Alice was recruited to spy for the OSS. Her mission was to renew contact with a Swiss banker, a former lover, and obtain Nazi financial data he possessed. Her mission was successful in that she found and relayed the information but was shot in the back by a Nazi agent for her efforts. She escaped, recovered, and returned to the U.S. where she continued her tennis expertise by teaching. Her OSS activities were never revealed until after her death.

Alice wrote a strong editorial in the July 1, 1950 magazine *American Lawn Tennis* urging desegregation of American women's tennis. She wrote, "If tennis is a game for ladies and gentlemen, it's also time we acted a little more like gentle-people and less like sanctimonious hypocrites..."

Although money was a great motivating factor, women across America cashed their paychecks with a sense of pride and dignity in what they were accomplishing. They had to overcome negativity from their male family members, job and racial discrimination in the workplace, resentful male co-workers, less pay than their male counterparts, and some fairly unglamorous job duties. Through it all, the women found a freedom and independence they had never known - the "We Can Do It" spirit with attitude. They became America's hidden army. The women's revolution was gaining momentum.

Chapter 9

The Eight-Hour Orphans

With all the Rosies, Wendys and Sallys flocking to war industry and production jobs, a great upheaval in American cultural society began to take place. For the first time during a war with American involvement, women kept industry humming. Nearly 19 million women worked in the shipyards, aircraft factories, steel mills, and munitions industries. Also for the first time, married women workers outnumbered single women workers by a wide margin. Married women usually had children, and those children needed care while mom was working.

Prior to the war, the woman's place was generally thought to be at home, raising the children and keeping the house and garden in order. As the husbands and fathers left for war duties, the societal shift began slowly then picked up at lightening speed. Women were torn between staying home as they had before the war, facing an uncertain financial future without a husband bringing home a paycheck, or heeding the government's call for patriotic war industry workers. Not having the financial support coming in from the man of the house, many families were placed in financial distress which in turn pushed the women to seek outside employment. The factories were paying wages never before dreamed of by American women or the man of the house.

Further complicating the women's dilemma were reports from social workers and child care advocates that the government propaganda encouraging women to go to work would undermine and harm family life. Their belief supported mothers staying home to care and nurture their children; mothers could not be expected to both work and tend to their families, it was unheard of! Placing a child in a care center would negatively affect the child due to the fact that some centers at that time had, purportedly, substandard care.

At first, the government was reluctant to push industries to hire women with young children, especially with all the reports and news articles supporting the negative affect it would have on home front families. But, as the war escalated, so did the demand for more aircraft, ships and munitions which increased the demand for workers. Everyone was feeling the pressure. Mothers were hired and went to work. End of discussion!

It didn't take long before stories began circulating that children were being cared for by aging grandparents often in poor health and physically unable to keep up with small children; children being left in parked cars outside the workplace for eight hours (the eight-hour orphans); or school age children home alone with younger siblings, often skipping school to care for them.

The term "Latch Key Kids" originated as school age children were given the house key on a string or ribbon to wear around their necks. The kids would get out of school before their mothers arrived home from the factory and let themselves in with their house key.

Factory absenteeism was also high for working mothers when a child became ill or older children began having problems at school. It quickly became obvious something had to be done.

Several government programs began distributing federal aid for child care programs in 1942. The Extended School Services programs helped pay for extended hours after school by offering organized, supervised activities run by qualified teachers. Grants were awarded to cities that offered supervised activities in local parks and playgrounds, summer camps and community centers. The Emergency Nursery School program was an older opportunity from the Depression era that updated nursery schools in low-income areas offering child care administered by childhood educators, not social workers. Nearly 2,000 schools of this type had 75,000 children enrolled.

The Lanham Act provided funding for a variety of wartime community services including child care programs. Matching funds from state and local governments resulted in child care centers springing up across the nation, especially in areas where war industries employed thousands and thousands of workers, the majority of which were women.

The West Coast had the highest percentage of female industrial workers in the country. In the San Francisco Bay Area and Portland, Oregon the Kaiser shipyards employed tens of thousands of women. In Seattle, Washington the Boeing plant also employed thousands of women who built B-17 bombers.

Henry J. Kaiser built a state-of-the-art hospital near his Portland shipyard to serve his shipyard workers and their families. With a little push from First Lady Eleanor Roosevelt, Mr. Kaiser also built state-of-the-art child care centers at his two Oregon shipyards. In the Bay Area, thirty-five child care centers of varying sizes were built providing care for mothers working in the shipyards nearby. The operation of his child care centers set a precedent for others across the country. Kaiser also strongly encouraged other businesses and war industry complexes to do the same.

By 1943, both Kaiser child care centers in Oregon were up and running near the workers' entrance to the shipyards. The huge wheel spoke design featured a large grassy courtyard at the hub surrounded by fifteen classrooms on the outer wheel. Each room measured thirty by fifteen feet and accommodated twenty-five children.

Kaiser child care center in Oregon.

The courtyard had swings, slides, teeter totters, monkey bars, and sand boxes for outdoor play and exercise. The classrooms had large picture windows, many of which faced the shipyards, so the children could see where their mothers were working. This was reassuring for the child to know "mommy" was close by. Each classroom had its own bathroom with child-sized sinks and toilets. The center also provided towels, bibs, toothbrush, and a comb for each child.

An infirmary was also on site for children who were "mildly ill" needing care while mothers worked. If the child became seriously ill or had a contagious disease, the mother was called from work to take the child home. Ten registered nurses worked in the infirmary and provided childhood immunizations, if and when needed, as well as first aid for minor cuts and scrapes.

A large kitchen provided all meals and snacks under the direction of five nutritionists specializing in the nutritional needs of growing children. The cooks also prepared pre-cooked, packaged take-home meals, another innovation of Kaiser, that mothers could pick up after work, take home, heat, and eat. The packages contained a well-balanced meal, enough for a mother and one child, at a cost of 50 cents. Larger meals for larger families were also available. The pre-cooked meal idea was very successful in reducing the stress, planning, shopping, and cooking for working mothers, thereby allowing them time with their families as well as rest for a refreshed return to work the next day. Not only were the children being cared for, but the mothers were also thought of - a totally new concept!

Daily activities in the care centers were well planned and supervised on a strict schedule. Each activity was an opportunity for learning skills and preparing the younger children for grade school. Drawing, coloring, working with clay, building blocks, listening to stories, music, and learning to get along with others were inside activities. Outside activities included tricycles, swings, sandbox play, jungle-gyms, and organized exercise games. Afternoon naps or "rest periods" for all!

The centers were designed to operate the same 24-hour schedule as the 24-hour shipyards. Initially, children of shipyard workers from two to six years old were eligible for the care center. Due to the demand, the age was soon lowered to eighteen months.

Children were welcomed at the beginning of each shipyard shift. Afternoon shift workers with school age children six to twelve years old were also accepted. Homework help was available for these children from the care workers, many of whom were teachers. Night shift workers dropped their children off in their pajamas, some already asleep, and care workers put them to bed on little cots in sleeping rooms. Parents were charged $5.00 per child, with additional children charged $3.75 each, for a six day week. Child care costs could be conveniently deducted from mom's paycheck.

With the success of the Kaiser Child Care Centers more mothers began taking jobs in the shipyards which increased production and decreased guilt. Mothers began feeling confident their children were being well cared for, fed properly, and kept busy with activities and learning with the added bonus of the children enjoying the experience. Child care centers across the country could not be built fast enough, especially centers near industrial areas. The earlier social worker, child advocate naysayers were quickly silenced.

From opening day of the two Oregon Kaiser Child Care centers in November 1943, until June 1945, the centers provided a total of just under 250,000 child care days. This allowed mothers to work almost two million hours in the shipyards or the equivalent amount of time it took to build six Liberty ships. The Bay Area shipyards had 24,500 women on the Kaiser payroll with 1,400 children attending child care centers daily. Similar successes and statistics were noted in other war industry locations supporting child care centers.

When the war ended and war production slowed or ceased altogether, the 3,100 federal and state funded centers across the country that had served from 600,000 to 1.6 million children, were closed and dismantled. Only California continued to operate publicly funded centers after the war.

The Kaiser method for child care centers was an exemplary demonstration of high quality, innovative child care during WWII, unmatched to this day. The model for superior child care in a setting with supportive care for the entire family remains a Henry Kaiser legacy. On-site child care in present day workplaces is rare, even at Kaiser facilities.

Chapter 10

WWII Women in Science

World War II presented opportunities for women never before available or so difficult to obtain they were simply discouraged. Men left gaping vacancies in every occupation, from bus drivers to scientists, as they left for war duties. The acute labor shortage was the catalyst for opening doors to women in science and technology. Since WWII was becoming a high technology war, the Army needed science-minded individuals with higher levels of education to work on a variety of their projects and experiments.

This became a challenge and an important transition period for colleges across the country. Colleges had to begin altering their curriculum to include more science, mathematics, chemistry, biological, medical, and engineering degree courses. All of these areas were previously discouraged for women; now the colleges were actively recruiting and admitting them.

The Office of Scientific Research and Development was formed in 1941 to keep a registry of men and women trained in the various science fields. The list included graduating students as well as those with previous science experience. The lists were carefully scrutinized by military and war production industries looking for the high achievers and most rounded individuals.

Besides utilizing the OSRD registry, military and civilian recruiters went directly to the colleges to obtain lists of students (men and women) nearing graduation in the needed fields, then began actively pursuing them. Both men and women were offered the choice of entering the Army as servicemen/women or as civilian employees. Most men accepted the offer instead of being drafted or going into combat overseas while the women chose a position as a WAC or civilian employee of the government.

The Army actively recruited women with training or degrees in engineering, chemistry, pharmacology, mathematics, toxicology, electronics, laboratory technology, and more.

Women scientific researchers usually worked under the direction of male scientists. In many cases, the women did all the research and development, wrote and published the papers, then the men stepped in to receive the accolades. These practices quickly faded as women increased their numbers in scientific fields making genuine contributions in areas of their expertise, and received their rightful recognition.

Women did not necessarily have to be scientists to affect change or see a problem then find a solution. The rationing of many household products as well as the simple needs of soldiers encouraged the invention of new or replacement products.

After receiving letters from her soldier son stating he was experiencing severe "jungle rot" on his feet, a mother working for Dow Chemical Company pushed Dow to come up with a solution. In 1942, polyvinylidene chloride (discovered by Dow Chemical Company in 1933) was used to make woven mesh ventilating insoles for the jungle boots of Army soldiers. The insoles drastically reduced blisters and tropical ulcers on soldiers' feet by keeping them dry.

Polyvinylidene chloride sheets were also used to wrap/cover guns and ammunition when preparing for overseas shipment (this kept moisture from damaging the military equipment). The spray version of polyvinylidene chloride was used on fighter planes to protect them from salty sea spray corrosion. For home front families, this product became a substitute for aluminum foil, which was no longer available due to the war. We recognize this product today as Saran Wrap!

Another mother with two sons serving in the Navy worked at the Green River Ordnance Plant in Illinois. Her job was to inspect and package cartridges used by the Army and Navy to launch rifle grenades. When the cartridges were packed, the boxes were sealed with a thin paper tape, then waxed for waterproofing. A tab of tape was left loose at the end of the box so the soldiers could pull it to release the wax coating and open the box. Unfortunately, the paper tape would become damp rendering it useless when the soldier yanked on it to open the box. A scramble for a knife or some type of sharp object to cut through the wax rendered the soldier vulnerable while under enemy attack. **Vesta Stoudt** did not want her sons to be killed over such a simple, fixable problem. Her solution was to use a strong, cloth-based waterproof tape to seal the ammunition boxes instead of the thin paper tape. She took the idea to her supervisors but no action or further experimentation was done.

Vesta Stoudt

Undaunted and anxious about her sons and the sons of other mothers, she wrote a letter to President Roosevelt February 10, 1943 explaining the problem and her idea for its solution. She wrote:

The enemy has time to kill hundreds of our men while they are trying to open the box to get the cartridges. We can't let them down by giving them a box of cartridges that takes a minute or two to open, enabling the enemy to take lives that might be saved had the box been taped with strong tape that can be opened in a split second.

Please, Mr. President, do something about this at once, not tomorrow or soon, but now. We packed nearly ten thousand today on my shift and all wrong.

In her letter she diagrammed the new way of taping the cartridge box leaving a tab of the sturdy cloth-based tape to pull, splitting the wax cover and easily opening the box.

The President promptly sent her letter to the War Production Board in Washington, D.C. In March, Vesta received word that her idea for the new type of tape had been approved and sent to Johnson & Johnson for production. Because Johnson & Johnson had experience making surgical adhesive tape, the WPB felt they would be more likely and able to fast track production of the new type of tape Vesta had suggested.

By using a medical type of tape as a base, adding a poly-coat adhesive to increase the stick-ability then a polyethylene coating for lamination of the tape to a cloth backing, the new tape increased the strength and flexibility of any previous products. This fit Vesta's original idea for a tape that could easily be ripped by hand yet be strong and waterproof to protect the packages of cartridges. Production began almost immediately. The new tape was called "Duck Tape" because it was waterproof like a duck and made out of cotton duck fabric. The original color was Army green.

 Once the soldiers had access to the tape, they used it for everything: repairing boots, rain gear, equipment, weapons such as handguns and rifles, closing wounds in the field, repairing jeeps, even repairing aircraft. Bombers returning from missions with bullet-riddled wings and fuselages were covered with duck tape and readied for the next mission.

Vesta Stoudt received a personal letter from President Roosevelt thanking her for her idea and contribution to the war effort. She also received the *Chicago Tribune* War Worker Award for her idea and persistence. After the war, the tape was used to seal ventilation ducts; therefore the name was changed from duck to duct. The color was also changed from Army green to silver.

Where would we be today without duct tape?

The flight nurses, discussed in a previous chapter, called attention to the need for research and discoveries in aviation medicine. Many women played important roles in experiments with long periods of high altitude flight needs as well as general flight safety. Supplemental oxygen, the appropriate levels and methods of delivery resulted from their work. The design and development of crash helmets, safety belts, night vision goggles, and more, resulted from WWII women's roles in aviation and their ongoing concerns for safety.

The following are a random sampling of other women who overcame obstacles to affect changes and claim their rightful places in American history during WWII:

An early volunteer for a position in the WAVES, **Florence Van Straten**, was assigned to the Naval Aerology Service as a weather forecaster. She had a Ph.D. in chemistry from M.I.T. and began analyzing the use of weather in combat operations in the Pacific. The results of her analysis  were utilized by Naval operations in preparing for battles using weather conditions to their advantage. An example of this was the American fleet using clouds and precipitation of a trailing frontal system to provide cover for their battleships, then staging a surprise sea attack on the Japanese ships.

By utilizing different types of weather phenomena, the Navy could plan ship maneuvers and carrier-based airplane flights. This would be a crucial concept used later in the war when the atomic bombs were dropped on Japan.

Ms. Van Straten also developed the technique to modify clouds and produce rain by injecting carbon black into the atmosphere - this technique was later modified and became known as "cloud seeding." She was also instrumental in working on the new technology known as "radar."

In 1946, working as a civilian atmospheric physicist for the Navy, her analytical work on upper atmospheric conditions assisted in the development of long-range missile technology.

Yvonne Brill was refused college admission in Canada to major in engineering so she studied mathematics and chemistry instead. She accepted a position at the Douglas Aircraft Company in Santa Monica, California while  attending USC evening classes; she wanted a Master's degree in chemistry. The Douglas plant was working on a satellite project at the time. Yvonne was intrigued with the project and quickly became involved. It is believed that she was the only woman in the U.S. researching rocket science in the mid-1940s. Brill invented the propulsion system that keeps communication satellites from falling out of orbit. Later, she developed the concept for a new rocket engine called a "hydrazine resistojet" - a method of spacecraft propulsion providing thrust by heating a non-reactive fluid.

Ms. Brill continued working as a rocket scientist for many years. She encouraged women to enter the many scientific fields then opening to them. In 2011, she was awarded the National Medal of Technology and Innovation, the nation's highest honor for engineers and innovators.

Gertrude "Trudy" Belle Elion loved science. She graduated from college at the age of nineteen with a major in chemistry. She was unable to find a lab-oratory job because she was a woman. When war was declared after the Pearl Harbor attack, she was eventually hired by a large pharmaceutical company and began research on the biochemistry between normal human cells and pathogens (disease causing agents). She was interested in how diseases affect the human body. From there, her research would enable the discovery of drugs that would block infections, both bacterial and viral. With her biochemist partner, Dr. George Hitchings, they developed drugs to combat leukemia, herpes, gout, malaria, meningitis, septicemia, bacterial infections, immuno-suppressive agents used in organ transplants to reduce the chances of rejection, and later, drugs used to treat AIDS.

In her career, Elion developed forty-five patents in medicine and was awarded twenty-three honorary degrees. Along with her partner, they were awarded the Nobel Prize for Medicine in 1988.

The first American woman to be awarded the 1947 Nobel Prize in Science was bio-chemist **Gerti Cori**.  She, along with her husband, discovered the mechanism by which glycogen, a derivative of glucose, is broken down in the muscle tissue to form lactic acid then later re-synthesized in the body and stored as a source of energy. This process is known as the Cori Cycle. She and her colleagues worked extensively investigating carbohydrate metabolism particularly how glucose was metabolized and the hormones that regulate the process - basically, what regulates blood sugar levels. Her research and discoveries had a profound effect on the treatment of diabetes.

Nutritionists **Lydia J. Roberts, Hazel K. Stiebeling** and **Helen S. Mitchell** developed the Recommended Dietary Allowances in 1941. The government used nutritionists to determine what the average person would need to maintain a healthy diet. The information researched and gathered by these women became the table known as the RDA. The initial table was not always correct and was revised many times due to increased knowledge of dietary requirements. The table was used by the government to determine what a nutritious diet should consist of in the wake of food rationing. The dietary requirements were also important in supplying the troops with adequate food.

Mary Sears had a Ph.D. in zoology when she joined the WAVES in 1943. Recognizing her education, the Navy sent her to Washington, D.C. to head the newly formed Oceanographic Unit of the Navy Hydrographic Office. She was the first  Oceanographer in the Navy quickly rising to the rank of Commander in the U.S. Naval Reserve. During her service, her research proved critical to the survivability of U.S. submarines during the war. Her intelligence reports predicted the presence of thermoclines (areas of rapid water temperature changes) under which submarines could hide to escape enemy detection by surface sonar.

The Oceanographic Survey Ship USNS Mary Sears was named in her honor.

Grace Hopper graduated from Vassar and Yale with degrees in mathematics and physics. She joined the WAVES in 1943 and was assigned to the Bureau of Ships Computation Project at Harvard University. Nicknamed "Amazing Grace" she was a pioneer in the infant field of computer science; one of the first programmers of the Automatic Sequence Controlled Calculator, otherwise known as the Harvard Mark I. She is credited with inventing the first compiler for a computer programming language as well as coining the term "debugging" for fixing computer glitches. While trouble-shooting a computer glitch, she found a dead moth inside a computer and debugged it!

Rachel Carson was a marine biologist for the U.S. Bureau of Fisheries as well as a writer and environmentalist. During WWII she was asked to participate in a program to investigate undersea sounds, life and terrain, the results of which would assist the Navy in developing technology and equipment for submarine detection. In the mid-1940s, Ms. Carson became concerned about the increasing use of synthetic pesticides developed through military funding in the war. Aerial spraying of DDT and other pesticides mixed with fuel oil could potentially cause environmental damage in the future. Since environmental abnormalities always present themselves in fish and wildlife first, the biologists were the first to see the impending dangers to the ecosystem. Her research and concerns were recognized by scientists and biologists across the country already documenting the physiological and environmental effects of the different pesticides on insects, birds, fish, and humans.

The battle lines were drawn as she fought government officials and politicians over pesticide use. She was frequently discouraged by the aggressive tactics of the chemical industry but more and more scientific research mounted in her favor proving the harmful effects of the pesticides on a variety of species.

Her book, *Silent Spring* published in 1962, provoked a monumental controversy with personal attacks on her professional integrity. The chemical and pesticide industries took aim at her by mounting a massive campaign to discredit her and her work. Although she made it clear that she was not advocating the ban of pesticides, she was educating the public and the government that more research was needed to ensure that pesticides were safe for the environment as well as humans. By following up that research, safer alternatives could be found to the more dangerous chemicals.

The federal government actually listened to the concerns and ordered a complete review of their pesticide policies. Carson and other witnesses were called to testify before a Congressional committee which ultimately resulted in the banning of DDT in the U.S. During an interview, Carson stated, "Man's endeavors to control nature by his powers to alter and to destroy would inevitably evolve into a war against himself, a war he would lose unless he came to terms with nature."

Rachel Carson is widely credited and recognized for launching the environmental movement.

The list of influential women of WWII and their achievements could go on and on. The above women are just a few that may have been over-looked or forgotten in todays history books. Think about where we would be today without their important contributions of yesterday.

Chapter 11

The Manhattan Project Women

The Manhattan Project is recognized as one of the most top secret projects in American and WWII history as well as the world's first large-scale, science based technological project. The end result of the Project was entry into the Atomic Age by way of nuclear weapons, namely the atomic bombs dropped on Japan in 1945.

The Manhattan Project or Manhattan was a code name used by the military personnel that created it. The initial office was located in Manhattan and called the Development of Substitute Materials Project of the Manhattan Engineering District. Too much of a mouthful for those involved, the name was shortened to the Manhattan Project or simply referred to as Manhattan. The Project ran from 1942 to 1946.

Three main sites were chosen by the military for their Project:

1. Oak Ridge, Tennessee - code named Site X.
2. Hanford, Washington - code named Site W.
3. Los Alamos, New Mexico -

code named Site Y or "The Hill."

The Oak Ridge plant processed uranium-235 then shipped it to Hanford. Hanford used the uranium-235 to produce plutonium which was then shipped to Los Alamos where it was placed in the assembled nuclear weapons. Each site had a code name for what was being produced: Oakridge used the term "tube alloy" or "product" for the uranium; Hanford also used the term "product" for the plutonium; Oak Ridge referred to the nuclear bomb as "the gadget."

Over 600,000 people were hired to work on the Manhattan Project. Figures varied, increased or decreased, with the work progress at each site. When the initial overall construction at each site was complete, the numbers dropped considerably.

Hanford and Oak Ridge had the highest turnover of construction employees due to the terrible environment at each location. Hanford had desert like conditions in the summer with horrific dust storms, snow and ice in the winter. Oak Ridge had unbearably high humidity, dust, dirt, and mud year round. Los Alamos also had dust, dirt, snow, and mud, but fewer employees on the site.

Approximately 5,600 military personnel were assigned to the three major sites. Of those, 422 were WACS serving in a variety of positions. Initially, the WACS served as clerical workers, stenographers, telephone operators, general clerks, and motor pool personnel. Many of the women became skilled in more technical duties and filled positions of classified information handlers, metallurgists, electronics technicians, scientific technicians, mathematicians, engineers, chemists, and cryptographic technicians. Army nurses were assigned duty at the site hospitals. Each site also had women physicists and scientists working on projects pertaining to that specific site.

Approximately eighty-five women were instrumental in designing and constructing the actual atomic bomb itself.

History books give little or no credit to the women of the Manhattan Project not only because the Project was highly classified, top secret, but also because of the commonly held, negative attitudes toward women in science at that time. Even after the Project ended, the women involved, in most cases, kept a very low profile about what they had done.

Whether the Manhattan Project women were military, civilian, or scientists they all had an eye opening experience as they passed through the security gates for the first time at either of the three sites. First they were required to pass vigorous reviews before receiving final job clearance consisting of complete physical exams, lie detector tests, fingerprinting, and urine testing.

Next step was photographs, front and side-to-side for the identification badges which were to be

worn at all times while inside the site. Each badge
was color coded limiting the wearer to certain
locations and boundaries within the site. Besides
the employee's photograph the badge also listed
the height, weight, age, hair, and eye color, along
with the date of issue. Badges were carefully
scrutinized by armed military security throughout
the site communities. Entrance into a restricted
area not allowed by the color code on the badge
led to strict and immediate disciplinary measures.

Entering or leaving the site for whatever
purpose subjected every individual, including high
ranking military officials, to search. Cars were
searched, packages, handbags, and briefcases were
opened and thoroughly inspected.

Absolutely no personal cameras were allowed
on any of the premises. Parents had very few
pictures of newborns or children living on site
during this time period; only if the parents took
their children to an off-site photographer were they
able to have the family scrapbook photos of early
childhood.

All outgoing mail to family members was
heavily censored. There could be no discussion of
the location, the weather, descriptions of the
terrain, the activities of the letter writer or the
family member working at the site. In turn,
incoming mail was censored if any war activities
or news of family members in the war was
mentioned. Folks receiving mail often opened
letters with heavy black marks blocking nearly

the entire contents. Mailed packages were routinely opened and inspected. There were non-specific return addresses at each site; all mail coming or going from Los Alamos, for example, listed P.O.Box 1663, Santa Fe, New Mexico as the address. Birth certificates and tax returns listed the P. O. Box as the residence. Tax returns did not have the taxpayer's name, only an identifying number.

The secrecy of the Project was continuously reiterated on a daily basis to all personnel. Before the bombs were dropped on Japan, only a few dozen men and women across the country knew exactly what was going on and what the Project entailed. The FBI planted men and women at each site to work among the people to watch their activities and listen to conversations. Workers were not to discuss anything about the jobs they were doing outside of the work areas and certainly not with their family members when they arrived home at the end of a long day. Homes of some workers (usually the scientists) were "bugged" with listening devices. Notes and papers were locked in files when the scientists left for the day and their briefcases searched when they left the building. Those found with questionable guilt were sent for lie detector testing. If found guilty of suspicious activity they were severely reprimanded, fired, escorted off the site, fined $10,000 or imprisoned for up to ten years, or all of the above!

For wives (or in a few cases, husbands) of the scientists and others involved in the project, frustration and anger levels were always high. They lived in the middle of nowhere, in disgusting conditions, every action and activity was closely scrutinized, and they couldn't have a discussion with their spouse about the work. Most of the women were young and adventurous doing what they could to make the best of it, while others fled the sites going home to live with family until their husbands could finish the project and join them.

Doing their part for the war effort, many of the wives took civilian positions within the compounds at each site. School teachers, daycare, beauticians, barbers, secretaries, bakers, cooks, janitorial...the list was endless and the pay was excellent. One woman at Hanford was hired as a civilian secretary in 1943 and did double duty as the cashier at the entertainment hall in the evenings. She took home a highly coveted paycheck of $60 per week!

The one woman often referred to as the "guardian of the Manhattan Project" and the gatekeeper at Los Alamos was civilian **Dorothy McKibbin**. Dorothy was hired as a secretary to J. Robert Oppenheimer, the director of the laboratory at Los Alamos and commonly recognized as the "father of

Los Alamos Main Gate -
aka Dorothy's office.

the atomic bomb." Nothing and no one passed through the security gates at Los Alamos without paperwork crossing her desk for inspection and approval.

New personnel were sent to her for security clearances, badges, housing assignments, and orientation to life on "the Hill." All equipment orders had to be authorized by her and personally inspected by her when they arrived.

At the end of the day, Dorothy shredded every piece of paper that had crossed her famous desk. She was charged with the highest levels of secrecy and responsibility and shouldered her responsibilities well. She was a mother or grandmother figure to many. Oppenheimer may have designed and produced the first atomic bomb, but Dorothy did almost everything else!

Rose Bethe arrived at Los Alamos with her scientist husband Hans Bethe. Soon after their arrival, Mr. Oppenheimer hired Rose to assist his secretary Dorothy. By taking the position of Housing Director, Rose alleviated some of  the work pressure on Dorothy. Her job was to find housing for everyone assigned to the Los Alamos Project. The task was difficult in the beginning as houses were scarce in the middle of Nowhere, New Mexico, as it was called by many. A nearby boys school had been purchased by the government for the Project and dormitories at the school were used to house singles. Quonset huts were placed in various locations for married couples and those with children. As government houses were built, the scientists with families were given first priority to the one and two bedroom homes. Rose directed the moving vans to the assigned apartments, dorms and houses then assisted the newcomers in locating laundry facilities, shopping, and activities on and off the site.

Each of the Manhattan Project sites had similar Dorothys and Roses by other names, but with the same duties.

Rosemary Maiers Lane was another civilian employee of the Project and was based at the Oak

Ridge site. Rosemary was a Registered Nurse hired for the position of Head Nurse of the Emergency Room at the Oak Ridge hospital. The promise of a high paying, government nursing job away from home, drew her to apply.

Each plant production facility at Oak Ridge had its own dispensary for minor accidents or first aid, but serious injuries were sent to the hospital ER. All physicians and nurses working in the ER were trained in treatment protocols and decontamination procedures for radiation exposure, even though the concept of radiation was not well known or understood by many of them. All physicians and nurses were required to wear radiation badges at all times while on hospital duty or outside within the compound. The badges were checked frequently for high levels of radiation using geiger counters. Patients arriving at the ER from one of the plants were checked with geiger counters before admittance to rule out radiation exposure or contamination.

Between the dispensaries, the clinics and the hospital, some one-thousand patients were seen each day at the Oak Ridge site. The same high number of patients were also seen at the much larger Hanford site. Most physicians and dentists working at the three Project sites were military, having been recruited or joined from their hometown private practices to avoid overseas duty. Hundreds of Army nurses were assigned duties at the various Project sites' medical facilities.

One of thousands of civilian employees hired for work at Oak Ridge was **Colleen Black**. She applied for a position in order to financially help her family. Ms. Black lived in a dormitory and payed $10 a month for her room and sixty cents a day for a hot meal with meat, two vegetables, drink, and dessert.

Her position was "general laborer" in the leak testing department. She tested the miles and miles of pipes for signs of leakage or moisture spots. Colleen and her fellow workers were never told what the pipes were for, where they came from, where they were going, or what they contained. "Everything was a big secret and you knew better than to ask about anything for fear of being fired," she recalled during a 2013 interview. Because Colleen and her female co-workers had to climb around the pipes, they wore pants. "Most women wore dresses or skirts in those days, so wearing pants or slacks was somewhat of a novelty. Women's pants were also very difficult to find," she mused.

Miriam White Campbell was an architecture student joining the WACS in 1943. The Army recognized her talent and sent her directly to Los Alamos. Her orders were to visually study, then draw the internal workings of "the Gadget," the atomic bomb, as the scientists built it. Since no cameras were allowed on the Project sites, reproductions of the intricate, internal pieces and parts were recorded by her drawings.

Before being recruited to work on the Project, **Nancy Farley Wood** taught calculus to Navy sailors while her husband cared for their five children. She also made radiation detector tubes commonly known as Geiger counters. Her designs were the most effective and used exclusively by the Project. After the war, she started her own company and called it the N. Wood Counter Laboratory. She used her first initial instead of her name for the company because she did not want potential customers to know the company was owned and run by a woman. Mrs. Wood was an early feminist who became one of the first national secretaries for the National Organization for Women (NOW). She was a strong proponent for women's rights until her death in March 2003 at the age of ninety-nine.

As briefly discussed in a previous chapter, thousands of civilian women with mathematic and analytical education, experience, and skills were recruited by the military to perform highly secret calculations in a variety of areas. The most experienced and highly skilled men and women were offered positions at Los Alamos and Hanford. **Naomi Livesay** began work at Los Alamos in

1944, supervising a team of "human calculators." Naomi was a civilian with a degree in mathematics, experience in working with the calculating machines, and experience in analysis of survey data. Her team was to conduct calculations tracking the blast wave of the conventional explosion through the fissile material at the core of the bomb and then track the shock wave of the fission detonation back out. Code words were used to describe the preceding terms so the human computers had no idea what exactly it was they were working on. The calculations were essential to the development phase of the bomb and needed to be done under extreme time constraints. The human computers worked in twenty-four hour shifts, six days a week to complete the task.

American women chemists, physicists, and scientists of the WWII era may have been influenced to pursue their careers by the early

work and spirit of **Lise Meitner**. An Austrian born physicist, she had a keen interest in radioactivity and nuclear physics with her work in the late 1930s. Working with Otto Han, she discovered the theory of how the nucleus of an atom could be split into smaller parts. She named it "nuclear

fission." In 1944, Otto Han was awarded the
Nobel Prize in Chemistry for the work and was
referred to as "the father of nuclear chemistry."
Meitner received no recognition for the major role
she played in this discovery. This became one of
the most glaring examples of women's historical
scientific achievements being overlooked by the
male dominated scientific community and the
Nobel committee. Women around the world
recognize her as the "mother of nuclear
chemistry." She did not work on the Manhattan
Project and had no direct role in developing
nuclear weapons, although without her discovery
of nuclear fission, the nuclear age would not have
progressed. She adamantly refused to be involved
with any phase of nuclear weaponry or bombs.
Although Meitner was not American, her work was
quickly recognized in the U.S. by physicists and
scientists embarking on further studies in the
nuclear field.

**Leona Woods Marshall
Libby** was a young physicist
working at the University of
Chicago when Enrico Fermi
and his colleagues began
work on the production of a
controlled, self-sustaining
nuclear fission chain reaction.
Libby helped construct
detectors for monitoring the

flux of neutrons in the stack of uranium and graphite blocks that would be used to construct the first nuclear reactor. On December 2, 1942 she participated in the first self-sustaining nuclear chain reaction releasing nuclear energy thus establishing the feasibility of developing nuclear weapons.

Libby and her husband, physicist John Marshall, moved to the Hanford site in 1944 to work on plutonium production. She was the only woman physicist on-site at that time and was thrilled to have her own bathroom at the reactor building! She joked with her coworkers that she was a "reactor babysitter." While she was babysitting - carefully watching the dials, bells and whistles of the reactors - she helped solve the mystery of the consistent failure of the reactor to maintain the chain reaction necessary for the process. It was xenon poisoning.

Once Libby recognized the xenon poisoning

problem, **Chien-Shiung Wu**, a Chinese American experimental physicist, contributed to solving the problem. She called it "reactor poisoning" and helped develop the process of separating uranium metal into Uranium-235 and Uranium-238 isotopes using gaseous diffusion.

Her extensive work with radiation led to the development of more sensitive geiger counters. Her colleagues nicknamed her the "First Lady of Physics." During the Manhattan Project she worked in the laboratory at the University of California in Berkely

One of the most recognized women working on the Manhattan Project was German-born American

 **Maria Goeppert Mayer** a theoretical physicist who later won the Nobel Prize in physics for her work. Her work for the Project focused on the development of the theory of nuclear shell structure as well as processes for uranium enrichment by separating

Uranium-235 from Uranium-238. After plutonium production was underway at Hanford, she went to Los Alamos to work on energy releases in nuclear explosions.

Several men and women continued to work on different methods of separating uranium isotopes during the Manhattan Project. Although the work was being done at several Project sites, all parties were communicating their findings in hopes of determining the best process for separation. The results of their research found the fission process best utilizes Uranium-238 to produce plutonium.

Another physicist working on this particular project was **Anne McKusick** at the Oak Ridge site. Her focus was on separating the U-235 from the U-238 by mass, using a strong magnetic and electrical field. She was an outspoken person and not afraid to voice her opinion when she recognized an injustice.

Her voice was heard loud and clear by Project superiors when she expressed her dismay at receiving less pay than her male counterparts; her request for equal pay was soundly denied by the Army. After she left Oak Ridge she also left the field of physics and explored the biomedical sciences receiving her M.D. in 1950 from Johns Hopkins University. She became a renowned specialist in rheumatology.

Czechoslovakian born chemist **Lilli Hornig** traveled to Los Alamos with her chemist husband who had been recruited to work on the Project. Lilli wanted to help the cause by taking a position in the secretarial pool. When word got out that she was a chemist, she was put to work as a staff scientist working with plutonium. She became concerned that the plutonium had the potential to cause reproductive damage in women so she transferred to the explosives group. After witnessing the powerful Trinity test, the world's first nuclear explosion on July 16, 1945, she and other Los Alamos scientists signed a petition to have a demonstration of the bomb's destructive power for the Japanese instead of dropping it directly on them. Their petition was quickly filed in an Army wastebasket.

Frances Dunne began her WWII work as an aircraft mechanic then was later recruited to work as an explosives technician at Los Alamos. She had very small hands and excellent manual dexterity which were needed to adjust the trigger mechanisms in the bombs. Her group field tested mock bomb assemblies until they were confident the mechanisms would work in "the Gadget." Along with her explosives team, she witnessed the Trinity test.

These women represent a very small group of Manhattan Project workers and a glimpse of the work done in total secrecy during WWII. Men and women worked together feverishly to produce the plutonium for the most devastating weapon ever created. The overall fear for Manhattan Project workers was that the Germans were working on the same project and Hitler was unpredictable.

The first bomb was dropped on Hiroshima August 6, 1945, the second bomb dropped on Nagasawki August 9, 1945. Both cities were devastated and thousands of lives were lost. The Manhattan Project women (and men) had differing reactions to the devastation and loss of life their creation caused. Some saw their work as a major contribution in ending the war that had already killed hundreds of thousands around the world.

Others were shocked, often distressed and felt guilty for having played a part in such horror. All agreed their efforts marked a significant moment in world history - the birth of the Atomic Age. They also wondered where it would lead the U.S. and the world.

Oak Ridge, TN one of the uranium separation plants on site.

Hanford, WA the "B" reactor where plutonium was produced in the world's first plutonium reactor.

"The Hill" at Los Alamos, NM where the atomic bomb was built.

The following lists are not complete but are presented as an interesting overview of the many women involved with the Manhattan Project and their top secret work:

Physicists		Work
Anderson, Elda	-	fission measurements
Argo, Mary Langs	-	nuclear fusion calculations
Engst, Joan Hinton	-	reactor design, construction
Ford, Mary Rose	-	health physics
Graves, Elizabeth	-	neutron scattering
Hall, Jane Hamilton	-	reactor supervisor
Jupnik, Helen	-	neutron absorption
Keck, Margaret R.	-	explosives/medical physics
Marshall, Leona W.	-	reactor design, detectors
Mayer, Maria G.	-	opacity calculations
Mooney-Slater, Rose	-	crystallography
Nordheim, Gertrud	-	neutron diffusion
Quimby, Edith	-	medical physics
Roberg, Jane	-	fusion weapon calculations
Rona, Elizabeth	-	Po-210 initiator prep.
Speck, Lyda	-	neutron spectra
Stewart, Leona	-	experimentalist
Way, Katharine	-	reactor design
Wu, Chien-Shiung	-	xenon in reactors

Chemists/Metallurgists   Work

Batchelder, Myrtle   - analytical chemistry
Baumbach, Nathalie   - plutonium chemistry
Berry, Yvette   - prep and analysis
Cortelyou, Ethaline   - plutonium chemistry
Evans, Marjorie   - plutonium chemistry
Failey, Hoylande Y.   - plutonium chemistry
Fortenberg, Rosellen   - analytical chemistry
Foster, Margaret   - U and Th analysis
Gavin, Kathleen   - plutonium chemistry
Goldowski, Nathalie   - fuel cladding
Greiff, Lottie   - chemistry
Herrick, Susan C.   - uranium chemistry
Hornig, Lilli   - chemistry, explosives
Karle, Isabella L.   - transuranic chemistry
Melhase, Margaret   - co-discoverer Cs-137
Miller, Mary L.   - supervisor chem. lab
Mooney-Slater, Rose   - crystallographer
Nachtrieb, Mary   - Pu chemistry
Newman, Mary H.   - U isotope separation
Novey, Elaine L.   - chemistry technician
Perley, Anne   - biochemical radiation
Perry, Ada Kirkley   - analytical chemistry
Rona, Elizabeth   - Po-210 initiator prep.
Shore, Roberta   - chemistry
Stuart, Marie   - radiochemistry
Wagner, Juanita   - analytical chemistry
Weaver, Ellen   - fission fragments

Biomedical Scientists	Work
Bernstein, Elaine K.	- biologist
Christian, Emily	- biologist
Finkel, Miriam Posner	- radiobiologist
Frisch, Rose	- biologist
Gordon, Pearl Leach	- radiation exposure nurse
Hamilton, Kay	- biologist
Happer, Gladys M.	- physician
Jones, Roberta H.	- radiation exposure nurse
Lenoff, Gladys	- radiation exposure nurse
Koshland, Marian E.	- immunologist
Nickson, Margaret H.	- physician
Painter, Elizabeth	- animal studies
Perley, Anne	- biochem./rad. exposure
Stroud, Agnes	- microbiologist

Technicians	Work
Adams, Gail	- plutonium chemistry
Boykin, Pearline	- Pu chemistry
Cahn, Ann	- laboratory technician
Calhoun, Opaline	- plutonium chemistry
Campbell, Miriam W.	- bomb assembly-plan drafting
Casler, Ruth	- plutonium chemistry
Daniels, Minnie	- plutonium chemistry
Dayton, Jean Klein	- bomb detonator design
Divan, Rebecca B.	- quartz fiber balances
Dunne, Frances	- explosives supervisor
Estabrook, Grace M.	- plant technician

Florin, Kay	-	plutonium chemistry
Foreman, Beatrice	-	plutonium chemistry
Fortenberg, Rosellen B.	-	analytical chemistry
Giacchetti, Olga	-	plutonium chemistry
Gilbreath, Rachel	-	plutonium chemistry
Koziolek, Winifred	-	plutonium chemistry
Meshke, Virginia	-	plutonium chemistry
Mokstad, Betty	-	plutonium chemistry
Novey, Elaine	-	plutonium chemistry
Nyden, Shirley	-	plutonium chemistry
Pellock, Helen	-	plutonium chemistry
Perlman, Ilsa	-	laboratory technician
Perry, Ada Kirkley	-	analytical chemistry
Pinckard, Marian	-	plutonium chemistry
Pomerance, Eleanor E.	-	calutrons
Rubinovich	-	detector assembly
Shupp, Selma	-	plutonium chemistry
Speck, Lyda	-	neutron spectra
Summers, Mildred	-	plutonium chemistry
Thomson, Helen	-	plutonium chemistry
Towle, Virginia	-	plutonium chemistry
Walker, Evelyn S.	-	metal oxides, plastics
Wood, Nancy F.	-	detector design/ assembly

Mathematicians/Computers   Work

Bacher, Jean	-	science assistant
Brode, Bernice	-	computations Grp 5
Carson, Lillian	-	theoretical group
Clark, Joan Robertson	-	math assistant

De le Vin, Emma	- theoretical div. Grp T-5
Ehrlich, Eleanor Ewing	- IBM calculations
Elliott, Josephine	- theoretical div. Grp T-5
Estabrook, Grace	- statistician
Frankel, Mary	- science assistant
French, Naomi L.	- theoretical div. Grp T-5
Goldberger, Mildred G.	- computations
Hudson, Hazel	- theoretical div. Grp 5
Inglis, Betty	- theoretical div. Grp T-5
Johnson, Margaret L.	- theoretical div. Grp T-5
Kenney, Ann	- equations
Kurath, Frances Wilson	- opacity calculations
Langer, Beatrice	- theoretical div. Grp T-5
Manley, Kay	- computations
Monk, Ardis	- computations
Noah, Frances	- theoretical div. Grp T-6
Rosenbluth, Arianna	- theoretical calculations
Sniegowski, Angeline	- computations
Taylor, Ethel	- computations
Teller, Augusta	- theoretical div. Grp T-5
Uchimayada	- theoretical division
Wright, Edith	- theoretical div. Grp T-5

Chapter 12

The Women's Land Army

Today's WWII history books often overlook one of the most critical groups of women workers of that time. They had several names: farm wives, farm daughters, farmerettes, land girls, and the Women's Land Army. They appeared on government posters as "America's soldiers in overalls." This mighty group of women played

crucial roles feeding the world by plowing the ground, planting the seeds, cultivating, and watering the crops, harvesting, tending to cattle, pigs, sheep, and chickens from 1942 through 1945.

Before Japan bombed Pearl Harbor in 1941, America was shipping foodstuffs to the British and other European allies. Their crops and farms were being destroyed by the Germans resulting in a scarcity of food. The agricultural heartland of America was unaffected by the war overseas at that time; production continued as usual with the government purchasing corn, wheat, and livestock for shipment overseas.

After Pearl Harbor and the Declaration of War, farmers lost the majority of their manpower to the draft and recruiting efforts. Farm prices began increasing as the government increased demands not only for the usual corn, wheat, and livestock, but also for fresh fruit and vegetables. Farmers across America were being asked to produce more and more with fewer workers. Something had to give.

Farmers wives and daughters took up the slack as husbands and sons went off to war. But even family loyalty to the farm could not keep women from the high paying factory defense jobs. Farmers paid around $50 per month plus room and board for hired hands, $3 a day for seasonal harvest workers while factory defense workers were receiving around $12 a day.

In December 1942, Secretary of Agriculture Claude R. Wickard challenged Americans with a speech in which he stated, "Farm production IS war production…The farm front is the warfront… farming is a battle as challenging as the one the soldiers are facing…" While different government officials debated agricultural issues along with the increasing needs for war, the farm labor shortage continued to grow, crops needed to be planted, tended, and harvested. The stress between farmers across America and the increasing government demands intensified.

The Woman's National Farm and Garden Association was an organization of farm and garden club women across America that had played a prominent role in establishing the Woman's Land Army of America during World War I. The group was very successful in its efforts to aid the agricultural needs during that War. Members began lobbying for support to revive it for the needs of WWII. First Lady Eleanor Roosevelt also lent her vocal support to the reformation of another Women's Land Army.

The women's lobbying efforts, along with the First Lady's support, were successful. An announcement came from the Office of Civilian Defense stating that emergency recruiting of women volunteers would begin immediately in order to harvest the nation's crops and assist with farm work.

Farm journals and women's magazines began publishing articles encouraging women to seek training from farm wives and their children in order to work summer, seasonal, or vacation jobs assisting with a variety of farm work including harvesting. Programs offered by schools and organizations began popping up across the U.S.

with short courses in planting, gardening, poultry raising, and dairying. Fruit and vegetable pickers were recruited from nearby high schools at harvest time; teen boys and girls from age fourteen to sixteen were too young for factory work, but legally able to work on the farms.

The 1942 farm labor crisis was relieved somewhat by the women's grassroots resurrection and recruitment efforts of the unofficial Land Army. Even so, there were many farms with a vast amount of acreage in wheat, corn and other products that could not be harvested due to lack of labor.

One young woman who had spent her summer of 1942 doing emergency farm work sent a letter to the *New York Times* in hopes of raising further awareness of women's abilities to do critically needed agricultural production jobs: "We can drive tractors. We can milk cows. We want to join up quickly in the farm production army. We are waiting to go. But we will not wait long, because there is too much to be done and we will find farms for ourselves. Let us get together and organize a Women's Land Army. Let us get together right away." Again, Eleanor Roosevelt promoted the idea of the Women's Land Army during a nationwide radio address.

Finally, in April of 1943, the United States Department of Agriculture announced the formal establishment of the Women's Land Army with **Florence Hall** as the appointed head official.

Ms. Hall announced to the media that the work of the WLA would not be easy, but women working together would bring "dexterity, speed, accuracy, patience, interest, curiosity, rivalry, and above all, patriotism to the tasks at hand." The WLA would  become a part of the U.S. Crop Corps which was responsible for ensuring the successful harvesting of crops.

(Author's note: The difference between the Civilian Defense recruitment and the Dept. of Agriculture's efforts was that Civilian Defense was all volunteer work.)

Requirements to enlist in the WLA were simply to be physically fit and a minimum eighteen years of age. The women's optional uniform consisted of navy blue denim overalls, a tailored powder-blue sports shirt, a denim jacket, and a visored cap or hat. They had to purchase their own uniforms; however, not enough were available so suitable field work clothing was acceptable. The price tag on the official blue denim overalls was about six dollars.

Another massive recruitment campaign began in the spring of 1943. Posters and advertisements began appearing as if overnight with the following themes:

"WAR TAKES FOOD -
FOOD FOR OUR FIGHTING MEN -
FOOD FOR OUR FIGHTING ALLIES -
FOOD FOR
WORKERS
AT HOME;

WE NEED MORE
HANDS -
ENROLL NOW IN
THE WOMEN'S
LAND ARMY!
THE NATION'S
CROPS NEED YOU!"

In the 1943 Sears, Roebuck & Co. catalog, a full page ad appeared with a picture of a farmer holding a pitch fork with a farm house and barn in the background. Under the picture was the following:

Soldier without uniform

You also serve - you who stand behind the plow, pledged to feed the Soldier, the Worker, the Ally, and, with God's help, all the hungry victims of the war! - You also serve - you who farm, you who pray and sacrifice. You'll feed the World even if it means plowing by lantern light, and harvesting by hand - even children's hands - even if it means putting up the trucks and going back to covered wagons once again. - You're Pioneers once more, with the best land on the globe to fight for - to keep free, and the best tools on earth with which to do the job. - You also serve - and America salutes you - not for stars like a General's pinned on your shoulders - but for the stars you'll help keep in our flag and in the clean sky overhead!

The U.S. Department of Agriculture Urges you to:
*See your County USDA War Board
Meet your 1943 farm goals
Take good care of your machinery
Conserve your trucks
Turn in your scrap
Buy War Bonds*

***Farmers must win the Battle of the Land
with the machinery they already have***

PRODUCE MORE FOOD FOR FREEDOM

Information booths were quickly set up in Macy's, Gimbel's, Bloomingdale's, and other well known department stores, encouraging women to volunteer. Women's magazines ran articles encouraging readers to volunteer their vacation time, weekends, or any spare time to help with farm and garden work. Teachers were a great source of help during the summer when school was out, and many encouraged their students to also join in the efforts.

The WLA boosted morale by consistently praising, "The farm woman is the unsung heroine of the food front…she works longer hours than ever before…at the double job of housekeeper and farm work." Many of the WLA volunteers with no experience in farming were still valuable as housekeepers, cooks, and babysitters for the farm wives working their own farms.

Recruits began streaming into the WLA centers across the U.S. to serve full or part time in paid positions. Depending on the region, women were planting, tending, and harvesting vegetable crops from the Atlantic Coast to the Pacific Coast, picking fruit, harvesting nuts in the West, picking cotton in the South, de-tasseling corn, and harvesting wheat across the Midwest. They were plowing, feeding and tending livestock, milking cows, and preparing cattle and pigs for shipment to slaughterhouses.

Some farmers were initially very reluctant to allow women without farming or equipment experience to work for them. Many of the women

WLA members learning
tractor mechanics

had completed short courses in operating the farm equipment and were more than capable of handling a tractor, a thresher, a combine, or even a horse drawn cultivator. When the reluctant farmers were faced with not having their usual laborers, becoming exhausted and sick trying to manage by themselves, watching their crops go unharvested and the consequent loss of income, they began to seek the help of the WLA. A total of 250,000 women were placed on farms across the U.S. during the 1943 crop/harvest season.

Wages for the WLA women were no incentive for enlisting when nearby defense plants were also clamoring for help and offering good wages. Most of the women received $25-50 a month including room and board for full time farm work; part time or seasonal workers earned twenty-five to ninety cents an hour. The chief motivating factor for these women, as the government viewed it, was the "desire to perform patriotic service in wartime."

A majority of the women also felt they were doing things they enjoyed: working outside, watching things grow, working with animals, operating the machinery. Some felt factory work was not for them, even though the money was enticing, it was much more satisfying to work the farms. In an interview about her 1945 farm work, one recruit stated, "No matter how heavy the hay we pitched, how our backs ached from weeding, or how stubborn the team we were driving, we always had the secret joy that we were helping the war effort." Another recruit finishing her work on a dairy farm stated she would never look at a bottle of milk quite the same again.

After their experience with the WLA, women raised in the city or towns away from farms, gained a new understanding and appreciation for farm wives. At the same time, farm wives were recognized for their wartime efforts of maintaining their family farms, increasing production, their bountiful Victory Gardens, operating machinery, tending livestock and harvesting their crops as well as maintaining their homes and children.

In 1945, as the WLA disbanded, grateful farmers across the U.S. praised the women and the work they had done. Many agreed the women had successfully come to the rescue of the crops and were more than capable of performing any type of farm work. A North Carolina farmer whose daughter was a WLA recruit remarked, "Men may have fought to defend the land but women toiled it. Women saved our heritage."

Approximately one-half million non-farm women participated in the Women's Land Army from 1943 through 1945.

WLA members proud of their harvests.

Chapter 13

The Red Cross & Doughnut Dollies

The American Red Cross was founded by
pioneer nurse and humanitarian, Clara Barton
in 1881. Its purpose was to provide national
and international disaster relief and mitigation,
especially in time of war, as well as assisting
families of armed forces personnel with
communications. Members staffed hospitals and
ambulances at home and abroad. The inter-
nationally known symbol of the organization is a
large red cross on a white background. The Red
Cross also introduced first aid, water safety and
public health nursing programs prior to World
War I. After WWI, the focus turned to providing
services to the veterans, safety training, accident
prevention, home care for the sick and many
educational programs.

As hostilities mounted in 1939 across Europe,
the American Red Cross provided relief supplies to
our allies and civilian victims of the conflict. In
February 1941, as tensions increased overseas, the
U.S. government requested the Red Cross begin
blood donor drives in order to stockpile plasma for
our armed forces. When Pearl Harbor was
attacked, the Red Cross was ready, quickly

mobilizing volunteers and staff to assist in aiding the sick, wounded, and "...in accord with the military and naval authorities, as a medium of communication between the people of the United States of America and their Army and Navy."

The American Red Cross is a civilian agency that works closely with all the military service branches. WWII put the Red Cross to test in a number of ways utilizing thousands of volunteers to provide needed services for our troops overseas.

One of the most remembered services, from the soldiers' viewpoint, was the **Clubmobile** staffed by the "Red Cross girls" to some, or the "Doughnut Dollies" to others. The idea for the Clubmobile came from Harvey Gibson, a prominent New York banker and the American Red Cross Commissioner to Great Britain. The Clubmobile's purpose was to reach troops in the

battlefields, the airfields and encampments providing the servicemen with food, entertainment, and a connection to home.

Clubmobile serving soldiers at an airfield.

The Clubmobiles, sometimes referred to as Clubs on Wheels, began serving the troops in late 1942 and operated until 1946 throughout Great Britain and Europe. They were often old remodeled London Green Line buses driven by an Englishman familiar with the area and operated by three young American Red Cross women volunteers. The clunky old buses traveled at the rear echelon of the Army Corps, receiving their assignments to station themselves where troops were at rest from the front. The next day found the old buses lumbering along the dusty, muddy roads to another assignment. Later in the war, large more reliable two-ton trucks were also put to work as Clubmobiles.

The three Clubmobile women worked in the makeshift kitchen aboard the bus with a built-in donut maker and a kerosene stove which heated water to make coffee in large 50-cup urns. One Clubmobile bus made and served over 75,000 donuts in just one week! Candy, gum and cigarettes  were also available as well as magazines, newspapers and paperback books. Donuts, coffee and other goodies were initially free to the troops.

On March 28, 1942 the Secretary of War, Henry Stimson, sent an order to the Red Cross stating all servicemen were to pay for what they received from the Clubmobiles. The Red Cross officials and volunteers adamantly opposed the order and protested vehemently to the Army, to no avail. The Army ordered the Red Cross to follow Stimson's order. There was one exception to the order - mobile units serving the front line soldiers were exempt from charging them anything.

(Author's note: To this day, thousands of WWII Veterans and/or their family members remain bitter about that directive. Many did not have a penny for the simple pleasure of a cup of hot coffee and a donut or a pack of chewing gum. Many of the Doughnut Dollies freely gave the soldiers the chargeable items, risking their volunteer positions by doing so. Those soldiers, now in their late 80s and 90s, have not and will not support any fund-raising efforts of the Red Cross. The majority of them had/have no idea the Red Cross was simply following orders from the Army!)

The American Red Cross Doughnut Dollies serving overseas were carefully chosen from recruiting teams traveling across America. Thousands of young women clamored for the job as a way to travel, see other countries and support the war effort. Applicants had to be college graduates, single and at least twenty-five years old. They had to be "physically hardy," able to lift heavy equipment and pass a physical exam. Besides their physical ability and agility, the women had to undergo a personal interview which focused mainly on attitude, character, and personality. References were required and closely scrutinized. The women had to know the right slang, have an appealing look, a sympathetic heart, a sense of humor, be sociable and entertaining, know how to deflect unwanted advances, yet laugh at bawdy jokes or songs.

From the thousands of women applying, less than twenty percent of the applications were accepted, then only one in six applicants were selected after the personal interview. Those lucky enough to be selected underwent a six week training course where they learned the history, policies and procedures of the American Red Cross as well as the military. There was a ten-page manual regarding the ARC's strict clothing requirements; the volunteers going overseas were allowed to wear regulation uniform trousers, boots, the shortened uniform "battle jacket," and a cap.

When demand for the overseas volunteers increased, their six week training course was condensed into a grueling two weeks. Some of the women viewed as potential leaders were sent for additional training in management skills, group dynamics, program planning, and organization of recreational activities.

Once trained, the volunteers were sent by ship across the Atlantic to allied ports where they received orientation in the areas they were to be assigned. The shipboard experience was a first for many of the women and seasickness overwhelmed most of them. They arrived at their destinations fifteen or more days later weak and exhausted but excited to begin their duties.

Over seven thousand women were assigned to eighteen-hundred Clubmobiles that traveled all over Europe. From 1941 to 1946, the American Red Cross Donut Dollies served over 1.6 million donuts. American donations to the ARC during the same time period totaled $784,992,995 which allowed the ARC to purchase 1.5 billion cigarettes, 31 million packs of gum, 17 million decks of cards, 121 million razor blades, and 58 million pounds of donut flour, all for military and naval relief.

Some buses also had a Victorola with loudspeakers playing a large selection of current and familiar music from home. After the long lines of servicemen had been served their hot

coffee and donuts, one or all of the girls would crank up the volume on the Victorola and step off the bus to dance or sing with them. Some of the young men talked about their families at home, showed battered and torn pictures, or shared letters from girlfriends or wives. Sometimes the girls would hear the horrific stories of the battles the men fought, the brutality of the war, or of seeing their combat buddies die. The girls just listened and did their best to boost morale and assure the men they were not forgotten back home.

Although the girls worked twelve to eighteen hours a day facing hardships, danger, and fatigue everyday, they loved what they were doing and felt they were making an important contribution to the soldiers themselves, as well as the war effort.

The Army began secret negotiations with the Red Cross in the spring of 1943 in preparation for the D-Day invasion at Normandy, France tentatively scheduled for June, 1944. The plan called for the Clubmobile service to move ten vehicles, five Clubmobiles and thirty Red Cross personnel to follow as close in the wake of the armed forces as military authorities would permit. The assigned personnel included Red Cross Donut Dollies and Red Cross nurses, most arriving four

Red Cross Donut Dollies landing on the Normandy beach, 1944.

Red Cross nurses arriving on the Normandy beach.

days after the initial invasion.

Clubmobiles lined up to serve the second front of servicemen near Normandy, 1944.

By the end of July 1944, five more Clubmobile groups had arrived at Normandy with their personnel. Over 75,000 doughnuts were served, thousands of personal supply kits provided as well as movies shown and live music enjoyed by the servicemen.

The Red Cross nurses worked alongside the Army nurses near Normandy in establishing field and evacuation hospitals to treat the injured and wounded servicemen.

Clubmobile volunteers continued their service until V-E Day (Victory in Europe Day) in May 1945. Limited service continued in Great Britain and Germany until 1946.

Not to be confused with the Red Cross Club-mobile was the **Red Cross Club Service.** The Clubs were non-mobile service facilities located in established buildings such as hotels or vacated buildings. The Clubs offered hot meals, recreational activities, overnight accommodations (in the larger facilities), barbershops, and laundry

facilities. They were a place for the military men to rest and relax (R & R) away from the pressures of war. Red Cross Naval clubs were referred to as Fleet Clubs while airmen sought Red Cross Aeroclubs.

The Red Cross operated nearly 2,000 Clubs overseas staffed by 5,000 Red Cross workers and approximately 140,000 volunteers who were usually American women and locals.

Rest homes were also available to servicemen through the Red Cross. The rest homes were most often private homes offered to the Red Cross in quiet, rural areas away from any active combat. They provided restful sleeping accommodations, hot meals, and recreational activities.

On the home front over 3.5 million women volunteered in a variety of Red Cross divisions. Although many women worked in factories, war industry jobs, or maintaining the family home, they still managed to volunteer their time in aiding the war effort with the Red Cross.

At train stations and airports, across America as well as ship docks on the East and West Coasts, the

Red Cross operated canteens staffed by women

Red Cross Canteen volunteers ready to greet soldiers with home-baked cookies and goodies.

volunteers serving coffee, cake and cookies. As soldiers gathered to board their transports for overseas assignments, the women offered their home baked goodies, a cup of coffee, and a cheerful smile. The canteens also offered magazines, newspapers, books, cigarettes, and toiletries. Chess and checkers games helped pass the time as they waited; many of the game pieces were proudly handmade by Junior Red Cross volunteers in their school wood shops.

The American Red Cross also trained nurses, as mentioned in a previous chapter. Before WWII, the ARC served as a nurse reserve for the Army Nurse Corps. On October 9, 1940 the Army Nurse Corps called upon those reserves for a commitment to one year of active duty. The nurses heeding the call underwent four weeks of training in military courtesy and practices, sanitation, ward management, camouflage, use of gas masks, map reading, as well as physical agility, and drills (the same training as required for Army Nurse Corps recruits). Once all training was completed and physical agility tests passed, the Red Cross nurses were officially sworn into the Army Nurse Corps as second lieutenants. They received initial officer status to "protect" them from the enlisted men - the Army had strict rules against fraternization between officers and enlisted personnel. Many of the women served longer than their one year

Red Cross nurses ready to serve.

commitment. From the Red Cross Nursing Service, a pool of 71,000 registered nurses were certified to serve overseas duties in the Army and Navy Nurse Corps.

The Red Cross Nursing Service recruited over 200,000 women to provide volunteer health care services to civilians on the home front. Registered nurses received their initial training from the Red Cross instead of colleges or nursing schools then were quickly hired by hospitals across the U.S. to fill positions left by the nurses volunteering for military services. Hundreds of registered nurses who had not been working in the nursing field for a period of time also received Red Cross training to bring them up-to-date on the current nursing practices.

Thousands of American women volunteered for the Nurse's Aide Corps training program through the Red Cross. Once completed, the women pledged to work a minimum of one hundred and fifty hours annually at a civilian or military hospital anywhere in the U.S. Duties of the Nurse's Aide included assisting the Registered Nurses in patient care and in other areas of non-technical nursing services. The aides were especially needed in the military hospitals as thousands of wounded soldiers arrived from overseas and the Pacific to recover from their wounds. The majority of the aides far exceeded their pledge of giving one hundred and fifty volunteer hours per year. They enjoyed their duties working with the soldiers' rehabilitation and encouraging their progress. Many went on to study nursing and receive a Registered Nurse license.

The Red Cross **Gray Ladies** were another group of volunteer women providing non-medical care and recreational services at military and veterans hospitals across the U.S. All volunteers were required to undergo a rigorous training program provided by medical professionals and the  Red Cross. They learned hospital organization, ethics, psychiatry, and occupational therapy. During the peak of WWII, over 50,000 women served as Gray Ladies in 1,000 military and veterans hospitals on the home front. The name, Gray Ladies, described their uniforms which were gray with a white collar and cuffs.

Gray Lady volunteers were young women, mothers, and wives. Many had fathers, sons, and/or husbands in the military and felt they were honoring their loved ones by serving, doing their part for the war effort. They also hoped that similar volunteers would care for their soldiers overseas. It was heartbreaking for the Gray Ladies to see so many wounded and maimed young men - many with little hope for a normal future. The ladies wrote letters for the soldiers, read to them, often just sat or held a trembling hand while the wounded young man cried about his condition.

The volunteers also supervised and assisted with recreational and occupational activities at the

Red Cross child volunteers packing comfort kits for soldiers.

rehabilitation centers. They worked at the information desks, delivered mail to the patients, and helped at the Red Cross Blood Centers.

Many of the Gray Ladies, as well as thousands of other Red Cross volunteers, rolled bandages and surgical dressings for use in military hospitals at home and in combat areas. The Red Cross estimates over 2.5 **billion** surgical dressings were produced by these volunteers.

Comfort kits or care packages were also prepared by Red Cross volunteers and other organizations. The packages contained a variety of goodies including hand-made sweaters, socks, and hats. Food stuffs may have included a can of Spam, margarine, bacon, lard, honey, raisins, powdered milk and eggs, chocolate, gum, and sugar.

Food and medical parcels were sent to prisoners-of-war in Europe, the Far East, and Japan. Under the Geneva Convention treaties and protocols for the humanitarian treatment of POWs, the German soldiers were required to provide food, clothing and hygiene products supplied by the

Red Cross volunteers packing parcels for soldiers.

American Red Cross. Although the Japanese also signed the Geneva Convention, they did not ratify it and reasoned they were not bound by its terms. The Japanese believed the POWs were all cowards because they had been captured alive. Many POWs were tortured, starved, or succumbed to their injuries and treatment by their Japanese captors.

Approximately 163,000 parcels were assembled each week by U.S. volunteers. Additional parcels were sent by Great Britain and Canada. All parcels were routed to Geneva, Switzerland where they were then distributed to the POW camps and other detention centers throughout Europe by the International Committee of the Red Cross.

A typical food parcel from the U.S. included:

* One pound can of powdered milk
* One package of ten assorted cookies

221

* One pound can of oleo margarine
* A half-pound package of sugar cubes
* A half-pound package of Kraft cheese
* Six-ounce package of K-ration biscuits
* Four-ounce can of coffee
* Two D-ration chocolate bars
* Six-ounce can of jam or peanut butter
* Twelve-ounce can of salmon or tuna
* One-pound can of Spam
* One-pound package of raisins or prunes
* Five packs of cigarettes
* Seven Vitamin-C tablets
* Two bars of soap
* Twelve ounces of C-ration vegetable soup concentrate

Medical parcels from the U.S. were labeled "Red Cross Prisoner-of-War First Aid Safety Kit" and contained the following:

* A twelve page booklet with instructions for use of the enclosed medical supplies printed in English, French, German, Polish and Yugoslav
* Ten packages of sterilized gauze
* One package of 500 laxative pills
* Two packages of 500 aspirin tablets each
* Twelve gauze bandages
* Two cans of insecticide powder
* Four tubes of boric acid antiseptic ointment

* Two packages of 500 sodium bicarbonate
  tablets each
* Two tubes of Salicylic ointment
* Two tubes of Mercuric antiseptic ointment
* Four tubes of sulphur ointment
* One box of 100 band-aids
* Two rolls of adhesive tape
* Two one-ounce packages of cotton
* Safety pins, forceps, soap, disinfectants
  and scissors

Special "release parcels" were provided by the American Red Cross to many of the Allied POWs upon their release from captivity. France received 71,400 release parcels, the Soviet Union received 10,000, Italy received 9,500, Egypt 5,000 and 4,000 were sent to the Philippines. Each parcel contained the following:

* Razor and razor blades
* Shaving cream
* Toothbrush and toothpaste
* Soap and a face cloth
* Pencil and stationery
* Comb
* Socks and handkerchiefs
* Playing cards
* Book
* Hard candy, chewing gum
* A cigarette case with the ARC
  emblem on it

In many of the German POW camps, the parcels were opened by the guards and all items were reportedly removed except for the cigarettes and chocolate. Food items were sent to the camp cook and combined to stretch meals. Toward the end of the war, food was scarce for everyone and the majority of food items were confiscated by the guards, often for their own consumption, while the prisoners starved.

The Japanese did not allow Red Cross parcels or the ships carrying them to enter their territories. Parcels for POWs held by Japan were stockpiled in Vladivostok, Russia. In November 1944, under pressure from the International Red Cross, the Japanese allowed one ship to transport parcels to Japan; however, it was not known if any of the POWs ever received them. The Japanese also sunk a Red Cross humanitarian aid ship after which no further shipments were sent to Japan.

The Red Cross also sent trained medical staff members to POW camps to check on the health and welfare of the prisoners. Warm clothing and shoes were always needed by the prisoners and provided by the Red Cross. The items were often confiscated by the guards for their own use after the Red Cross team left. The quality of the food was a constant complaint from the prisoners as well as their Red Cross parcels being ransacked by the guards. Red Cross officials reported their findings to the appropriate authorities but little, if

International Red Cross mail room in Geneva.

anything, was done to remedy the problems. The Red Cross also provided the camps with books, textbooks, records, some musical instruments, and softball equipment.

The Japanese refused Red Cross access to any of their POW camps and would not share the names of American or Allied troops held there. The Russians were also difficult for the Red Cross to deal with. American families of POWs held in Japanese and Russian camps spent agonizing years waiting for news of their loved ones. The best the military could do was notify them that their loved ones were "missing in action."

While the Red Cross teams visited the POW camps, they made lists of the prisoners being held so notifications could be made to the military and the prisoners' families. Prisoners were allowed to write to their families once a month but the letter could only contain twenty-five words. Likewise, family members could send letters but they could only contain twenty-five words and only convey family news. All letters were sent to the International Red Cross in Geneva then on to their addressees. By 1945, twenty-four million messages had been processed for POWs and their families.

At the peak of Red Cross WWII activity, nearly every family in America had a member or two who had volunteered to serve in any number of the Red Cross divisions; even children participated in volunteering under the direction of the Red Cross organization. Americans not able to physically participate in a volunteer activity felt they helped the cause by donating what money they could (monetary donations totaled over $784 million). Over 6,600,000 Americans donated 13,400,000 pints of blood for military use. Red Cross volunteers and staff operated in more than fifty countries around the world.

By the time WWII ended in 1945, the Red Cross published the following statistics:

* Volunteers   7,500,000
* Adult members   36,645,333
* Junior members   19,905,400
* Paid staff   39,000
* Certified nurses
  serving the military   71,000

* Service personnel
  receiving aid   16,113,000
* Messages between
  servicemen/families   42,000,000
* Tons of supplies
  shipped overseas   300,460
* Families aided by
  home service   1,700,000

Sadly, fifty-two female Red Cross workers, and thirty-four male workers, were killed during their wartime, volunteer service.

General Dwight Eisenhower addressed Congress June 18, 1945, regarding the actions of the American Red Cross during WWII:

The Red Cross, with its clubs for recreation, its coffee and doughnuts in the forward areas, its readiness to meet the needs of the well and to help minister to the wounded...has often seemed to be the friendly hand of this nation, reaching across the seas to sustain its fighting men.

Chapter 14

First Lady Eleanor Roosevelt

Anna Eleanor Roosevelt preferred to be called "Eleanor" by her friends and family. When her husband, Franklin D. Roosevelt, was elected President of the United States in March 1933, and served four terms to April 1945, she became First Lady Eleanor. Recognized as the longest serving First Lady of the United States, she became a leader in her own right by shaping the role of First Lady for her future successors.

First Lady Eleanor Roosevelt with President Franklin D. Roosevelt.

Previous First Ladies remained in the background of their Presidential husbands and focused on the domestic and hostess type duties of the position. Eleanor changed that by quickly becoming the most controversial First Lady in U.S. history. No other First Lady had served their terms through two nationally traumatic events - the Great Depression and World War II.

Eleanor was denounced by many as naive, undignified, neglectful of her family, and subversive because she did not fit the mold for women of that era; very few married women with children (she had six children) had careers and even fewer were as outspoken as she was. One of her early quotes previewed her ideals:

> *We make our own history. It is more intelligent to hope, to try, rather than not try. Nothing is achieved by the person who says it can't be done.*

Later, she wrote:

> *In order to be useful we must stand for the things we feel are right, and we must work for those things wherever we find ourselves. It does very little good to believe in something unless you tell your friends and associates of your beliefs.*

Eleanor dedicated her life to human rights, civil rights, and international rights. She divided her wartime work into three categories: refugee issues, home front issues, and soldiers' concerns. She was an outspoken champion of expanded roles for women in the workplace, the civil rights of African Americans, Asian Americans, and the rights of WWII refugees - primarily children. She expressed many of her political, foreign and war views through her daily newspaper column titled, *My Day* published in 180 newspapers nationwide with readers numbering over four million. Her columns also allowed readers an inside look at her daily life, her travels, her humanitarian concerns, and how she handled the pressures of public life. She encouraged readers to write to her expressing their concerns on topics they felt were important. Within the first year that her column appeared, she received an avalanche of over 300,000 letters to which she gave personal replies to as many as she could.

She was a prolific writer penning more than 2,500 columns as well as 200 articles in various publications, published six books, and gave at least seventy speeches a year. In many of her columns and articles, Eleanor did not mince words. She was often very blunt when expressing her concerns in order to get her point across.

The outspoken First Lady was not afraid to utilize the media, in fact Eleanor was the first presidential spouse to hold a press conference.

She also gave an impromptu speech at the 1940 Democratic National Convention which helped her husband win an unprecedented third term. While President Roosevelt held office, his wife held 348 press conferences of her own. Women reporters had been barred from White House press conferences prior to Roosevelt's term. Eleanor promptly called for one press conference a week with her in which only women reporters were allowed access. Her first press conference consisted of thirty-five women reporters! Consequently, the news media rushed to hire more women reporters at a time when there were very few.

Historian Doris Kearns Goodwin in her book, *No Ordinary Time*, recounts the White House activity on December 7, 1941. Around 1:30 in the afternoon, President Roosevelt was in his study meeting with advisor, Harry Hopkins, when Secretary of the Navy Frank Knox burst into the room announcing the Japanese attack on Pearl Harbor and the destruction of the U.S. Naval Fleet.

First Lady Eleanor had just finished hosting a luncheon and stopped at the President's study at the same time he had finished a phone call confirming the attack. While Presidential aides and secretaries dashed in and out of the room, Eleanor recalled her husband as visibly appearing "deadly calm" but "inside he was incensed by the attack." Both the President and First Lady realized it would only be a matter of time before Germany would declare war on the United States. They also realized the U.S. would be hard pressed to fight a war on two fronts, especially with the Pacific Fleet in near ruins. Military advisors were consulted and the President placed a call to British Prime Minister Winston Churchill. "We are all in the same boat now," was Churchill's reply to the President.

That evening, the President dictated a speech to his secretary which he would deliver to Congress the next day, now known as the "Infamy Speech." First Lady Eleanor had her regularly scheduled radio broadcast that evening for the Pan-American Coffee Bureau. She pre-empted her scheduled broadcast with an address regarding the attack, thus becoming the first public figure to speak to the Nation about the attack on Pearl Harbor. She urged her listeners to rally behind the President and his Cabinet as the nation was lead to war, then called on women and young people to support the war effort. She also sought to calm fears. Her entire radio address follows:

Good evening, ladies and gentlemen, I am speaking to you tonight at a very serious moment in our history. The Cabinet is convening and the leaders in Congress are

meeting with the President. The State Department and Army and Navy officials have been with the President all afternoon. In fact, the Japanese ambassador was talking to the President at the very time that Japan airships were bombing our citizens in Hawaii and the Philippines and sinking one of our transports loaded with lumber on its way to Hawaii.

By tomorrow morning the members of Congress will have a full report and be ready for action.

In the meantime, we the people are already prepared for action. For months now the knowledge that something of this kind might happen has been hanging over our heads and yet it seemed impossible to believe, impossible to drop the everyday things of life and feel that there was only one thing which was important - preparation to meet an enemy no matter where he struck. That is all over now and there is no more uncertainty.

We know what we have to face and we know that we are ready to face it.

I should like to say just a word to the women in the country tonight. I have a boy at sea on a destroyer, for all I know he may be on his way to the Pacific. Two of my children are in coast cities on the Pacific. Many of you all over this country have boys in the services who will now be called upon to go into action. You have friends and families in what has suddenly become a danger zone. You cannot escape anxiety. You cannot escape a clutch of fear at your heart and yet I hope that the certainty of what we have to meet will make you rise above these fears.

We must go about our daily business more determined than ever to do the ordinary things as well as we can and when we find a way to do anything more in our communities to help others, to build morale, to give a feeling of security, we must do it. Whatever is asked of us I am sure we can accomplish it. We are the free and unconquerable people of the United States of America.

To the young people of the nation, I must speak a word tonight. You are going to have a great opportunity. There will be high moments in which your strength and your ability will be tested. I have faith in you. I feel as though I was standing upon a rock and that rock is my faith in my fellow citizens.

Now we will go back to the program we had arranged...

In March 1941, Eleanor visited the Tuskegee Institute's hospital in Alabama. As she was leaving with her entourage of secret service men and media, she spotted two airplanes flying overhead and watched as they landed at the nearby airfield. There were two young black men flying one of the bright yellow Cub airplanes and a black women flying the other plane (previously described in Chpt. 4, Mildred Carter). Eleanor was a strong supporter of African-American rights which made her very unpopular with the southern whites. Seeing the young black men flying the plane intrigued her. She instructed her group to take her to the airfield.

That field was the Tuskegee Army Air Field. After speaking with a few of the surprised young men about their Civilian Pilot Training Program, organized by the nearby Tuskegee Institute, she

 asked to go for a plane ride. Her secret service men strongly advised against it but she insisted, instructing them to photograph and film the event. They were to have all the photographs and film developed and printed before their return to Washington.

She had an idea!

Charles Alfred Anderson, "Chief," was the first African American to earn his pilot's license and the first flight instructor at the Tuskegee Institute. He is well known in aviation history as "The Father of Black Aviation." He welcomed Eleanor aboard, posed for photographs and off they went into the blue Alabama sky. Eleanor was thrilled with the one hour flight and loved seeing the countryside below.

Back on the ground, she thanked Mr. Anderson for the wonderful flight and chatted again with each of the young men who were present. She urged them to continue with their instruction and assured them of her full support. All of those present that day were left dumbfounded by the sudden, unannounced visit by the First Lady of the United States.

Back in Washington, D.C. armed with her photographs and film, Eleanor mounted her campaign to convince the President of the need to support the Tuskegee Airmen program and utilize the fighter pilots in North Africa and the European Theater. The rest is history. The Tuskegee Airmen flew more than 15,000 sorties, completed over 1,500 missions and never lost an escorted bomber to the enemy. No other escort unit could claim that record. The Airmen were awarded one hundred fifty Distinguished Flying Crosses, Legions of Merit and the Red Star of Yugoslavia at the end of the war. The success of the group contributed to the integration of the U.S. military. All thanks to a plane ride with the First Lady!

Continuing to emphasize her dislike for segregation through her newspaper columns, Eleanor wrote: "Freedom must be universal and all men must be assured that there will be respect for the individual human being regardless of his race, his creed, or his color." Following the bombing of Pearl Harbor, she was concerned about the war hysteria that would inevitably occur causing prejudice toward Japanese-Americans and warned against it. As war was declared on Germany,

Eleanor also foresaw prejudice occurring toward German-Americans.

Eleanor argued heatedly with her husband against his proposed Executive Order 9066 which would give the Secretary of War the power to establish military zones in which to intern Japanese-Americans as well as German and Italian-American citizens. Unfortunately, she lost her argument and was widely criticized for her views. The *Los Angeles Times* called for her to ..."retire from public life."

Over 120,000 men, women, and children of Japanese ancestry were sent to internment camps - 70,000 of those were American born citizens. Eleven thousand German-American citizens were also sent to internment camps, along with 3,000 Italians. They all lost their homes, businesses, savings, and property. Eleanor did not back down from her public and private stand against racial injustice. She visited the camps to show her support and frequently expressed the need for racial tolerance among all Americans. She repeatedly announced that it was wrong for innocent people to have to suffer for a guilty few.

In October 1942, Queen Elizabeth invited Eleanor for a visit to Great Britain. Eleanor studied the British home front efforts, visited the American and British troops, inspected factories, shipyards, hospitals, schools, bomb shelters, Red Cross clubs, and military installations in England, Scotland and Ireland. The First Lady was greeted by huge crowds wherever she went and never failed to personalize her visits by talking directly to individuals in the crowd. She was especially interested in what the women were doing to aid in the war effort. She found the British had organized on-site child care and factory canteens for the women which in turn boosted morale, daily attendance, and increased factory productivity.

While visiting the American troops she heard many complaints about their late paychecks, the lack of timely mail from home, etc. The First Lady fired off a letter to the President expressing her displeasure and disappointment and requested his immediate attention.

Eleanor wore her Red Cross uniform wherever

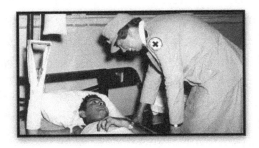

she went on tour. While visiting many of the Red Cross Clubs and Clubmobiles she learned of the controversy surrounding the volunteers' dis-pleasure with the military ruling of charging the troops for their coffee and donuts. She also learned the Red Cross workers noted many of the soldiers were developing blisters and infected sores on their feet from the Army issued cotton socks. Another letter was fired off to the President regarding the charges for coffee and donuts while another letter went directly to General Eisenhower strongly urging him to issue the men socks made of wool in an effort to control the foot sores and infections (shortly thereafter General Eisenhower issued the order for distribution of wool socks to the soldiers; however, the charges for coffee and donuts remained unchanged).

While on tour Eleanor collected the names and  addresses of the Red Cross workers and soldiers in military hospitals she met. When she returned to the White House she sent personal letters to each of the families stating how proud she was to have met their sons or daughters.

Chalmers Roberts, an employee of the Office of War Information at that time, accompanied the First Lady to Great Britain. Reporting to his superiors he stated the First Lady, "…literally wore us down, both officials and the press." She began her days promptly at eight in the morning and often went until well after midnight. When she returned to the U.S. in November, Mr. Roberts reported, "Mrs. Roosevelt has done more to bring real understanding of the spirit of the United States to the people of Great Britain than any other single American who has ever visited the islands."

Eleanor ventured into the South Pacific war zone in August, 1943. She was anxious to visit Australia and New Zealand to observe their home front activities as well as visit American service-men. She also wanted to visit Guadalcanal where the first major offensive against the Japanese had finally ended in victory that February. Although there were still scattered skirmishes, the President was reluctant to let her go into an actual war zone. She went anyway.

Traveling as the President's representative and in her official Red Cross delegate uniform, Eleanor visited seventeen islands plus Hawaii, Australia, and New Zealand. In Australia and New Zealand she met members of the Women's Air Force Auxiliary weather forecasters and marveled at their knowledge and reporting skills. She also met an all woman ambulance crew who did their own maintenance work on the vehicles and were able to easily lift the heavy stretchers loaded with sick or injured in and out of the ambulance.

Just as in her visit to Great Britain, Eleanor kept a grueling pace and tried to make each encounter a personal one. She also wrote down names and addresses of the Red Cross volunteers and wounded American servicemen so she could contact their families when she arrived back in the States. She visited hospitals, military camps, war and civilian factories as well as the many Red Cross Clubs. It is estimated she saw over 400,000 troops during her month long visit.

Everyday, no matter how exhausted, she set up her typewriter and pecked out her *"My Day"* column in about thirty minutes. She discussed the realities of life in a war zone and shared her many observations, one of which was, "No one out here has any pity for the Japanese. They have seen them do too many things which we consider beyond the pale of civilized practice."

She also expressed her sadness over the thousands of casualties and the wounded, some maimed for life. After a personal visit from the First Lady, many of the soldiers were uplifted by her kindness and compassion. Many of them felt they had just received a visit from their own mom. With her own four sons serving in the military, she simply talked and treated the servicemen as she would have liked her own sons to be treated. She was definitely a morale booster for the weary servicemen and women.

After her visit, Admiral William Halsey admitted, "She alone had accomplished more good than any other person or any group of civilians who had passed through my area."

This particular trip left the First Lady disturbed and depressed after seeing the devastation and carnage of war. She urged the President to redraft the telegram/letters sent to families of servicemen killed in action. They needed to be less cold and formal, more sympathetic and humane, she implored. The letters' wording was immediately changed.

Back home after Eleanor's travels abroad she resumed her wartime, volunteer efforts. She had many ideas for home front activities from the British and Australian/New Zealand trips she wanted to encourage on her own home front. She had always supported increasing roles for women and African-Americans in the war effort by encouraging war factories to hire them. Now she pushed harder by urging all women to learn a trade or skill to become useful and productive citizens while also aiding the war effort.

Once women began filling the thousands of factory jobs across the country, Eleanor learned of the high absenteeism among the working mothers due to the lack of dependable child care. She pressured the shipbuilding, aircraft and munitions factories to provide day care centers for their workers. Since the factories were under contract with the government, it seemed reasonable to provide government sponsored or assisted day care programs on the factory sites. Government approval was accomplished rather quickly and the building began (refer back to Chapter 9 The Eight-Hour Orphans).

Eleanor also lobbied long and hard for equal pay for women workers but was unable to successfully prompt any federal law or intervention. She was an early outspoken advocate of women serving in supportive military roles including piloting aircraft - the end result was the formation of the WAC, WAVES, SPAR and WASP.

At the White House she insisted the daily operations mirror that of all Americans with regard to food and gas rationing. A Victory Garden was planted on the South Lawn and utilized by the White House cook staff. The First Lady frequently checked the garden's bounty and gave extras to local charitable organizations.

Eleanor had been a long time supporter and volunteer of the American Red Cross serving as an honorary delegate for several years. She was instrumental in organizing internal improvements to the organization, especially after her trips abroad seeing first-hand how operations were carried out. Her regularly scheduled radio broadcasts were often peppered with pleas to support the Red Cross by donating blood, volunteering, or contributing cash donations.

The First Lady wanted to set an example for American women and their involvement in the nation's war efforts. She believed that actions speak louder than words so her actions were duly noted in the media. Pictures of the First Lady tending her Victory Garden, visiting Veteran's hospitals, visiting factories, day care centers or volunteering at a blood drive, were frequently splashed over newspapers across America. In Washington, D.C. she volunteered at the Union Station Red Cross Canteen where she made sandwiches and coffee, then distributed them to the thousands of servicemen awaiting train transport to seaport locations for overseas duties. She was not adverse to washing dishes as hundreds of coffee cups were quickly needed to serve thousands of servicemen passing through.

During one of her volunteer days at the train station, she was approached by a Navy Chaplain and was asked to inspect a nearby government run medical care facility for mentally ill servicemen returning from the war. The Chaplain was appalled at the conditions of the hospital and the way the patients were being treated. Eleanor toured the facility unannounced and found the conditions even worse than what the Chaplain had discussed with her. She noted the deteriorating conditions of the out-of-date facility, the lack of professionalism in caring for patients and inadequate supplies for proper care.

She successfully lobbied the creation of a commission to investigate and improve the facility and its services as well as other Veterans hospitals across the country. With the huge influx of servicemen returning from war, she felt it was important for the government to upgrade and maintain their facilities. The First Lady also encouraged the Red Cross to participate in setting up and overseeing recreation centers within or adjacent to the hospitals.

First Lady Eleanor Roosevelt is recognized for many things, perhaps most famous for redefining the role of First Lady to the President of the United States. She was one of the greatest social workers of the 20th Century, one of the great ladies in the history of America with visions she deemed worth fighting for. She is credited with expanding numerous opportunities for women and empowering them to move forward with those opportunities. Although Eleanor was faced with many challenges as First Lady during war time and often criticized for her outspoken ways, she did not stand down in her beliefs, "Do what you feel in your heart to be right - for you'll be criticized anyway. You'll be damned if you do, and damned if you don't."

She also remained humble about her achievements stating, "As for accomplishments, I just did what I had to do as things came along." Winston Churchill reflected, "She left golden footprints behind her."

Eleanor Roosevelt died November 7, 1962 at the age of 78 from aplastic anemia, bone marrow tuberculosis, and heart failure.

Chapter 15

Boosting Wartime Spirits - Radio and Music

Radio

On December 7, 1941 at 2:31 P.M. Eastern Standard Time, East Coast sports fans listening to the New York Giants vs the Brooklyn Dodgers football game heard the following Emergency Broadcast: *"We interrupt this program to bring you a special news bulletin - the Japanese have attacked Pearl Harbor, Hawaii by air. President Roosevelt has just announced. The details are not yet available. The attack also was made on all military and naval activities on the principle island of Oahu."* Within minutes radio stations across America also interrupted their broadcasts to deliver the news. All promised to deliver details as they became available.

An NBC reporter in Honolulu telephoned this report to New York: *"Hello, NBC. Hello, NBC. This is KGU in Honolulu, Hawaii. I am speaking from the roof of the Advertiser Publishing Company Building. We have witnessed this morning from a distance, a view of a brief full battle of Pearl Harbor and the severe bombing of*

Pearl Harbor by enemy planes, undoubtedly Japanese. The city of Honolulu has also been attacked and considerable damage done. This battle has been going on for nearly three hours. One of the bombs dropped within fifty feet of KGU tower. It is no joke. It is a real war. The public of Honolulu has been advised to keep in their homes and away from the Army and Navy. There has been serious fighting going on in the air and in the sea. The heavy shooting seems to be... a little interruption. We cannot estimate just how much damage has been done, but it has been a very severe attack. The Navy and Army appear now to have the air and the sea under control." His report was then interrupted by a telephone operator for an emergency call.

1940's family gathered in front of the radio.

In the 1940s, nearly 80% of American households owned at least one radio. Radio was a lifeline for Americans that brought news, music and entertainment from far away places right into their living rooms. Soap operas, quiz shows, children's shows, comedy, drama, and sports brought families together at the end of the day as they gathered around their radio. Never before had recordings of music and live musical performances been broadcast to so many millions of Americans. Before the war, 7% of radio airtime was devoted to news. During the war, radio sales increased boosting ownership across America into the 90% range. The number of news and human interest stories filled 25% of radio airtime as Americans tuned in for any hopeful word the war was nearing an end.

Radio brought the war into American living rooms by broadcasting live and recorded reports from battlefronts in Europe and the Pacific. Radio also brought news from home and the music our troops loved, as they fought in places around the world.

Radio commercials in the 1940s were most often aimed at women listeners. Kellogg's Corn Flakes gave listeners an "American Breakfast," and Lux Flakes helped wash the dishes "while leaving hands soft and smooth." Halo shampoo from Colgate "glorified your hair." Clean your hands with Lava soap from Proctor & Gamble after working in your Victory Garden, then enjoy a Lucky Strike cigarette. After a stressful day, try a Bromo-Seltzer to "fight your headache in three ways" unless you have the "American Stomach" of heartburn, indigestion, feelings of fullness, BiSoDol mints are the answer for you!

Programming was educational and informative especially for women faced with trying to prepare nutritious meals under food rationing restrictions. The *"Housekeeper's Chat"* featuring Aunt Sammy (Uncle Sam's wife) was extremely popular for many pre- and post war years. The program name was changed to *"Homemaker's Chat"* in 1934 and aired until 1944. The broadcast was an early creation of the U.S. Agriculture Department, Bureau of Home Economics featuring advice on what to feed the family for dinner, how to effectively clean house, fix a leaky faucet, sew a dress, plant a garden, and helpful hints for baby care. Aunt Sammy's recipes were the most popular shows with thousands of requests for printed copies. The Agriculture Department published the first recipe booklet in May 1931 simply titled, *"Aunt Sammy's Radio Recipes,"* with updated versions through the years.

Aunt Sammy was not the voice of a single woman, but the voices of hundreds of women across America reading from scripts prepared by the Home Economics Bureau then sent to a variety of radio stations. The radio stations not only hired women for the role of Aunt Sammy, but also for commercials that targeted women purchasing products for their homes and families. Programs such as *"The Heinz Magazine of the Air"* were hosted by women with commercials featuring the named companies products.

The Office of War Information along with the Radio Bureau wrote, produced and aired short commercial spots between radio programs promoting volunteerism for the war effort. Americans were encouraged to donate blood for our troops, contribute scrap metal to build planes, and ships or buy war bonds. Popular patriotic singer Kate Smith made fifty-seven commercial appeals between radio programs one day in February, 1944. She was able to raise $112 million for the war effort that day alone.

The OWI also launched the *"Womanpower"* campaign in 1942 that made a concerted effort to recruit women into wartime service at home. The following programs had those efforts in mind: *"Place of Women in War," "Women's Part in the War," "Women's Contribution to the War Effort," "Women in Railroading," "Detroit Woman War Worker."* Other OWI programs included, *"American Women Speak,"* and *"Women Can Take It"* which consisted of interviews and personal stories of women describing their contributions to the war effort. The commander of the WAACs (Women's Army Auxiliary Corps), Oveta Culp Hobby, was a frequent guest on the programs; she described the role of women in wartime at home and in the military.

The War Department created the Armed Forces Radio Service (AFRS) in May, 1942. After World

War I the military realized the importance of recreation and entertainment for the troops. Battle fatigue was a common occurrence among the troops often leaving them incapacitated, unable to continue their duties (now known as Post Traumatic Stress Disorder). Soldiers experienced boredom ninety percent of the time with disruptions of sheer terror the rest of the time. Radio and entertainment would be the answer for WWII soldiers.

From 1942-1949 *Command Performance* was broadcast over AFRS utilizing a direct shortwave transmission to the troops overseas. Produced in Hollywood before a live audience, the program boasted a military audience of over ninety-five million. Performers included celebrities, comedians, singers, and big band sounds. Jack Benny, Frank Sinatra, Bob Hope, Ginger Rogers, Ann Miller, Judy Garland, and The Andrews Sisters were frequently requested by the troops and performed without pay. A series of 415 episodes were recorded by the celebrities.

Another popular AFRS radio show during the same time period was *Mail Call*. This program also featured popular entertainers of the day to boost troop morale and remind them of their loved-ones at home. Lighthearted news pieces were often read between performers. Comedian Bob Hope had the troops laughing at his jokes and one-liners while Bing Crosby, Dinah Shore, Judy Garland, and other singers performed upbeat, familiar songs. The program was also produced in Los Angeles which hosted a majority of these shows due to the close proximity of the entertainers. Three male announcers, Ken Carpenter, Harry Von Zell, and Don Wilson began the broadcast by cheerfully greeting the troops:

> *"Mail Call from the United States of America! Stand by Americans! Here's Mail Call, one big package of words and music and laughter delivered to you by the stars from whom you want to hear in answer to the requests you send to the Armed Forces Radio Service in Los Angeles, USA."*

From 1942-1953, an all black radio variety show was created by a widespread Federal effort to recognize black Americans through cultural programs. The show was broadcast over AFRS as a morale booster for the black military members, but all troops enjoyed hearing the performances of the black entertainers and musicians. The show was *Jubilee* featuring Louis Armstrong, Scatman Carruthers and his orchestra, the "Duke" Duke Ellington, the "Count" Count Basie, the Mills Brothers, Lena Horne, Nat King Cole, and others. The programs were highly praised by blacks and whites alike for the best jazz performances of that time.

As many of the radio men were drafted or volunteered for military service, more and more women took their places and were regularly heard on the radio. The men who remained were most often utilized to broadcast daily news and any word from the battlefronts. Two women's voices were recognized by thousands and thousands of home front listeners and G.I.'s abroad for boosting morale: Jean Ruth Hay and Martha Wilkerson.

Jean Ruth Hay is said to have been the world's first global disc jockey. At the age of twenty-four, while living in Colorado near Fort Logan, she heard many complaints from soldiers about being awakened by the 5:30 A.M. bugle blast for reveille. She convinced the manager of the local radio station to allow her to do a 5:30 A.M. wake-up show six days a week with soldiers as her primary listening audience. She called her show *"Reveille with Beverly"* and became an overnight sensation.

"Beverly" (because it rhymed with reveille) began each broadcast at precisely 5:30 with the pop and fizzy sound of an ice cold bottle of Coca-Cola being opened followed by her signature line, "Hi there boys of the U.S.A..." She played popular music of the day featuring Duke Ellington, Benny Goodman, Nat King Cole, Artie Shaw, and more. She also took requests and often read notes from GIs, always with the (voice) appeal of the girl next door. Occasionally she was given scripts to read over the air with strict instructions to read "word for word as it is written…no ad libs," or she was given a list of songs to be played that did not exist. In June, 1944 she was given a song list dedicated to "America's Allies." The list she was to read included the following non-existent songs: "Opening Night," "Torpedo Junction," "I Dug a Ditch," and "Knocking One Out of (Uncle) Sam." That list contained secret messages to the French Underground, most likely in preparation for the D-Day invasion.

The *"Reveille with Beverly"* show was soon picked up by CBS and the Armed Forces Radio Service. The shows were recorded on vinyl and shipped overseas to be rebroadcast in nearly fifty-four countries reaching an estimated eleven million servicemen. In the Pacific Theater, some referred to "Beverly" as a counterweight to "Tokyo Rose" who broadcast anti-American propaganda. In 1943, Columbia Pictures produced a movie version of her story featuring Ann Miller in the title role.

Martha Wilkerson was a young twenty-five year old mother who had worked with the Office of War Information. The Armed

Forces Radio Service hired her to be the regular DJ host of their daily fifteen minute radio program, *"GI Jive."* The program was recorded in Los Angeles then shipped overseas for broadcast to the servicemen. Martha was known on the air as "GI Jill" and quickly became the sweetheart of homesick servicemen far from home. Her program was a combination of music and cheerful conversation which reminded the soldiers of their girls and families back home - the reason they were fighting in the war. Because her fifteen minute program was so popular and in demand, the AFRS granted her a second program, *"Jill's All-Time Jukebox,"* which aired for thirty minutes. GI Jill encouraged her listeners to send her requests for their favorite music or interviews with their favorite celebrities. She also added a personal touch by replying to as many letters from soldiers as she could, often enclosing an autographed photo of herself.

Although she was often referred to as America's answer to Tokyo Rose and Axis Sally, GI Jill's programs never had any hint of propaganda. Her goal was to boost morale not tear it down. It is estimated the number of *"GI Jive"* programs recorded and played for the troops numbered over two thousand.

Many Hollywood and Broadway women celebrities also recorded spots for the Armed Forces Radio Service during WWII. Lena Horne,

Doris Day, Rita Hayworth, Betty Grable, Linda Darnell, Jo Stafford, Billie Holiday, and Peggy Lee were all favorites of the servicemen as well as home front folks. These singers would say a few words of encouragement to their soldier listeners then sing one or two of their most requested songs.

Music

The most popular music of the 1940s was swing and jazz, but country, western swing, rhythm, and blues music were also popular across America. The Big Band sounds of Glenn Miller, Tommy Dorsey, Duke Ellington, and Benny Goodman got people on their feet dancing after the Depression.

A new dance craze, the jitterbug, was sweeping the clubs and dance halls as exuberant dancers flipped, skipped, twirled, and swung their partners in a fast paced, sometimes acrobatic, two-step pattern. A new form and style of jazz music also evolved during this time as young jazz musicians tweaked swing music a bit and called it "bebop."

Popular singers with the Big Bands were Bing Crosby, Frank Sinatra, Dinah Shore, Kate Smith, and Perry Como, all of whom eventually struck out on their own to record a variety of music and increase their popularity with listeners.

Music and song have always captured emotion no matter what the era or social climate. World War II music and song seemed to have focused on romance, strength and patriotism. It also had various purposes, usually influenced by the government. For example: *"I'll Be Seeing You"* and *"Praise the Lord and Pass the Ammunition,"* were songs that kept the home front folks calm and hopeful for the return of their loved ones, but for the soldiers, these songs brought loneliness and made them homesick. The most patriotic song of WWII was Irving Berlin's *God Bless America* sung by Kate Smith.

Music played by the AFRS, mentioned above, had to be approved by the War Department Office of Information and was always upbeat and morale boosting. It has been argued that music composed during the 1940s, placed emphasis on the home front listeners' perception they were a part of the war effort. For the soldiers perception, the music was patriotic and reminded them why they were fighting.

The creation of military bands during this time also served the home front listeners as well as the troops abroad by boosting patriotism and morale to both groups. Many of the musicians were drafted or volunteered to serve in the war effort. Over sixty Big Band leaders enlisted; however, many did not qualify due to health or age restrictions. Benny Goodman did not qualify but volunteered his talents to entertain the troops by making special recordings for the AFRS or touring with the United Service Organization - USO, as did others (the USO was, and still is, a nonprofit organization whose mission is to support U.S. troops and their families by providing programs, services and live entertainment to boost morale).

With so many bands losing their musicians, the women stepped up to fill those empty places. All-women jazz bands became popular and helped de-segregate music. In the beginning bands were racially segregated mainly because of the variation in music styles. There were many popular African-American women singers and just as many successful instrumentalists. These women had been playing and singing for years, often forming their own jazz bands then playing in clubs and private settings where they were welcomed. The war changed that.

The International Sweethearts of Rhythm was the first integrated all women's band in the

U.S. The fifteen member band travelled by bus across the U.S. playing swing and jazz at such venues as the famous Apollo Theater in New York

City, the Regal Theater in Chicago and the Howard Theater in Washington, D.C. The group received national acclaim as "the most prominent and probably best female aggregation of the Big Band era" and "one of the hottest stage shows that ever raised the roof of the theater!" At the Howard Theater the Sweethearts set a box office record of 35,000 patrons in just one week during 1941. In Hollywood, California the group recorded short films to be used in movie theaters as "fillers" between presentations. For the first time, female musicians proved they could play trumpets, saxophones, piano, and drums as well as the men.

Because they were an integrated group, they encountered segregation laws in many of the regions they toured. They ate, slept and rehearsed on the bus to avoid trouble in restaurants, stores, and hotels. The women were paid very little: $8 a week to start, a raise after several years to $15 a week and then to $15 a night, three nights a week, just before they broke up.

In 1945 the Sweethearts traveled to Europe with the USO for a six-month tour visiting troops in France and Germany. That trip gave them credit as the first black women entertainers to travel with the USO. When they returned to the States the group began to slowly disband. Some of the women moved on to other bands, some were just tired of the traveling, others were disappointed with the amount of pay for the effort, health, safety and family issues… The Sweethearts had a major impact on the music of the 1940s, but they were repeatedly ignored in popular jazz history.

One of the most celebrated African-American singers of the twentieth century was **Marian Anderson**. Her singing career began at an early age when she was awarded a first place contest prize to sing with the New York Philharmonic orchestra. In  the early to mid 1930s, Marian toured Europe, South America and the Soviet Union, then returned to the United States to make several cross country tours. Her engagements were booked up to two years in advance as she sang her way through seventy concerts over five months, traveling twenty-six thousand miles, the longest tour in concert history. But there were still places in America, at that time, where a black artist - man or woman - was not welcome, no matter how famous they were.

Marian was not only recognized for her beautiful operatic voice but also as a pioneer in the Civil Rights Movement before the Movement even existed. In April 1939, the DAR - Daughters of the American Revolution - refused to allow Marian to perform at Constitution Hall in Washington, D.C.

because of her ethnicity. What an uproar the DAR women encountered! First Lady Eleanor Roosevelt promptly cancelled her membership by submitting the following letter to the president general of the DAR:

"I am afraid that I have never been a very useful member of the Daughters of the American Revolution, so I know it will make very little difference to you whether I resign, or whether I continue to be a member of your organization.

However, I am in complete disagreement with the attitude taken in refusing Constitution Hall to a great artist. You have set an example which seems to me unfortunate, and I feel obliged to send in to you my resignation. You had an opportunity to lead in an enlightened way and it seems to me that your organization has failed.

I realize that many people will not agree with me, but feeling as I do this seems to me the only proper procedure to follow."

The First Lady wasn't the only DAR member to resign in protest of the discrimination; hundreds followed her lead. Mrs. Roosevelt and others quietly planned an outdoor concert to be held at the Lincoln Memorial. With permission and an invitation from the Interior Secretary, the concert was set for Easter Sunday, April 9, 1939. When

Interior Secretary Harold Ickes introduced Marian to the crowd and radio audience, he declared that, "genius knows no color line."

Marian took her place at the podium standing between Lincoln's famous words on the exterior wall of the Memorial - "with malice toward none; with charity for all…let us strive on to finish the work we are in; to bind up the nation's wounds" - and a diverse crowd of 75,000, as well as a live radio audience of millions, Marion Anderson's beautiful voice sang out across the country's color barriers as no other event or voice had ever done.

She began by singing *America (My Country 'tis of Thee)* and watched as the sea of people in front of her, blacks and whites, young and old, hats in hand, hands over hearts, sang along with her. She concluded the first half of her concert by singing

Ave Maria then returned for the second half to sing a selection of African-American spirituals. After a thunderous ovation she chose as her encore, *Nobody Knows the Trouble I've Seen.*

Marian Anderson showed all of America the transformative power of music - the sound of freedom and equality. Her Lincoln Memorial concert has been recognized as a crucial turning point in civil rights history. She also opened doors, literally, to other African-American women singers: Julia Lee, Lena Horn, Ella Fitzgerald, Sarah Vaughan, Billie Holiday, Etta James, and many more.

During WWII and the Korean War, Marian entertained troops in hospitals and military bases at home and abroad. As a frequent guest at the White House, she entertained visiting dignitaries with her powerful voice. Marian sang at the presidential inaugurations of Dwight D. Eisenhower and John F. Kennedy and was the first African-American to sing at New York's Metropolitan Opera House since it opened in 1883.

Marian Anderson died in 1993 at the age of 96.

Many popular Big Bands of the late 1930s and 1940s featured solo singers who then went on to perform on their own. There were few male or female vocal groups during that time, but one group stood out as the most successful female vocal group of the first half of the 20th Century, often times synonymous with the musical hits during WWII. **The Andrews Sisters** had a style all of their own that differed from the con-temporary sounds of the day. Sisters LaVerne, Maxene, and Patricia Andrews sang upbeat rhythm and blues, often labeled as "jump blues." Their trademark style was lightning-quick vocal syncopations which produced major hits

with each record release. They liked to think of their voices as the harmonizing of three blaring trumpets in front of a full big band behind them. Several band leaders felt the sisters took the focus away from the band and did not want to share the spotlight playing backup to a girl trio of singers. Nevertheless, the Andrews Sisters were very popular and in high demand across the country. Their music was perfect for jitterbug dancing which was the craze with teens and young adults at that time.

During WWII the Sisters toured and entertained extensively across America, Africa, and Italy. They visited Army, Navy, Marine, and Coast Guard bases, war zones, hospitals, and war production factories. They recorded messages encouraging the purchase of war bonds and blood donations as well as recording their musical hits to Victory Discs for the Armed Forces Radio. In Hollywood, the Sisters worked with Bette Davis

and John Garfield to establish the Hollywood
Canteen, a club for servicemen to enjoy food,
dancing and entertainment before being shipped
out for overseas duties. The Andrews Sisters
performed there regularly, danced with the
servicemen, served food, washed dishes, and
helped where needed. The Stage Door Canteen
in New York City was very similar to the Hollywood Canteen; the Andrews Sisters performed
and helped out there as well.

The Andrews Sisters were so popular during the
war years that their records were being smuggled
into Germany. To get the records into the country,
the smugglers changed the record label to read,
"Hitler's Marching Songs." The smuggled records
often found their way to several of the Prisoners of
War camps giving the American prisoners a sense
of hope. The Sisters' previous million record
seller, *Bei Mir Bist DuSchon* (To Me You're
Beautiful) was a favorite of the Nazis until they
learned it was a popular Yiddish song whose
composers were of Jewish descent. It was
promptly banned!

At the peak of their career, the Sisters were
averaging more than eight chart topping hits per
year selling 75-100 million records. They had 113
charted Billboard hits with 46 reaching Top 10
status (more than Elvis or The Beatles). Not only
did they sing swing and boogie-woogie songs but
also released jazz, folk, country western, seasonal,
and religious hits. Only Bing Crosby had sold

more records in the 1940s than the Andrews Sisters. The Sisters actually recorded 47 songs with Mr. Crosby of which 23 charted on Billboard making the team of Andrews and Crosby the most successful pairing of recording studio acts in show business history. Their million seller recordings with Crosby were: *Pistol Packin' Mama, Don't Fence Me In, South America, Take It Away,* and *Jingle Bells.*

The Andrews Sisters also appeared in seventeen Hollywood films. The film *Buck Privates* featured them singing their best-known song (to this day), *Boogie Woogie Bugle Boy* which was nominated for Best Song at the 1941 Academy Awards ceremony. Other hit records during the war years included: *(I'll Be With You) In Apple Blossom Time, Sonny Boy, Don't Sit Under The Apple Tree, Pennsylvania Polka, Here Comes The Navy, Shoo-Shoo Baby, A Hot Time in The Town of Berlin, Don't Fence Me In, Rum and Coca Cola, Accentuate The Positive, Get Your Kicks On Route 66, Hit The Road,* and many more.

LaVerne, Maxene and Patty left America with a legacy of music that continues to be popular even today. The Andrews Sisters have been the most imitated of all female singing groups in musical history. Their style continues to influence singers and composers alike including: The Four Freshmen, The McGuire Sisters, The Lennon Sisters, The Pointer Sisters, The Manhattan Transfer, Bette Midler, Mel Torme, Elvis, and Barry Manilow.

LaVerne died in 1967, at the age of 55; Maxene died in 1995, at the age of 79; Patty died in 2013, at the age of 94.

In any discussion of WWII radio and music, the name **Kate Smith** consistently pops up. Born Kathryn Elizabeth Smith, Kate has long been known as The First Lady of Radio. Her singing career spanned a total of five decades and included radio, recording, and television. During the Great Depression and WWII her popular patriotic songs and contributions to the war effort  endeared her to Americans at home and abroad. She recorded nearly 3,000 songs and introduced more new songs than any other performer, ever.

Kate's theme song was *When the Moon Comes Over the Mountain* followed by her signature

greeting to the radio audience in her folksy, southern accented voice, "Hello, every-body!" and her sign-off, "Thanks for listenin'."

The Kate Smith Hour was one of the leading radio variety shows from 1937 to 1945. The show featured comedy, music, drama, as well as appearances by film and theater personalities. Team Abbott and Costello along with Henny Youngman got their show business starts on her radio program as the featured comedians.

Kate loved to help people and was very patriotic. During WWII Kate was an Honorary member of the Red Cross raising more than $4 million for their work. After multiple marathon

War Bond sales efforts she raised over $600 million; no show-business figure ever raised close to that amount. She traveled over 520,000 miles entertaining troops at home and abroad. Even though she did not like to travel overseas, she says she did it "for our boys."

Perhaps the song she is best identified with is *God Bless America* written by the famous songwriter, Irving Berlin. Kate approached Mr. Berlin and asked him to write a song for her that would lift the spirits of Americans struggling with the after-effects of the Depression and the fear of impending war. He wrote a song nearly twenty-two years earlier but never published it or had it recorded. He found it deep within his files and presented it to her thinking it would be just what she was looking for. The two of them changed a few of the lyrics then presented the music to the Jack Miller Orchestra along with a huge choir and began rehearsals.

On Armistice Day (now known as Veteran's Day), November 11, 1938, during her regular radio program, *The Kate Smith Hour*, she introduced the song by saying:

> *"This year, with the war clouds of Europe so lately threatening the peace of the entire world, I felt I wanted to do something special - something that would not only be a memorial to our soldiers - but would also emphasize just how much America means to each and every one of us...The song is 'God Bless America;' the composer, Mr. Irving Berlin. When I first tried it over, I felt, here is a song that will be timeless - it will never die - others will thrill to its beauty long after we are gone. In my humble estimation, this is the greatest song Irving Berlin has ever composed...As I stand before the microphone and sing it with all my*

heart, I'll be thinking of our veterans and I'll be praying with every breath I draw that we shall never have another war..."

As the orchestral instruments blended together with the choir in the background, Kate Smith's powerful voice lifted in song as *God Bless America* crossed the microphone to her radio and studio listeners for the first time. Her song floated across America causing a momentary pause in activities as people stilled to listen. It was magical and magnificent! There was not a dry eye in the studio audience when the song ended, followed by thunderous applause and a standing ovation. From then on, *God Bless America* closed each of her radio broadcasts. The song and music became an instant hit selling over 400,000 pieces of sheet music over a short period of time. Many Americans refer to it (even today) as "the other National Anthem."

Both Irving and Kate agreed to waive all royalties to themselves from the performances of the song, instead assigning the royalties to the Boy and Girl Scouts of America - that designation continues to this day.

Singer-songwriter Woody Guthrie was so inspired by Kate Smith's *God Bless America* that he wrote his response, *This Land Is Your Land*, which has also become an American patriotic favorite.

A recording of Kate singing *God Bless America* was used as the last wake-up call for the space shuttle Atlantis July 21, 2011, ending the thirty year shuttle program.

Kate Smith had been overweight from an early age; she loved to eat and was a great cook. Remarks about her size (she was 5'10" weighing over 235 pounds at the age of 30) did not discourage or embarrass her. Instead, she is often thought to be the inspiration for the saying, "It ain't over 'til the fat lady sings," most likely referring to how she closed all performances with a song *(most often God Bless America)*.

Ms. Smith leaves a long legacy of awards and honors including:

* The only private citizen ever awarded the Legion of Valor medal from the Red Cross.

* Received the Presidential Medal of Freedom, America's highest civilian honor, October 26, 1982 bestowed by President Ronald Reagan.

* The only radio artist to be listed among the ten leading American women by the publication *American Women.*

* Grammy Award for *"How Great Thou Art"* - 1966.

* One of only four women ever awarded the

Patriotic Service Cross by the United Flag Association.

* Awarded two stars on the Hollywood Walk of Fame for recording and for radio.

* Posthumously inducted into the Radio Hall of Fame in 1999.

Kate Smith died June 17, 1986 at the age of 79 due to severe complications from diabetes.

Chapter 16

Boosting Wartime Spirits - Film

In 1943, President Franklin Roosevelt stated, "Entertainment is always a national asset. Invaluable in time of peace, it is indispensable in wartime." Whether entertainment was through radio, music, or film, it took the edge off wartime tensions for both the troops and the home front civilians. Film was also used for recruitment, military training and propaganda purposes. In wartime, the entertainment industry was often controlled by the country's government. The belief was to keep the civilian home front supportive and to remind the soldiers what they were fighting for. This required government regulation and some censorship during WWII as the new technology in media was able to get news, as well as entertainment, to the listeners faster than ever before. Few people could afford a television, but almost every household had a radio or access to a nearby movie theater. Newspapers and radio news stories were presented daily while weekly newsreels preceded government released films at the movie theaters. Ninety million Americans went to movie theaters each week during WWII.

The **First Motion Picture Unit** was the primary film production unit of the U.S. Army Air Forces during WWII. The military Unit was made up of film industry professionals including veteran actors Clark Gable, William Holden, Alan Ladd, James Stewart, and Ronald Reagan. Because the Army Air Corps was in desperate need of pilots, the Unit was contracted with Warner Brothers Studio to produce a recruitment film targeting young men as potential pilots. *Winning Your Wings* was produced in two weeks and featured the handsome James Stewart in the lead role as a pilot who served his country in wartime. The short film was quickly released to movie theaters across the U.S. in May, 1942 and changed the perception of military pilots. Over 150,000 young men were recruited as a direct result of the film.

Other films promoting military service included *Men of the Sky, Beyond the Line of Duty,* and *The Rear Gunner*. A surge in enlistment numbers was noted after the government release of each film.

Another segment of the Unit was training combat cameramen. There were sixteen combat units with twenty to thirty enlisted men in each unit. They were trained to operate a variety of photographic equipment in battle conditions as well as developing the film they shot on location. Since the photographers would be on the front lines filming, they were also given weapons and combat training. Training also included learning aerial battle tactics with enemy aircraft. Much of the WWII aerial photography still shown today was filmed by these men.

Perhaps one of the most difficult assignments given to the Unit was the construction of a large-scale, topographic and navigational model of Japan's islands. The top secret project was code-named "Special Film Project 152" and included every landmark, check point, every radar center, every Japanese naval vessel in a harbor, every railroad, buildings, forests, and rice paddies that would be viewed by pilots flying overhead at 30,000 feet. The project was to be completed within forty days, filmed and packaged for B-29 aircraft crews in preparation for the final assault, the atomic bomb drops, on the Japanese. The First Motion Picture Unit produced four hundred films during WWII. Most of the films featured male actors portraying military roles, training films, propaganda, or recruitment films.

Animation became more popular during WWII. **Walt Disney** and the U.S. Army began working together the day after Pearl Harbor was attacked. The Army wanted animated films to reach a variety of audiences for education, training and propaganda while the State Department wanted health films. Army personnel were stationed at the Disney Studios for the duration of the war to protect the facilities as well as oversee and approve the work being done there. Just as the large motion picture studios, the aircraft and shipyards, the Disney Studios were heavily camouflaged against enemy aerial sightings. The camouflage, when viewed from high overhead, appeared as a quiet California suburb.

The purchase of war bonds was a high priority. Animated cartoons were quickly developed to encourage their purchase and spread the word in an entertaining way. Bugs Bunny sang and danced happily in his cartoon feature *Bugs Bunny Bond Rally;* Donald Duck quacked out his approval of bond sales in *Donald's Decision;* the Seven Dwarfs and Three Little Pigs were not to be outdone, staring in their own cartoons - *7 Wise Dwarfs,* and *The Thrifty Pig.* In all of these short film cartoon features, the characters sent messages to spend less, save more, buy war bonds, and invest in victory by supporting the war effort. Daffy Duck, Pluto, and Minnie Mouse encouraged Americans to collect scrap metal to help build ships and planes and recycle their cooking grease to be used for making explosives - *Scrap Happy Daffy, Out of the Frying Pan Into the Firing Line*.

The government's agricultural division commissioned Disney Studios to produce films highlighting the importance of the American farmer, food production, and to encourage folks to grow their family food in Victory Gardens - *Food Will Win the War; The Grain that Built a Hemisphere.*

Animation was also used for training pilots, ground crew, weathermen, and navy personnel. Short cartoon features, as part of training, taught ordinary G.I.s how to behave, safety briefs, sexually transmitted diseases, and encounters with women who may be German spies.

The Army and Navy also requested Disney Studios to produce cartoon-type characters as insignias for their equipment. Over 1,200

were created including the famous mosquito riding a torpedo placed on PT boats; a winged flying tiger graced the Flying Tiger aircraft as well as the shark faced nose on their fighter planes.

Over ninety percent of Disney employees, during the war years, worked on the production of the animated training and propaganda films turning out over 400,000 feet of film. Women were often overlooked as animators but held positions in the Ink & Paint Department. Men created the animated celluloid sheets, or cels, then the women inked the cels coloring the characters and background according to the animators specifications. Over one hundred women worked exhausting double shifts in the Ink & Paint Department suffering eye strain and muscle cramps in order to meet deadlines for the thousands of cels needed for a single animated cartoon. I & P girls were paid $18 per week while top animators were paid $300 per week.

One of the "girls" perks in the I & P Depart-ment was "Tea Time" breaks twice a day; a uniformed maid would serve tea and Lorna Doone cookies in a designated and decorated tea room. This gave the girls a pleasant break away from their tedious work.

As in other production facilities, the loss of men to war duties opened many doors to women. Disney Studios was no different as the draft called many of their lead animators. The studio asked the women members of the I & P Department to submit samples of their artwork to be considered for jobs in the animation department. Ten women were accepted and trained for animation.

Retta Davidson was one of the first ten women selected for an animation position. She began her career at the age of seventeen right out of high school. Retta was hired as a painter and worked on *Pinocchio*, *Bambi,* and *Fantasia*. She worked in  the animation position for a year then took leave to enlist in the Navy, served four years then returned to Disney and resumed her work as an assistant animator.

 **Retta Scott** grew up in Washington State and moved to Los Angeles, California after she received a scholarship to an art institute there. She relaxed in her spare time

by visiting Griffith Park Zoo sketching the wild animals and their surroundings. Retta was hired by Disney to work in the Story Department on the Bambi project. Later moved to the animation department, Retta was tasked with animating scenes of the hunting dogs chasing Faline in the Bambi project. She also worked on *Fantasia, Dumbo,* and *The Wind in the Willows* (production of *The Wind in the Willows* was set aside during WWII to free employees for work on war projects). During WWII Retta worked primarily on the animated propaganda films.

Hazel Sewell Cottrell was Walt Disney's sister-in-law. She was very talented, with a sharp eye for detail and color utilizing different techniques. Mr. Disney quickly appointed Hazel as head of the Ink & Paint Department where her eye for color and

Walt Disney & Hazel Cottrell

detail along with her ability to work well with animators gained her respect from both departments' personnel. She was again promoted to Art Director and worked on the animated film *Snow White and the Seven Dwarfs.*

In 1941, Hazel along with her husband Bill Cottrell and a total of seventeen senior artists and animators, travelled to Latin America with Walt

Disney. The U.S. government asked Mr. Disney to undertake a goodwill tour to the area to counter a suspected Nazi influence. The three month long trip was a great success resulting in two feature films, *The Three Caballeros* and *Saludos Amigos,* as well as several short subject films.

Mary Blair and her artist husband, Lee Blair, were two of the artists traveling with Walt Disney on the above mentioned goodwill tour. Mary was a graduate of the Chouinard Art Institute in Los Angeles and was quickly hired as an artist and animator by Disney Studios. Her dramatic  and bold color designs were ground-breaking and inspirational. She worked on the art for *Dumbo, Lady and the Tramp,* and *Fantasia* before the trip then developed the art for *Saludos Amigos* and *The Three Caballeros* after the trip. After the war Mary worked on several popular films receiving credit for the color styling on *Cinderella, Alice in Wonderland,* and *Peter Pan.*

Her art and graphic design were in high demand outside the Disney Studios as well. She worked as a freelance graphic designer creating advertisements for Nabisco, Pepsodent, Maxwell House, and others. She also illustrated many of the Little Golden Books for publisher Simon and Schuster.

Walt Disney beckoned her back to design a Pepsi-Cola sponsored pavilion for the 1964 New York World's Fair. After the fair, the attraction was moved to Disneyland where it continues as a major attraction to this day - "It's A Small World."

There were many other artists, animators, and inkers as well as other cartoon studios during the war. The above is just a small sample of what these American women were doing during the war years.

Although many of the films during WWII depicted men in battle, there were many films starring women celebrities of the day. These women seemed to pull double duty by filming and actively participating in the war efforts. Here are just a few famous female names and what they did:

Betty Grable was the number one female box office star in 1942, '43, '44, then remained in the top ten for the next ten years. She posed hundreds of times for publicity shots in the early 1940s but it was her swimsuit shot in a 1943 pin-up photograph where  she was looking back over her shoulder that captured the hearts of GIs. It is estimated that over five million copies of the swimsuit pose were in the hands of soldiers around the world.

The term "pin-up" was coined earlier by *Life* magazine. When the Grable photo was released, the term became more widely used as soldiers pinned her picture up wherever they could. She was the number one pin-up girl of WWII representing the girl back home waiting for the return of the soldiers and end of the war. On one occasion she received 54,000 letters from soldiers requesting a photo as they prepared to ship out overseas from their base at Camp Robinson, Arkansas. She happily autographed 54,000 photos and sent them back to the soldiers. Her fan mail averaged over 10,000 cards and letters each week, many thanking her for her wartime efforts.

Betty never toured outside the United States to entertain the troops, instead she traveled across the U.S. visiting military units and war bond rallies. At one rally she is said to have auctioned off a pair of her nylon stockings for $40,000 and another pair at a different rally for $110,000. She was a frequent volunteer at the Hollywood Canteen, a popular club for servicemen,  managed and staffed by movie stars and studio workers. Betty loved to dance so she was a very popular girl to jitterbug with! The servicemen patiently waited their turn with her on the dance floor.

Bette Davis was one of America's most

celebrated leading ladies best known for her forceful and intense style in the roles she played. She stated that her "bitchy" style is what drew her fans to see her films. Her real persona was not bitchy at all when WWII was declared. She was one of the first Hollywood stars to step up and sell war bonds in early 1942. Bette sold $2 million in the first two days then sold an autographed photo of herself in character from her hit movie *Jezebel* for $250,000.

In the fall of 1942, Bette, Carey Grant, John Garfield, and Jules Stein transformed an abandoned Hollywood nightclub into the Hollywood Canteen. Bette devoted countless

hours to insure the success of the Canteen by soliciting donations of labor and money from the

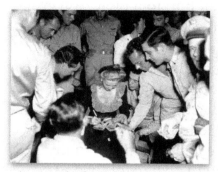
Autographs for the boys.

entertainment industry. The Canteen was a military nightclub for any member, man or woman, of the armed services where they could relax and enjoy themselves before leaving for European or Pacific duties. A sign over the entrance proclaimed, "Through these portals pass the most beautiful uniforms in the world."

No liquor was served, just coffee, juice, sodas, sandwiches, cookies, cakes and pies. The staff of 50,000 volunteers were primarily from the entertainment community featuring stars, dancers, singers, producers, directors, musicians, even hairstylists, make-up artists, secretaries, cameramen, radio personalities, and more. Bette made sure there were big name entertainers every night for the soldiers to meet, share a dance, autograph a photo, have a soda or coffee and not have to worry about what they were about to face on the front lines. Shortly after opening, the Canteen had fed over 300,000 servicemen, brewed 3,000 pounds of coffee, served 60,000 gallons of orange juice, and gave out 150,000 packs of cigarettes.

On September 15, 1943 the one millionth serviceman entered the famous Hollywood Canteen. Betty Grable greeted him with a kiss and

Marlene Dietrich escorted him to a table. Over three million servicemen enjoyed mingling with the stars at the Canteen during the war. In 1944, Warner Brothers Studio made a film titled *Hollywood Canteen* incorporating many of the stars in the film that had actually volunteered at the Canteen, including Bette Davis. Davis later stated, "There are few accomplishments in my life that I am sincerely proud of. The Hollywood Canteen is one of them."

Carole Landis spent more time visiting troops, especially hospitalized troops, than any other actress. She toured the U.S. selling war bonds and visited more than 260 military bases across America. She collected packs of cigarettes from the tobacco companies then donated them to the many volunteer groups preparing care/comfort packages for the troops overseas.

Carole was a member of the Hollywood Victory Committee as well as a tireless volunteer for the Red Cross. She gave blood as often as allowed and encouraged others to do the same through media reports and film of her donating at Red Cross collection sites. She taught basic Red Cross first aid and rolled bandages while enjoying the time spent with fans. She was a regular at the Hollywood Canteen when not touring the country.

In November 1942, along with Mitzi Mayfair and Martha Raye, the stars ventured out for a five month tour of bases in Europe and Africa. Carole visited thousands of wounded soldiers in field hospitals. She sang and danced for them and wrote letters home to their families.

While on a two month tour of the South Pacific bases, Carole became ill with malaria, amoebic dysentery, and near-fatal pneumonia. She was hospitalized for several weeks and lost fifteen pounds; her health was compromised from then on. Even so, she continued to volunteer for the Red Cross, became an Air Raid Warden, raised money for war bonds, and donated several movie projectors to bases overseas. All totaled, Carole traveled over 125,000 miles during the war visiting Australia, Brazil, Algeria, Bermuda, Scotland, Ireland, Guam, New Zealand, as well as multiple trips across America. Jack Benny remembered Carole by stating, "You soon forgot she was Carole Landis, the sex symbol, the Hollywood star, the sweater girl, because she was a real human being and had a warm heart that spilled over with kindness."

Because of the popularity of actors and actresses, they were a natural choice to solicit the sale of war bonds. Home front folks clamored to see them in person and gladly purchased what they were able toward the bonds. In so doing, the entertainers boosted morale and public support of the war effort. Here are just a few of the actresses and the generous amounts they collected:

Hedy Lamarr - $17 million in one day. She sold kisses for $25,000 a smooch. Hedy also volunteered at the Canteen by washing dishes and waiting tables.

Dorothy Lamour - $30 million in four days and a total of $350 million from kisses and autographs.

Carole Lombard - $2 million in one evening while attending a war bond rally in her home state of Indiana. Sadly, as she and family members were returning to California, her plane crashed into a mountain just after takeoff from Las Vegas on January 16, 1942. All aboard were killed. President Roosevelt honored her patriotic spirit by declaring her the first woman killed in the line of duty during the war. He posthumously awarded her the Presidential Medal of Freedom.

The February 1943 issue of *Modern Screen* magazine lauded the movie stars and movie industry for their bond efforts with the following:

...war bond sales amount to $838,250,000! Among the things this sum can bring are eight battleships for your sons! Or twenty-four cruisers

for your brothers! Six hundred-seventy sub chasers, one hundred-twenty subs, or tanks, bombers or freighters! Our boys aren't going to die for lack of equipment, ever again, and we can thank our "stars" for much of the good work!

Many other actresses contributed to the war effort by publicly demonstrating to Americans, "If we can do it, so can you." **Rita Hayworth** was the icon for scrap metal drives. She had the bumpers removed from her car and replaced with a sign reading, "PLEASE DRIVE CAREFULLY - MY BUMPERS ARE ON THE SCRAP HEAP."

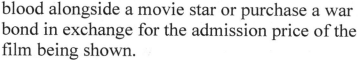

Theaters across America offered movie goers the chance to donate blood alongside a movie star or purchase a war bond in exchange for the admission price of the film being shown.

Huge, highly publicized tours of celebrities crisscrossing America raised vast sums of money for war bonds and entertained troops. The **Stars Over America** tour boasted over three hundred actors and actresses traveling to over three hundred cities and towns for the war bond drive. The group raised $775 million on their highly publicized tour with another $86 million collected on their final stop at Madison Square Garden in New York.

The Hollywood Victory Caravan was a smaller group headed by Bob Hope and twenty-one of his celebrity friends. Bing Crosby, Desi Arnaz, Cary Grant, Claudette Colbert, Olivia de Havillan, and Groucho Marx were a few performers presenting shows across America at military bases for the Army and Navy Relief Funds.

The U.S.O. tours also traveled to military bases across America as well as overseas. The travel was often dangerous and/or hazardous due to weather conditions or enemy fire. Bob Hope is synonymous with U.S.O. shows performed for hundreds of thousands of troops during WWII and beyond. Many of the young women on the overseas tours had never been abroad and viewed their trip as an adventure. Instead of a well-lit soundstage, the women found themselves singing, dancing, telling jokes in ankle deep mud, pouring rain, blistering heat, big buzzing bugs in their hair and clothing, or even gun fire. When the women saw the sea of servicemen and women, the looks on their faces and the thunderous applause given, it humbled them.

Visiting hospitals was the hardest for the women. The maimed bodies and frightened eyes were heartbreaking to see but a kind word, a song, a joke or two that brought a smile to the wounded made the trip worthwhile, meaningful and never forgotten.

Twenty-eight performers died on U.S.O. tours from plane crashes, illness, or diseases contracted while on the tour.

Several women movie stars aided the war effort by enlisting. **Myrna Loy** was disappointed to learn she was too old to serve in an active duty role so she quit making movies and served with the Red Cross. Her service with the Red Cross launched what she called her second career, becoming an activist and philanthropist.

Martha Ray was a singer and a comedian best known for her travels with the U.S.O. during WWII, Korea, and Vietnam. The troops lovingly referred to her as "Colonel Maggie" and bestowed the honorary rank of Lt. Colonel Green Beret Special Forces upon her as well as honorary Colonel in the U.S. Marine Corps. Martha was awarded the Presidential Medal of Freedom by President Clinton in 1993. She is the only woman buried in the Special Forces section of the cemetery at Fort Bragg, North Carolina.

Bea Arthur was one of the first women to become an active duty U.S. Marine in the Marine Corps Women's Reserve. Bea served as a truck driver and a typist while stationed at Marine bases in Virginia and North Carolina. She began her service as a private and quickly rose  through the ranks to staff sergeant, received an honorable discharge in 1945, and continued her acting career.

Hollywood actresses were not the only women stars to participate in the war efforts. In New York's theater district, women banded together to re-establish the Stage Women's War Relief which originally formed in WWI. The name was changed to American Theatre Wing for War Service; the focus also changed from knitting socks and sweaters to opening a recreation center where servicemen could gather, relax, enjoy entertainment, dancing, and snacks. In March 1942, the **Stage Door Canteen** held an open house for the public prior to opening for the servicemen. The price of admission: donations of food supplies for the kitchen. Over half a ton of sugar was donated as well as coffee and sandwich materials.

A local radio station repeatedly asked for donations throughout the Canteen's service which were gladly met by local citizens and businesses.

The remodeled basement was small, accommodating only 500 at a time, but the volunteers admitted the servicemen in shifts which then allowed a crowd of 2,000 each evening to enjoy the club, seven nights a week.

All volunteers were Broadway show people, actors, actresses, comedians, dancers, singers - all committed to seeing that the servicemen and women had a good time. Gertrude Lawrence, Talulah Bankhead, Helen Hayes, Katherine Hepburn, Gypsy Rose Lee, Ethel Merman, Bette Davis, and a relative newcomer, Lauren Bacall, all volunteered to sing, dance, make sandwiches, wait tables, serve coffee (no liquor allowed), wash dishes, and sweep floors. Bette Davis was so impressed with the New York Canteen, she took the idea to Hollywood and opened the Hollywood Canteen that same year (discussed earlier). Other cities across the U.S. quickly followed suit opening their own Canteens; however, the most famous and most popular were the New York and Hollywood Canteens.

The film industry played an important role in helping Americans at home and fighting in the farthest reaches abroad, to pull together and support one another. New technology in filming and recording made it possible for Americans to actually see what their soldiers were up against as well as allowing the soldiers reminders of why they were fighting. Some of the most inspirational and memorable films were produced during WWII and featured many of our most beloved actors and actresses.

Entertainers worked tirelessly to raise money for war bonds or traveled into hostile combat areas to remind the soldiers America awaits their return, they have not been forgotten. These entertainers' lives were also changed by their experiences in the war effort. Perhaps Bob Hope said it best for all involved, *"Thanks for the memories!"*

Chapter 17

Boosting Wartime Spirits - Entertainment

Baseball, the All-American sport and national pastime, was also greatly affected by WWII. Professional ballplayers were known for their physical strength, good health and abilities which also made them the best candidates for the draft. Over five hundred major league and more than two thousand minor league players were either drafted or volunteered to serve in the military. This left the teams scrambling to find players and some Americans wondering if it was really necessary to continue with professional baseball during wartime.

While home front families sent their loved ones off to war, many felt a bit resentful that some professional athletes were not being asked to also serve - they were fit to play baseball, but not fit for war duty? A flurry of letters to the editor appeared in newspapers across the states with a variety of responses. Baseball's response: players classified as 4-F were found to be unfit for service by Army and Navy doctors, not baseball's doctors.

In January 1942, with spring training camp just a few months away and the increasing public tension regarding players, baseball commissioner Judge Kenesaw Landis sent a personal letter to President Franklin Roosevelt asking his opinion on whether major league baseball should be suspended for the duration of the war. The President loved baseball (although he was a terrible player during his school years), attended eight opening day appearances during his time in office, and often threw out the first pitch. His response to Landis' letter was immediate:

> *My dear Judge:*
> *Thank you for yours of January fourteenth. As you will, of course, realize the final decision about the baseball season must rest with you and the Baseball Club owners - so what I am going to say is solely a personal and not an official point of view.*
> *I honestly feel that it would be best for the country to keep baseball going. There will be fewer people unemployed and everybody will work longer hours and harder than ever before.*
> *And that means that they ought to have a chance for recreation and for taking their minds off their work even more than before. Baseball provides a recreation which does not last over two hours or two hours and a half, and which can be got for very little cost. And, incidentally, I hope that night games can be extended because it gives an opportunity to the day shift to see a game occasionally.*

As to the players themselves, I know you agree with me that the individual players who are active military or naval age should go, without question, into the services. Even if the actual quality to the teams is lowered by the greater use of older players, this will not dampen the popularity of the sport. Of course, if an individual has some particular aptitude in a trade or profession, he ought to serve the Government. That, however, is a matter which I know you can handle with complete justice.

Here is another way of looking at it - if 300 teams use 5,000 or 6,000 players, these players are a definite recreational asset to at least 20,000,000 of the fellow citizens - and that in my judgment is thoroughly worthwhile.

With every best wish,
Very sincerely yours,
Franklin D. Roosevelt

The *Chicago Sun* dubbed the President's letter the *Green Light Letter* calling it "the most notable contribution to baseball in our time." The 1942 baseball season opened as scheduled. The teams hardest hit by the war were the minor league teams. In 1940 there were 44 minor leagues with 310 clubs; by 1943 there were just 9 leagues with 66 clubs.

The major league had two leagues with eight teams in ten cities, most in the Northeast and Midwest. The quality of the team players, for both minor and major league teams, dropped considerably as contracts were offered to older players, younger players classified 4-F by the military, and disabled players (a one-armed outfielder and a pitcher with an artificial leg were amazing to watch). So major league baseball continued, although not quite the same.

Philip Wrigley owned the Wrigley's Chewing Gum empire as well as the Chicago Cubs Major League Baseball team. He wanted to maintain baseball in the public's eye during the war years and utilize the many baseball parks going unused due to the loss of teams. Along with a group of Midwestern businessmen, Wrigley started a new professional league of all woman ballplayers - **The All-American Girls Professional Baseball League.** He believed that baseball's ultimate survival during the war years depended on women.

Wrigley sent baseball scouts and recruiters across the country and into Canada to look for good ball players in high schools, industrial leagues, organized ball teams, even church leagues. Two hundred-eighty women were invited to tryouts in Chicago from May 17-26, 1943 for sixty positions on four teams. The women were carefully chosen for their throwing, catching, running, sliding, hitting, and ability to play their field position. Those making the rosters were the first sixty women to ever play professional baseball. Contracts were signed with strict clauses for compliance and adherence to the rules, not only of baseball rules but also moral standards and rules of conduct on and off the playing field.

The first players to sign were **Clara Schillace, Ann Harnett, Edie Perlick** and **Shirley Jameson**. Starting salaries ranged from $45 to $85 a week then up to $125 in later years, plus bonuses.

Back L-R: Clara, Ann, Edie
Seated: Shirley

One of the contractual agreements was the requirement to attend Helena Rubenstein's Beauty Salon and Charm School classes. The women were taught the proper etiquette for every situation since they would be constantly in the public eye and media. Personal hygiene, dress code and makeup were also presented. Each woman was given a beauty kit full of cosmetics, creams and skin lotions with instructions on how to apply and use them. Lipstick (preferably bright red) was to be worn at all times. The women were not allowed to smoke or drink in public. Hair fashions and self-styling techniques were also discussed; short hair, cut above the shoulders, was not permitted. The ballplayers were expected to look and act like women but play like men.

Uniforms were belted, short-sleeved tunic styled dresses with a flare of the skirt to allow for running and fielding. Their design was modeled after figure skaters' dresses of the day. They were not to be more than six inches above the knee. A team logo was sewn on the front of each dress; dress colors varied by team. Satin shorts were worn under the dress, knee-high baseball socks and a baseball cap with an elastic band across the back completed the uniform. Each woman purchased their own cleats and baseball mitts or gloves. Fines for not following the rules were five dollars for the first offense, ten for the second and suspension for the third.

When not playing or practicing, the teams were expected to visit wounded veterans at nearby hospitals, volunteer, sell war bonds or participate in exhibition games in support of the Red Cross.

Rules of the game itself had to be defined since women played softball, not baseball. To make the games more appealing to the crowds, increase hitting, spotlight base running and fielding, the base paths utilized in softball were extended as well as the pitching distance to home plate from a mound instead of flat ground. The size of the ball also changed - smaller, more like a baseball instead of a softball. Pitching changed from underhand windmill (softball) to overhand pitching (baseball).

Softball had ten players, this new game would have nine, although team rosters consisted of fifteen players.

A total of 108 games were played in a regular season which ran from mid-May to the first of September. The team with the most wins became the pennant winner then went on to a series play-off to determine the League Champion.

The first four cities selected to have a team were located close to each other and near Chicago due to travel restrictions - no travel by vehicle at night due to black out regulations and gas rationing. Gas rationing also affected how far the fans could travel to see the games. Gas was limited to three gallons a week with most vehicles of that time easily able to travel forty miles on three gallons.

The cities selected to have a team(s) were: South Bend, Indiana; Kenosha and Racine, Wisconsin; and Rockford, Illinois. The team names included the Kenosha Comets, Racine Belles, Rockford Peaches, South Bend Blue Sox, Milwaukee Chicks, Minneapolis Millerettes, Fort Wayne Daisies, Grand Rapids Chicks, Muskegon Lassies, Kalamazoo Lassies, Peoria Redwings, Chicago Colleens, Springfield Sallies, Battle Creek Belles and the Muskegon Belles.

League play was officially underway on May 30, 1943. Along with the roster of fifteen players, each team had a team manager, a business manager and a female chaperone. Before the start of each game, the two teams formed a line along the first and third base lines in the shape of a V for "Victory for the Troops." As the National Anthem played, the women ballplayers removed their caps, placed them over their hearts and bowed their heads until the Anthem was complete, then it was PLAY BALL!

The All-American Girls Professional Baseball League was a hit with the baseball fans. Ticket prices ranged from fifty cents or less for bleacher seats and a dollar or more for reserved/box seats. The 1943 season saw attendance figures of over 176,000. Local newspapers in the smaller towns reported on all the games, posted stats, interviews and photographs of the teams which increased interest and boosted attendance. Loyal fans appreciated their favorite players, often giving them gifts of watches, money, radios, record players, etc. for well played games. As the teams' popularity spread, it was not uncommon to have two or three thousand fans in attendance. During the 1948 season with ten teams playing, 910,000 fans enjoyed the games.

Here is a peek at a few of the AAGPBL players and their accomplishments:

Dorothy "Dottie" Kamenshek was often referred to as one of the finest female baseball players of that time period. She was only seventeen when she signed her contract to become a member of the Rockford Peaches team in 1943. Dottie was considered an "all-around" player, comfortable playing any position. She held the league's batting title twice and was named to seven All-Star teams. Her professional baseball career spanned ten years and included the following accomplishments: 657 stolen bases; in 3,736 at-bats, she struck out only 81 times; her lifetime batting average was .292, the highest ever in the women's league.

A League of Their Own, a movie released in 1992 starring Geena Davis playing a baseball character named Dottie Hinson, was said to have been roughly based on Dorothy Kamenshek's career as well as another player, Pepper Paire Davis. Dorothy was a consultant for the film and spent two days teaching the actresses how to throw the ball and turn a double play. The film also starred Tom Hanks, Madonna, Rosie O'Donnell and was directed by Penny Marshall.

In 1999, *Sports Illustrated* magazine named Dottie one of the 100 greatest female athletes of all time. Dottie died at the age of 84 in Palm Desert, California following complications from a stroke.

Pepper Paire was just 5' 4" and twenty years old when she signed her contract in 1944 to play for the Minneapolis

Millerettes. She was an aggressive catcher with a strong throwing arm and a compact swing at the plate. She also played shortstop, third base and pitched when called upon. Pepper had a lifetime batting average of .225 with 400 runs batted in. Although she suffered numerous injuries, including a fractured collarbone, she continued to play. Along with Nalda Bird, Pepper wrote the official theme song of the All-American Girls Professional Baseball League - *Victory Song*. From the movie, *A League of Their Own,* the song became popular once again. Pepper also served as a technical advisor for the film. In 2009 she published her book, *Dirt in the Skirt*, about her years playing on the AAGPBL. She is also included in a permanent display of 'Women in Baseball' at the Baseball Hall of Fame in Cooperstown, New York. She died of natural causes in Van Nuys, California at the age of 88.

Elizabeth "Lib" Mahon was twenty-five years old when she was spotted by one of Wrigley's scouts playing fast-pitch softball in college. She aced the tryouts and signed with the Minneapolis Millerettes in 1944 but was traded shortly thereafter to the Kenosha Comets. She played outfield positions and occasionally infield when she was needed. Elizabeth was a powerful hitter

with a career batting average of .248, including 432 scored runs; in 837 games she had 400 runs batted in. She tied the RBI record with Pepper Paire for fourth best in the AAGPBL and played on two All-Star teams as well as two Championship Teams. Elizabeth died in South Bend, Indiana at the age of 81.

Thelma Eisen was another 5'4" powerhouse who batted and threw right handed. She signed her contract with the Milwaukee Chicks in 1944 then played on a variety of teams for nine seasons. Thelma was an excellent defensive player and favored center field but played  any position where needed. She was the team authority on rules of the game for any team she played on. Thelma was also a very fast runner which made her a speedy base runner in stealing bases. She also robbed hitters of base hits by quickly snagging their outfield fly balls. Her career totals of stolen bases numbered 674 in 966 career games. In 1946 Thelma became the first female manager in AAGPBL history as she briefly guided the Peoria Redwings. She died in Pacific Palisades, California on her 92nd birthday.

June Peppas was a late comer to AAGPBL. The 5'5" left-hander signed with the Fort Wayne

Daisies in 1948 and also played with the Racine Belles, the Battle Creek Belles and the Kalamazoo Lassies. She played first base, outfield and also pitched. June had a difficult time transitioning and perfecting the required overhand pitch rather than the underhanded softball-style pitch. She had control problems and walked more batters than striking them out. She eventually mastered her control problems and became a winning pitcher playing on two All Star Teams. Her baseball career ended in 1954 when the leagues disbanded. June is currently living in Florida.

Poster featuring the 1946 AAGPBL All-Stars

Popularity of the games dwindled after the war ended and in 1954 the All-American Girls Professional Baseball League disbanded. Many of the players kept in touch with each other, often gathering for reunions. The public soon forgot about the feats of the women's teams and their wartime efforts - they quickly became another neglected (sports) history factoid.

In the early 1980s a group of former AAGPBL players, led by June Peppas, organized a retired players association then lobbied for recognition in the National Baseball Hall of Fame and Museum at Cooperstown, New York. All six hundred of the AAGPBL players are now listed in the designated area, "Women in Baseball" at the Cooperstown museum along with a display featuring the original uniforms worn by the players. After the film *A League of Their Own,* interest peaked in the Museum's display as well as the importance of these women during WWII.

Women also participated in other sports during the war. **Basketball** was popular across the country, especially in the war production factories. Over ten thousand companies boasted about their

A YMCA women's basketball team

organized women's teams. The teams often played each other in games which led to tournaments and bragging rights. The teams promoted camaraderie among the workers, while the games instilled uniformity in a time of uncertainty. Friends and families enjoyed watching the games which were usually played in local high school gymnasiums; an entertaining couple of hours to take their minds off of war news and worries.

Japanese-American women sent to relocation centers organized basketball teams within the centers and challenged local high school girls' teams. This was popular entertainment for the men, women and children held in the centers.

In 1940 there were 12 million bowlers in America. By 1948 there were 20 million. **Bowling** became a great inexpensive family sport and entertainment during the war. Although wooden pins became scarce due to the rationing of wood, most bowling establishments made due with what was available.

Women's interest in bowling surged during the war years as war production plants formed industrial leagues as an intramural, morale booster. As with the basketball leagues, the bowling leagues featured team competitions and tournaments. Many women had never bowled before nor had the opportunity. The Professional Women's Bowling Association formed after the war, most likely from the women who were introduced to the sport while working in the war production plants.

Women's tennis increased in popularity during WWII. **Pauline Betz Addie** was the dominant female tennis player from 1941 through 1946, winning the U.S. National Champion-ship (now called the U.S. Open) four times. She was a five-time Grand Slam singles champion and the world's top-ranked

woman player. As the war raged on, no tournaments were held in Europe but that did not keep her from playing in the U.S. *Time* magazine featured Pauline on its front cover of the September, 1946 issue. Somewhat of a media sports darling, she was described in the article as, "The first lady of tennis…a trim 5 ft. 5 in.; her hair is strawberry blonde, sun bleached and wiry. Principally because of her green eyes she seems to have a ready-to-pounce, feline quality. A straightening of her shoulders is a characteristic mannerism - a squaring away that seems to symbolize in an otherwise relaxed girl, a won't-be-beat spirit."

Early in 1947, at the age of twenty-seven, she openly considered playing professionally which caused the U.S. Lawn Tennis Association to immediately bar her from any further amateur matches. This decision caused quite a furor in the sports media as well as with fans who used words of "unjust" and "premature" simply based on a verbal "consideration." Not being able to compete any further on the amateur level, she abandoned her Grand Slam career and began a professional career from 1947 to 1960. She earned $10,000 her first year and was undefeated. The pro tour was much less challenging to her than the amateurs.

Pauline was inducted into the International Tennis Hall of Fame in 1965. She marched in the U.S. Open Parade of Champions in 1997 to help christen the Arthur Ashe Stadium in Flushing Meadows, New York. Pauline died May 31, 2011 in Potomac, Md. at the age of 91.

Without a doubt, the greatest American female athlete of that time was **Mildred Ella "Babe" Didrikson Zaharias**. Babe first gained world fame in track and field during the 1932 Los Angeles Olympics where

she won two gold medals and one silver. She was an AAU Championship basketball player, played organized baseball and softball, was an expert diver, roller-skater, and bowler. She started playing golf in 1935 quickly becoming America's first female golf celebrity and the leading player of the 1940s and early 1950s. Formally turning professional in 1947, she dominated the Women's Professional Golf Association and later the Ladies Professional Golf Association. She was a founding member of the LPGA along with twelve other women golfers in 1950. She was also the first woman to attempt to qualify for the U.S. Open in 1948; however, her application was rejected by the USGA which stated the event was open to men only. Undaunted, by 1950, Zaharias had won every golf title available at that time. Amateur and professional wins totaled eighty-two.

Although Babe is best known for her athletic skills, she was also an excellent seamstress. She made most of her own clothing including her golf clothes.

ESPN named her the 10th Greatest North American Athlete of the 20th Century, while the Associated Press named her the 9th Greatest Athlete of the 20th Century. She was inducted into the Hall of Fame of Women's Golf in 1951, then posthumously in 1957, received the highest honor given by the USGA in recognition of distinguished sportsmanship in golf - the Bob Jones Award. When the LPGA Hall of Fame was opened in

1977, Babe Zaharias was the first of six women inducted.

Babe was an inspiration to young girls and women during the war years. She pushed her way into a male dominated professional sport and made a name for herself. One reporter wrote, "Except perhaps for Arnold Palmer, no golfer has ever been more beloved by the gallery." Babe died from cancer September 27, 1956 in Galveston, Texas at the age of 45.

World War II opened many doors for American women in sports, especially women in professional sports. Once they were confident of their abilities as well as their rightful place in competition, there was no stopping them!

Chapter 18

Women War Correspondents

The American women newscasters and journalists of today number in the thousands. They cover the news around the world, interview political and world leaders, entertainers, musicians, and the man-on-the-street. All of them owe their present livelihood to the women correspondents of WWII.

When Pearl Harbor was attacked, 1,600 reporters were accredited as war correspondents; only 127 of those were women who had fought for the right to the title. Several of these women were already working as journalists and writers for newspapers and magazines, but when war was declared, they wanted a piece of the action.

The military did not want women anywhere near the front lines and used a variety of excuses to keep them away. The most common excuse was the bathroom facilities (there usually weren't any); one General denied permission for a woman correspondent to follow his unit due to the lack of bathroom facilities. The General stated he would not have his thousands of Marines pulling up their pants because there was a woman nearby. The woman's reply, "That won't bother me one bit. My object is to cover the war!"

Needless to say, those curious and adventurous women jumped through razor wired hoops and miles of red tape to obtain the title of WWII War Correspondent. At the time, twenty-five newspapers, over twenty-five magazines, eight wire services, and five radio networks sent their women writers and reporters to the War Department to undergo the accreditation process for becoming an official war correspondent.

The process began with interrogation of the individual, usually by a male military person. Some of the questions asked of the women: Are you athletic? How fast can you run? Do you like camping? Can you carry a heavy pack? Are you afraid of firearms, loud noises? Can you shoot a gun? Can you keep a secret? Do you like being uncomfortable? How do you handle seeing unpleasant things? If the appropriate answers were given, the paperwork was then passed along for a security clearance.

After passing interrogation and security, next came the inoculations: tetanus, typhoid, typhus and smallpox. These usually made the women sick with low-grade fevers, aching muscles and sore arms for several days. While recovering, they anxiously awaited their approval notices as well as passports and immunization certificates.

With final approval by the War Department, the women were issued their AGO card, their official identification from the Adjutant General's Office. With card in hand they were issued the standard military equipment for their job - a helmet, musette bag, fatigues, green overalls with a white hood, gloves that had been treated for gas exposure, a gas mask, insect powder, sunglasses, mosquito netting and a canteen (cameras, note-books and type-writers were the correspondents responsibility and may or may not have been provided by their media employers). Instructions were given on the proper use of a gas mask. Uniforms consisted of an officer style jacket, two skirts, khaki shirts, ties, and a cap. Pants were added later. A green armband with a large **C** for **C**orres-pondent was to be worn at all times. The color green was an identifier of a non-combatant. An identifying patch was later developed and sewn on the sleeve to replace the armband.

Ruth Cowan, war correspondent in regulation uniform.

The women were assigned the rank of Captain to insure their protection if captured by enemy forces. Assignments were given, usually far from any front lines or in such desolate areas that the women would be dis-couraged and (hopefully) go home. The correspondents and photographers had to secure their own passage overseas which often led to some very creative arrangements in boarding ships or planes.

Generals in the field had their own rules about reporters, men or women, and were not overly accommodating to either one. One woman, a member of the Associated Press and a regular at First Lady Eleanor Roosevelt's weekly women-only press conferences, was disappointed at being sent to Algiers. She was to follow a group of WACs from training to overseas duties (the WACs were also disappointed with this first assignment). All of the women were treated poorly and were frequently subjected to misogynist attitudes while trying to accomplish their jobs. The AP reporter, Ruth Cowan, wrote a telegram to be sent to her friend Eleanor Roosevelt that stated, "Don't encourage more women to come to Africa. The men don't want us here..." She submitted the telegram to the PRO (Public Relations Officer) on base suspecting it would be censored and not sent. She was right! Word quickly spread about the telegram; the atmosphere suddenly seemed to improve for all the women. Ruth played her cards right - it would not look good for a friend of the First Lady, wife of the Commander-In-Chief, to be treated poorly by military personnel while doing her assigned job.

Initially, the women correspondents were denied access to battle areas and front lines, especially areas in the Pacific Theater. They wanted to write about the fierce fighting, the battles and the front line activities, but instead resigned themselves to stories focusing on the day-to-day activities of the soldiers, the nurses and physicians, the wounded, recovering soldiers, local people, and how the war affected them. Their stories were submitted to the magazines or newspapers they worked for and most often published as human interest war stories. The stories were well received by the soldiers' families at home but that was not enough for the daring and adventurous who were looking for the big story with the big glory - a front page spread or feature article. The following are a few of those daring and adventurous women who did make that front page spread or feature article:

Annalee Whitmore Jacoby and **Shelley Smith Mydans**, along with their husbands, were staying

Annalee & Mel
say "I do"

at the Bay View Hotel in Manila when Pearl Harbor was attacked, followed by the attack on the Philippines. Annalee and her husband, Mel, had just married and were honeymooning between assignments - he was a correspondent for *Time* magazine, she a recent correspondent for *Liberty* magazine. Annalee submitted her story to *Liberty* describing the city under siege, searchlights in the sky overhead, the roar of airplanes, exploding bombs, hotel blackouts at night, the frenzied buying of food and medical supplies, more bombing, fires, fear and fleeing.

Shelley was a writer and researcher, often submitting articles to *Life* magazine. She interviewed two young sergeants who had been on duty and wounded when the Japanese attacked Clark Field near Manila, wrote her story then quickly cabled it to *Life* where it was published.

Shelly Smith Mydans

The two women's articles clearly depicted the serious actions taking place in the Philippines and were a wake-up call to Americans - there really was a war going on in the Pacific. The question, along with the fear, arose - if the Japanese could take Pearl Harbor and the Philippines, could they take the West Coast as well? These two women's articles may have been the first written/published by women correspondents in a war zone, although inadvertently.

Shortly after their articles were sent in cablese (a style of press messages sent uncoded and highly condensed) the Japanese overtook Manila and no further messages could be sent. The two couples were among the 3,500 American civilians ordered to the detention center at the University of Santo Tomas (refer back to Chapter 6). Living conditions were deplorable, food scarce, tempers hot and hostile, people sick and dying. Shelley wrote articles about the people, the conditions, their hopes and fears. Even though she could not send them out, she saved them and submitted them upon her release. Shelley published *Open City* in 1945 in which she described her time as a Japanese prisoner-of-war. Shelley and her husband were finally released in a prisoner exchange December 1943, after two years in the detention center.

Annalee and her husband elected to escape to Bataan where 83,000 American and Filipino soldiers, plus 26,000 civilians were living in the tunnels. She also wrote articles describing the conditions, the suffering, lack of food and supplies, the wounded and dying soldiers being cared for by the Army nurses in the jungle. She worked with the medical teams doing whatever she could to help and recorded what she witnessed…"hundreds of wounded soldiers coming in everyday over-whelming the physicians and nurses, the infected, gangrenous wounds, the dysentery, lack of medicine, the mosquitos, snakes, and constant bombing. Nurses were often hit with shrapnel, sick with dysentery, fatigue and exhaustion but they continued to do the best they could to care for their patients."

Annalee described it all as a "subdivision of hell." She and her husband finally escaped by boat for a month long, dangerous sea voyage to Australia. Upon arrival in Australia, she submitted the articles for publication that gave readers an uncensored view of conditions in the Philippines. The magazine, however, censored some of her more gruesome descriptions in an effort to avoid upsetting its readers.

Margaret Bourke-White had a love of photography from an early age. After graduating from Cornell University she moved to Cleveland, Ohio and established a commercial photography studio featuring architectural and industrial photography. Margaret quickly established herself as the best-known photographer of the day after many of her industrial photos were published in a variety of magazines. In 1930 she was invited to photograph Soviet industry and become the first Western photographer allowed to do so.

Life magazine hired her in 1936 as their first female photojournalist promptly publishing one of her photos as the front cover on its first issue.

Margaret returned to the Soviet Union in 1941 just as the Germans broke their pact of non-aggression toward them. When the Germans invaded Moscow, she fled to the U.S. Embassy, climbed up on the roof and captured the fire fighting over the Kremlin on film. Her photographs were published around the world even though the Soviets declared anyone taking photographs would be shot. Now, with a taste for filming the increasing war tensions, Margaret pushed for access to the danger zones. She repeatedly heard the excuse that it was too dangerous for a woman to travel overseas during wartime. Undaunted, she stowed away on a troop freighter which was torpedoed in the Mediterranean.

Along with a group of Army nurses, she escaped the sinking ship in a lifeboat with all of her cameras and gear; she left all her personal belongings and clothing on the sinking ship. As the remaining troops escaped via lifeboats, she

Lifeboat with Army nurses & troops escaping sinking ship.

clicked photos of their rescue efforts from her own lifeboat. Once all aboard had been rescued by a nearby destroyer, the ship rolled over and slipped to its watery grave. Margaret submitted a photojournalistic piece to *Life* magazine on the dangers of wartime travel at sea.

In 1943, General Doolittle asked Margaret if she wanted to go on a bombing mission in a B-17. He was impressed with her photography and her ability to capture the true sense of war activities. She took the time to become familiar with the inside of the bomber, the  positions of the crew members and their jobs, scoped out the best placement of her cameras and gear as well as the best locations for shooting. She also had to practice operating her cameras while wearing the heavy, high-altitude flight suit, bulky electric mittens, and oxygen mask. Once the mission was complete, Margaret became the first woman to fly with a U.S. combat crew over enemy soil.

Her colleagues at *Life* called her "Maggie the Indestructible" as she survived being strafed by the Luftwaffe, dragging her cameras through sniper fire, being stranded on an Arctic island, and tramping through North Africa, Italy and Germany.

In 1945, she traveled with General George Patton throughout the fall of Germany. Perhaps the most difficult photographs she shot during all of her war travels were the horrific, shocking scenes at the Buchenwald concentration camp when liberated by the Allies. The 20,000 survivors were barely alive, skin and bones, so weak they could barely lift their heads, clothed in rags or naked, suffering from starvation, dehydration, and diseases. The smell throughout the camp was unbearable as many of the toughest soldiers were overcome with nausea and vomiting. The survivors wept without tears at the sight of their American saviors. Margaret commented about filming the camp by stating, "Using a camera was almost a relief. It interposed a slight barrier between myself and the horror in front of me."

Following the war, Margaret published her book *Dear Fatherland, Rest Quietly* in an effort to help her recover and heal from the brutality of war she had witnessed through her own eyes and the eye of her camera lens.

Her war photos were incredible and are still highly regarded today. Margaret Bourke-White died in 1971 at the age of 67 due to Parkinson's disease.

Martha Gellhorn is considered to be one of the greatest war correspondents of the 20th century. Her writing was clear, clever and precise due to her sharp eye for significant details. She also had a sharp tongue!

During her sixty year career she reported on nearly

every major world conflict, often writing powerful anti-war articles for *Collier's Weekly* magazine. During the Great Depression, she traveled across America reporting on how small towns and their people were affected. Working with famed photographer, Dorothea Lange, the two women documented the Depression for government files and investigated topics not usually open to women. The work these women accomplished marked them as major contributors to the history of America.

In the late 1930s, while Gellhorn was in Germany, she reported on the rise of Adolf Hitler and speculated what might result. As unrest escalated, Gellhorn began fighting for the right to report activities from established front lines which were strictly off limits to women at that time. She fired off an angry letter to chief military figures as well as her close friends, President and First Lady Roosevelt stating, "I have too frequently received the impression that women war correspondents were an irritating nuisance. I wish to point out that none of us would have our jobs unless we knew how to do them and this curious condescending treatment is as ridiculous as it is undignified. It is necessary that I report on this war. I do not feel there is any need to beg as a favor for the right to serve as the eyes for millions of people in America who are desperately in need of seeing, but cannot see for themselves."

As WWII spread across Europe she traveled to Britain, Finland, Hong Kong, Burma, and Singapore reporting war activities in each location. In Italy, she traveled with French troops who were more accommodating to women correspondents. She managed to accompany a night combat flight mission over Germany with exploding flak threatening her aircraft.

When Martha heard of plans for the Normandy invasion and that no women correspondents were allowed access, she boarded a hospital ship and hid in a bathroom. When the ship landed she pretended to be a stretcher bearer and waded to shore in waist deep water. She was the only woman correspondent on Normandy beach D-Day, June 6, 1944. Other reporters, men and women, were anxiously waiting in nearby cities for access. The women journalists submitting their photos and stories of that historic day became known as the **"D-Day Dames."**

Martha was among the first journalists to submit reports from the liberation of the Dachau concentration camp. Her reports were heartbreaking and deeply affected her, just as Buchenwald affected Margaret Bourke-White. As a result, she was one of several women journalists covering the Nuremberg trials which began in Nuremberg, Germany November 20, 1945 and ended October 1, 1946. *(Author's note: The Nuremberg trials have been described as "the greatest trial in history." The trials were a series of military tribunals held by Allied forces after WWII for the prosecution of twenty-three of the most prominent political and military leaders of the Third Reich for war crimes.)*

Martha had a tabloid-style personal life. She was the third wife of novelist Ernest Hemingway. The stormy, unconventional marriage lasted from 1940 to 1945. Hemingway taught her how to ride horses, fish and shoot. They were also avid tennis players. He was not happy with his wife's long absences especially in dangerous, war-torn areas. Although he frequently traveled with her, he tried to block her planned trips as often as he could. He admired her writing, which was much like his own, and often critiqued her reports before she submitted them. When her early interests in writing turned to the subject of war, he asked her, "Why aren't you writing about the war?" She replied, "I don't know about weapons and battles." With a chuckle he replied, "Write about what you do know and that is people." That is exactly what she did! Her signature writing from then on focused on civilians, soldiers and the casualties of war throughout her career.

Hemingway was well known for his philandering which came as no surprise to his wife; she also had many dalliances. She divorced him in 1945.

Despite her personal life, her frontline journalism set new standards for war reporting. She wrote several novels about her war and other experiences including: *A Stricken Field* (1940), *The Face of War* (1959), *The Lowest Trees Have Tops (1967), Travels With Myself and Another (1978),* and *The View From the Ground (1988).*

Martha also covered the Vietnam War, the Six-Day War in the Middle East and the civil wars in Central America. When the Bosnian War broke out in the 1990s, while in her early 80s, she decided she was not "nimble" enough to go.

Nearly blind and suffering from ovarian and liver cancer, Martha took her own life by drug overdose. She died in London in 1998 at the age of 89.

Dickey Chapelle, birth named Georgette Louise Meyer, was born in Milwaukee, Wisconsin. She was a high spirited, adventure seeking, risk taker during her early childhood. She had her eye on the sky from the age of  fourteen. At the age of sixteen she attended aeronautical engineering and design classes at MIT but later decided she would rather fly the airplanes than design them. After meeting Admiral Richard Byrd, nicknamed Dickey Byrd, she changed her first name to Dickey. Her love of aviation landed her a job with Trans World Airlines as a photographer and writer.

Although her photojournalist credentials were mediocre at best, *National Geographic* hired her to cover WWII assignments. She was just a tiny woman, but was not easily pushed around or overlooked, even by high ranking military men. Her signature uniform, (fatigues, Correspondent armband, an Australian bush hat, large black Harlequin eyeglasses, pearl earrings, camera) short

stature and fast talking gained her access to dangerous front line battles.

Her first assignments were with the Marines during the battles of Iwo Jima and Okinawa where she photographed and described the bloodiest fighting of WWII. While on the island of Iwo Jima she climbed to the top of a ridge at the frontline to photograph the surrounding panoramic view. She kept hearing loud buzzing all around her, assuming they were large bee-like insects, she swatted at them to keep them away from her camera. When she returned to camp, the Lieutenant in charge screamed at her, "That was the goddamndest thing I ever saw anybody do in my life! Do you realize all the artillery and half the snipers on both sides of this f**king war had ten full minutes to make up their mind about you?" Evidently those buzzing insects were actually sniper bullets!

Dickey continued her photojournalist career for nearly three decades. After WWII she traveled around the world covering news and war stories. During the Hungarian Revolution of 1956, she was captured and jailed for over seven weeks.

She learned to jump with paratroopers, shooting pictures as she fell to earth under her canopy. Her assignments most often had her traveling with Marine troops on various missions.

Dickey's work garnered her frequent awards which she was proud of, but earning the respect of the journalistic community, as well as the military community, were her greatest achievements. She published her autobiography, *What's A Woman Doing Here?* in 1962, then appeared as a radio guest interviewed by Mike Wallace. He asked her if jumping out of airplanes, putting herself in harm's way on front lines, or going on dangerous assignments with Marines was a good place for a woman; was it really a "woman's job?" Dickey's quick reply, "It is not a woman's place. There's no question about it. There's only one other species on earth for whom a war zone is no place, and that's men. But as long as men continue to fight wars, I think observers of both sexes will be sent to see what happens."

On November 4, 1965, while on patrol in Vietnam with a Marine platoon, the lieutenant in front of Dickey kicked a tripwire boobytrap that sent a piece of shrapnel flying into her neck, severing her carotid artery. She died moments later. Dickey Chapelle was the first American woman reporter to be killed in the line of duty. She was given full military honors. The United States Marine Corps honors her memory each year with the Dickey Chapelle Award recognizing the woman who contributed most to the morale, welfare and well-being of the men and women of the United States Marine Corps.

Elizabeth "Lee" Miller began her career in the 1920s as a New York City fashion model with a keen interest in photography. She traveled to Paris in 1929 in hopes of learning more about photo- graphy from the famous artist and photographer Man Ray. She then returned to New York  to establish her own photo studio. When WWII broke out she was living in London doing fashion photography for *Vogue* magazine. She began sending photos to *Vogue* documenting the Blitz and the devastation suffered by the city and its people, thus becoming the magazine's first official war photojournalist.

When she received her official war correspondent accreditation from the U.S. Army, she was teamed with an American photographer, David Scherman, who was on assignment for *Life* magazine. Together the two submitted photos and stories to both *Life* and *Conde Nast Publications*. On assignment, Lee wore a stylish helmet she designed herself with a slitted visor that could be pulled down or pushed up. It did not interfere with her photography, but it was a bit bizarre to see her wearing.

Her photographs revealed the horrors of war including the aftermath of bombs dropped on cities large and small, the townspeople, the soldiers, the bloody field hospitals, even German officers surrendering. One iconic photo taken by Scherman is of Lee bathing in the Munich apartment bathtub of Adolf Hitler.

She also recorded the first use of napalm at the siege of St. Malo. Perhaps her most disturbing photos of the war where those of the Nazi concentration camps, particularly Buchenwald and Dachau. The tall piles of human bodies and bones were incomprehensible and grievous to her *Vogue* editors who held back publishing them. Lee chastised and cajoled them into publishing the photos along with the story and bold caption, "BELIEVE IT!"

After witnessing the horrors of war through her camera lens, she returned to England where she suffered severe bouts of depression - now known and recognized as post-traumatic stress disorder. Of all the war photos she shot, the concentration camp images haunted her the most, for the rest of her life.

She continued to take an occasional photo shoot assignment for *Vogue* but later found an interest in gourmet cooking and pursued it with great accomplishment. Lee Miller died in 1977 at the age of 70 from cancer.

Dorothea Lange was not a war correspondent as the aforementioned women were. Instead, Dorothea recorded Americans responding to the tragedies of the Great Depression and WWII here at home. She was a photographer and photojournalist who greatly influenced the development of documentary photography.

She contracted polio at the age of seven leaving her with a weakened right leg that caused her to limp severely for the rest of her life. It did not hamper her in her pursuits, instead she said, "It formed me, guided me, instructed me, helped me and humiliated me. I've never gotten over it, and I am aware of the force and power of it."

She received her photography education from Columbia University in New York City then opened her own portrait studio in San Francisco, California. During the Great Depression she studied the unemployed and homeless with her camera and captured the plight and indignities in stark black and white photos. The government took notice and hired her to work for the Federal Resettlement Administration, later named the Farm Security Administration. Her photos of migrant workers, sharecroppers, and homeless farm families became icons of the Depression era. Perhaps the most iconic photo was, and remains today, the "Migrant Mother," the image of a

"Migrant Mother"

desperate, weary, thirty-two year old mother who appeared older than her stated years, with two children clinging to her, as she peers from their lean-to tent, hungry, haggard, and hopeless.

After Pearl Harbor was attacked, President Roosevelt ordered all Japanese-Americans into armed relocation camps. The War Relocation Authority assigned Dorothea to photographically cover the internment in California. She traveled throughout California photographing families preparing to leave their beloved homes and belongings, packing suitcases, trunks, and boxes with clothing and valuables. Next she traveled to assembly centers where she captured anxious men, women and children being tagged for identification then waiting for hours in the baking desert sun to be transported to their camp at Manzanar.

An entire family as new arrivals at a Japanese internment camp, tagged and waiting to be transported.

Families were assigned housing in tar-paper covered barracks without plumbing or cooking facilities. Food was rationed; groups of 250-300 internees at a time were served in large mess halls after waiting in long lines for hours.

Lange's images of life in the camps were heartbreaking. To see the photos of detained

Food lines.

Japanese-Americans, many of whom were prominent businessmen, physicians and lawyers, as well as infants and small children, being treated like criminals because of their ancestry, without charging them with any crime, caused Lange to wonder how her employer, the government, could be so callous.

Her images so clearly depicted the treatment of the internees that the federal government censored and impounded them, perhaps conflicted by their own actions. The photographs were not seen in print or publicly for more than fifty years. Most of the photographs may now be viewed in the National Archives and at the Bancroft Library at the University of California Berkeley in Berkeley, California.

In 1945, Dorothea was invited by Ansel Adams to accept a faculty position at the California School of Fine Arts, which she accepted. In 1952, she co-founded *Aperture* magazine, dedicated to photography and photographers.

Dorothea Lange died of esophageal cancer in San Francisco, October 11, 1965 at the age 70.

Many other women correspondents also left their mark in magazines, newspapers, and newsreels during the war years. Even though they were all discouraged, discriminated against, shunned, and even prevented from doing their jobs in the beginning, the women persisted and consistently turned in quality work. Those women dared to do what none had done before. WWII was a historic turning point for women reporting war news and being able to report from war zones.

Some correspondents continued to record the postwar activities of recovery and rebuilding across Europe and the Pacific. Others returned to their home newspapers and magazines often feeling a great letdown after following the sights and sounds of war. Those sights and sounds haunted them for the rest of their lives. Several wrote books about their experiences in hopes of appeasing their haunted visions while others found solace in their families and gardens.

All in all, some of the best war coverage of WWII came from the work of women war correspondents and photographers. They set the stage and standards for future women pursuing photojournalistic opportunities.

Chapter 19

Home Front Soldiers-Without-Uniforms

Although war had been raging in Europe for two years, the majority of Americans felt WWII began for them when Pearl Harbor was attacked. Life in America changed forever as the news spread swiftly across the country via radio, then newspaper. It didn't take long for even the tiniest of towns in the most remote locations to

realize that America, as they knew it, would never be the same. The Declaration of War would have a profound affect on American government, the economy and our society as a whole.

As sixteen million men enlisted for battle on the front lines, Americans left at home were urged to become "soldiers-without-uniforms" or "soldiers-without-guns" and begin the battle on the home front. The majority of those left at home were women and children - America's other soldiers.

The government's massive propaganda machines quickly spewed then distributed hundreds of thousands of posters and flyers across the nation urging everything from enlisting in the various military branches to working in war industry jobs, conserving resources, planting gardens, buying war bonds, and more.

Everyday life decisions during this period for American civilians were influenced by the government and the needs of the military - what to wear, what to eat, what to grow, how far to drive, lighting the home at night, what volunteer organizations to work for, how to buy, what to buy, what not to buy, etc. Of course the majority of the concerns and decisions fell to the women whose husbands, fathers, and sons where off fighting overseas or in the Pacific.

As discussed in previous chapters, the government's demands for farm production more than doubled for wheat, corn, and other foods. At the same time, farmers faced labor shortages, less fuel and old outdated machinery to produce the commodities. Farm wives, their young children, older men not fit for military service and the Women's Land Army kept production of the nation's foodstuffs at all time record highs. American farms fed eight million U.S. soldiers a day as well as millions of civilians starving in Great Britain and Russia, not to mention the millions of American citizens still hungry and recovering from the Great Depression.

The government Office of Price Administration began **rationing** and price regulations almost immediately after Japan's attack. Due to the loss of rubber supplies from Southeast Asia cut off by Japan, tires were the first to be rationed in early January 1942. Along with tires came the halt of new car manufacturing and sales which, in turn, brought the order for gasoline rationing. New cars remaining on sales lots could only be purchased by physicians, police and fire officials, civil defense workers, railroad workers and ministers. By February 1942 auto makers had shifted production to military vehicles, tanks and aircraft.

Rubber was desperately needed for the manufacture of aircraft tires as well as military vehicles. Although 450,000 tons of scrap rubber was collected during a one-time, nationwide rubber drive in June 1942, there was no efficient way to recycle rubber and it was found to be of poor quality for military use. Because of that, synthetic rubber production was increased in the U.S. from 3,721 tons in 1942, to 756,042 tons by 1945.

Applying for gas rationing cards & stickers.

Gasoline cards/stickers were distributed in May 1942. Those owning a drivable vehicle needing fuel had to appear before a local War Price and Rationing Board to explain their job classification which then determined their allotment of gasoline. Those applying also had to certify the ownership of their vehicle and that there were no more than five tires for that vehicle. Any more than five tires per vehicle owned by an individual were confiscated by the government due to the severe rubber shortage. Falsifying information to the Board was a punishable offense with a fine of $10,000 and ten years in jail.

Once obtained, gasoline stickers were placed on the driver's side, lower front windshield easily sight accessible by the female gas station attendants who would fill the tank with the appropriate amount and not a drop more. The sticker allotments were as follows:

A sticker = issued to non-essential drivers, the
lowest priority. This group
usually consisted of the head of
household who owned a vehicle.
The allotment was 3-4 gallons per week.

B sticker = issued to drivers deemed essential;
war industry workers.
The allotment was up to 8 gallons per week.

C sticker = issued to drivers deemed very
essential; physicians, ministers,
postal workers, railroad workers
and farmers.
The allotment was 8 gallons per week
(in some areas wheat farmers were issued
T or X stickers due to the urgent need for
wheat and the machinery used to harvest it).

T sticker = issued to (commercial) truck
drivers.
The allotment was unlimited.

X sticker = issued to police, firemen, civil
defense workers and those deemed
VIPs (usually government officials).
The allotment was unlimited.

Public outcry over government officials
receiving unlimited allotments was loud and long.

A Senate resolution was introduced requiring members to renounce their special privilege for gas allotment. The resolution failed when the defiant Senators voted against it. The public and the press took the legislators to task over not setting a good example for Americans who were struggling to abide by the new rules - to no avail, the X stickers remained on the Senator's vehicles.

To conserve tires and fuel, a national speed limit was set at 35 mph. The speed limit was often

ignored on open roads with little or no traffic but considered unpatriotic by most when not obeyed. Sunday drives in the country or leisurely sightseeing drives were banned, and all automobile racing was strictly prohibited.

Ration books for food, clothing and other items were issued in May, 1942 by local ration boards. Over 5,500 local boards had hundreds of volunteers selected by local officials and trained under the guidelines set by the War Price and Rationing Board. Each

man, woman and child living under one roof considered a household, received a ration book.

Stamps were issued and distributed each month in books which were identified by each family member's name, physical description and occupation (even the children). Each book was good for six months however, some of the stamps in the books were only good for one month. Stamps were color coded and had a "point" value. Tokens of the same color were used by merchants to make change. Red stamps were for meat, butter and fats. Red tokens were issued as change for red

stamp purchases. Blue stamps were for canned goods; blue tokens for change. White stamps for flour, sugar and bread. Green stamps for a variety of goods. Each stamp had a value of one point or

more. The shopper selected the items needed based on how many points she had available plus the cost in cash.

343

For example, one pound of quality steak might cost 12 points, while a pound of low quality hamburger or stew meat would cost only 7 points. A pound of butter might cost 16 points while a pound of oleo margarine would cost only 4 points. One jar of baby food would only be 1 point, but a

Walt Disney poster of famed characters shopping with their new ration books.

small bottle of ketchup would be 15 points. Only babies and small children up to a certain age were entitled to canned milk with the appropriate ration stamp. Of course cash was also needed to purchase items however, no amount of cash could purchase more than the ration stamp/coupon allowed. A bit confusing, to say the least, which infuriated many homemakers trying to make the best of it while planning meals.

Sugar was the first food item to be rationed in May 1942, with a limit of one-half pound per

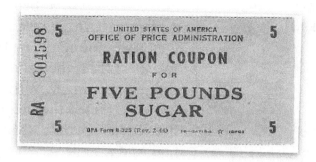

person per week. Commercial bakeries and other food processors also had their sugar supplies reduced by 30% of normal. That caused a bit of panic in trying to maintain a quality product for customers. As the war progressed, their allotments were cut again forcing many to close shops altogether.

Since sugar was in such high demand, the crops of sugar beets were increased in many areas. Cane sugar (the most popular) supplies from Hawaii fell short of demand and could not be exported to the U.S. due to the attacks on supply ships. Sugar beets have a high concentration of sucrose in their roots (the beet) and can be quickly processed into granulated sugar. Sugar beet farms were primarily located in California and Oregon near the Japanese internment camps. The internees planted, tended and harvested the thousands and thousands of acres of sugar beets then sent the beets to nearby processing plants.

Coffee was rationed on November 29, 1942.

Do with less— so they'll have enough!

RATIONING GIVES YOU YOUR FAIR SHARE

German U-boats repeatedly attacked ships from Brazil that carried coffee beans to America. Coffee rations were one pound every five weeks. Of all the products rationed during WWII, coffee affected the most home front people. Many had to cut their consumption from three cups per day down to one. To stretch their allotments, one pot may have been brewed several times. During this period coffee companies began adding fillers that changed the quality and taste of the coffee which made folks even more grumpy!

Retailers began experiencing a variety of shortages throughout 1942 due to the loss of imported goods. To them, rationing was a good thing - to everyone else, especially homemakers, it was a nightmare. Meat, lard, shortening, cooking oils, cheese, butter, margarine, canned, bottled, and frozen processed foods, dried fruits, jams, and jellies were all rationed. It was not unheard of to stand in line for two hours or more for a quarter pound of real butter or a one pound cut of real cheddar cheese. Typewriters, bicycles, shoes, silk, nylon, cotton fabric, home heating oil, firewood, and coal were also on the ration lists.

Many everyday products were difficult, if not impossible, to obtain due to the War Production Board severely curtailing their manufacture. Items curtailed included baby strollers, hot water heaters, hairpins, light bulbs, jewelry, cooking utensils, pots and pans, razors, sewing machines, vacuum cleaners, electric stoves, lawn mowers, washing machines, waffle irons, toasters, and alarm clocks. Stainless steel tableware was no longer available. Most of these items were made of metal which was needed for the war industries.

The metal alarm clock shortage was lifted after too many war factory employees arrived late to their jobs. The government authorized the production of a new type of clock which used less metal. The "Victory" clock could be purchased at work by factory employees with the cost withdrawn from their paychecks.

Medical supplies were also in short supply on the home front. Bandaging material was in high demand for military use. As mentioned earlier, the Red Cross volunteers rolled thousands of miles of cotton bandages which, in turn, caused vast shortages of cotton. Penicillin was not yet mass-produced for civilian use so any amount of it in civilian hospitals on the home front was considered golden treasure, rationed out by triage officers to the sickest in need. Sulfa supplies were diminished by the enormous amounts needed for the military. Morphine was also in short supply.

Blackmarkets quickly developed for gasoline, beef, sugar, and coffee. Counterfeit ration stamps quickly began popping up across America. Cattle rustling was common in many areas. Beef was a prime source of protein and, to many, defined the menu for a proper meal. Sugar was needed for bread making and other foods. Housewives traded ration stamps among themselves or sold them when money was short. Of course this was against the law; however, in the early stages of rationing it was difficult for the government to prosecute the offenders. Many of the retailers were not aware of the differences in stamps (real vs counterfeit) or that the entire coupon book had to be presented at the time of purchase. Some retailers accepted the ration stamp along with a larger cash amount for a higher prime cut of meat - this practice was also illegal. One in every four retail transactions during the war was illegal.

Spam, from the Hormel Foods Corporation, was one of the first canned meat products made popular during WWII. From 1941 to 1945, over 270 million pounds of Spam were shipped

overseas and fed American and Allied forces. The original recipe consisted of just five ingredients: pork shoulder meat, water, salt, sugar, and sodium nitrate (for coloring and preservative). Later, potato starch was added to soak up the gelatinous goo formed as the meat was cooked in the sealed can.

The military contracted with Hormel to provide the meat in six pound cans. It was nutritious for the troops, filling, cheap, had a long shelf life, and easy to transport. By the end of the war the soldiers were sick of it! They often had it served to them three times a day or it was the last thing to eat in their mess kits. Many soldiers used Spam to lubricate their guns, waterproof their boots and tents, or mixed it with a little lighter fluid or gasoline for a candle. Once they arrived home it may have been forbidden in the house!

On the other hand, home front wives and mothers scooped it up as a cheap, nutritious meat source for family dinners. The seven ounce can of Spam was considered a "canned good" not a meat, so the premium ration stamps for meat did not have to be used. The family cook devised any number of ways to prepare it so the children and other adults were kept guessing as to what it really was hence the term "mystery meat." By the

war's end, families were sick of it too!

Shopping for the home front housewife was not an easy, quick run in the family car to the corner market for milk and bread. In fact, for a short period of time, the government declared a ban on sliced bread. The goal was to keep bread prices down even though wheat prices were rising due to demand by our allies. The ban was short lived due to mounting protests from angry housewives across America as well as a major drop in bread sales. The saying, "the greatest thing since sliced bread" came from this time period and circumstances.

Some ration stamps were only good for a month, and in most cases, could not be carried over to the next month. As mentioned earlier, the number of points available and the amount of cash on hand determined what the shopping lists would consist of, so planning was essential. Many housewives had never before planned meals for a week or month at a time. They did not understand nutrition values, or know how to cook a nutritious, balanced meal.

The government came to the rescue - actually, the ulterior motive was to keep America producing war goods by keeping citizens well fed so they could work. To do that, the soldiers-without-uniforms had to be educated about food, nutrition and how to utilize ration stamps for the best nutritional value.

Government sponsored radio programs such as the *Homemakers Chat* and *Aunt Sammy's Radio Recipes* were mentioned earlier. The *Coupon Cookery* booklet was published in 1943 and featured 128 pages of nutritious recipes from Prudence Penny that could be prepared with food purchased using ration stamps. There  were cartoon-like illustrations with catchy bylines, captions and patriotic poetry throughout the booklet. The cost was $1.50. The dedication in the front of the booklet read:

> *To the housewives of America*
> *Those soldiers, tried and true,*
> *Who are struggling on the home front*
> *To serve good meals to you!*

Under a cartoon featuring a perky, apron wearing housewife pulling a rabbit out of a hat on the family dinner table, the caption read:

> *It may not be convenient*
> *But we don't admit defeat*
> *For in spite of War and Rationing*
> *America must eat*
> *It may take a deal of cunning*

And a bit of laughter too
To keep the meal-time pleasant
When the coupons are too few!"

Prudence Penny was a pseudonym for
hundreds of cooking instructors and writers for the
Los Angeles Times initially, then later, all Hearst
newspapers. The fictional domestic goddesses
created recipes, solved cooking problems, and
gave hints with tips on how to stretch ration
stamps. Pork knuckles, liver, tripe, beef tongue,
kidney, heart, brains… the poorest cuts of meat or
organ meats found a place in Prudence's
publications with "delicious" ways to prepare
them.

The different faces of Betty Crocker from 1936 to 1996.

Betty Crocker was another pseudonym dating
from 1921. She was created by Marjorie Husted,
a home economist who worked for a flour milling

company which eventually became General Mills. Betty was chosen as the first name because it was thought to be wholesome and cheerful. Crocker was the last name of a recently retired director of one of the original flour milling companies. The name Betty Crocker became a recognized name for helpfulness, trust- worthiness and quality in kitchens across America. Betty Crocker was known as the First Lady of Food. *Fortune* magazine named Betty Crocker the second most popular American woman in 1945 - First Lady Eleanor Roosevelt was named first.

During WWII, the Office of War Information utilized Betty's popularity for home defense radio broadcasts on a variety of topics including planting, managing, and harvesting a Victory garden, managing ration points, and sending messages to soldiers. They also used her name to distribute over seven million copies of the

government published booklet *Your Share* to familiarize Americans with wartime protocol.

From 1941 through 1945 the *Betty Crocker Cook Book of All-Purpose Baking* was published as an aid to wartime home cooking and baking. Recipes in the cookbooks were modified due to sugar and flour rationing often using substitutes such as honey or oat flour. Many of these recipes are still used today for their reduced sugar and flour dietary requirements.

Once the home front housewives had their shopping lists, their ration books and cash in hand, it was time for a trip to the grocery store, butcher shop, bakery, and dairy. For those living in the city, public transportation or walking was the method of choice for shopping trips. Country dwellers usually had a distance to travel but had to consider the amount of fuel available in their automobiles. It was not uncommon to see a carload of farm wives, sharing one of their vehicles, driving into town for their shopping needs once a week. They would take turns sharing a vehicle and chip in gasoline ration stamps.

The biggest source of fresh food, which helped alleviate some of the ration stamp difficulties, was

the **Victory Garden**. The name originated from the Secretary of Agriculture, Claude Wickard, who strongly urged Americans to plant and grow their own fruit and vegetables in backyard plots or any unused spots of land. The government quickly cranked out booklets, posters and radio spots with detailed instructions on how to plant, maintain and harvest a garden.

YOU CAN USE
the land you have
to grow the foods you need

The Victory Garden idea was a tremendous success across America. In 1943 an estimated 20.5 million gardens were planted in backyards, small acreages on farms, window sills in the city, abandoned parking lots, horse racing tracks, even the Portland, Oregon zoo! The harvest that year from those gardens accounted for at least one-third of all the vegetables consumed in the United States, not to mention the harvest of various fruit, nuts, and berries.

From the success of the garden harvests came

CAN ALL YOU CAN

IT'S A REAL WAR JOB!

the increased popularity of canning and preserving. "Canning" is a misnomer, since cans were not used due to the shortage of tin. Glass jars in a variety of sizes were most commonly used. Manufacturing demands for the jars increased as the popularity of the gardens increased. Gardens produced bountiful harvests of corn, peas, beans, carrots, tomatoes, potatoes, peaches, apples, apricots, blackberries, raspberries, rhubarb, cherries, nuts… the list goes on and on. Pickles and olives were cured, jams, jellies and pie fillings were "put up" in pantries across America. County fairs awarded blue ribbons for the most beautiful and tasty canned goods.

Gardeners took great pride in their Victory Gardens. Morale and a sense of accomplishment were also boosted for the soldiers-without-uniforms across the nation. The availability of fresh fruit and vegetables also saved ration stamps for other needed items such as shoes and clothing.

Those living on farms also saved ration stamps by owning their own livestock. Cows provided milk, cream, and butter. Chickens provided eggs and Sunday dinner. Beef cattle and pigs provided meat for the family and was often shared or traded with neighbors. From nearby lakes and rivers came fresh fish in bountiful numbers.

Clothing items became scarce during the war

years, too. The military needed cotton and wool for the millions of uniforms needed by their soldiers. Thread, buttons, zippers, even pins and needles were scarce for the home front women. Ration stamps were also needed to purchase clothing and shoes. The government strongly encouraged Americans to mend and patch worn items. Hand-me-downs were passed between family members and even neighbors, especially infant and children's clothes. Just as canning interests peaked during the war, so did sewing, knitting, and crocheting. Sewing machines were scarce and often shared with neighbors. Wool and cotton yarn was difficult to find; sweaters that became too small were unraveled and the yarn used to make something else.

Women's silk stockings all but disappeared due to the war. Silk came from Japan, so nylon became a popular replacement however, nylon was also needed to make parachutes. Women were embarrassed to go barelegged in those days so many began drawing a brown or black line up the back of their legs to simulate silk stockings. First Lady Eleanor Roosevelt began wearing heavy black cotton stockings instead of silk, and encouraged American women to do the same.

The rubber shortage even effected the manufacture of women's girdles; production was extremely limited and availability all but disappeared. The government campaigned the suggestion that women "grow their own muscular girdles by exercising" to save the rubber for war needs. This did not go over well with American women! Patriotism had limits especially when it came to women's under-garments. One female journalist, Marion Dixon, took a stand by writing, "Neither exercise nor any other known remedy could restore aging muscles to their original youthful tautness. Without proper support from well-fitted foundation garments to hold the abdomen in place, there was no way a woman past thirty could keep her posture erect or do physical work without tiring. Certainly Uncle Sam does not want American women to wear garments that would menace their health or hamper their efficiency, especially during wartime, when every ounce of energy and effort is needed."

The War Production Board quickly changed their stance on girdles announcing the foundation was an essential part of a woman's health and wardrobe. Manufacturing would quickly resume with availability restored despite the need for rubber!

Apparel fashions changed due to the fabric shortages. Women's dresses became shorter, hems more narrow, skirts became more slim instead of flared or full, fewer pockets, cuffs, fabric belts no wider than two inches, no more ruffles, pleats, attached hoods or shawls or full length sleeves. Since metal zippers were difficult to find, wraparound dresses and skirts became popular.

Fabric exemptions were made for maternity clothing, religious vestments, and bridal gowns. Women often shared bridal gowns due to the extremely high costs of purchasing one and the unavailability of silk.

Men's suits were also difficult to obtain and were manufactured with fewer pockets, no vests, only one pair of trousers instead of the usual two and slimmer trousers with no cuffs at the ankles. "Victory Suits," as they were called for both men and women were single-breasted, had narrow lapels, a bit more fitted and no pocket flaps.

With so many women joining the work force, slacks became more stylish, more slim and fitted;  some were tapered and tighter at the ankles to keep from getting caught in the machinery. "Rosie the Riveter" coveralls were extremely popular. Made of blue denim or a heavy weight cotton canvas, the coveralls were ideal for factory work as well as working in the home Victory Garden. When the coveralls became too worn-out to work in the factory, the legs were "cut-off" to make shorts.

Doing your Bit...
and a little Bit More?

The use of cosmetics during the war clashed with the shortages and rationing, but women can be very resourceful when need be. Vegetable dyes and lemons were used for hair coloring, beef gravy as a self-tanning agent, especially on the legs without stockings, and beet juice for staining the lips. Lipstick came in cardboard tubes if it could be found at all. Deep, dark red colors were used primarily by the military nurses and the factory Rosies. The colors even had patriotic names such as Victory Red or Fighting Red.

Hairstyles also changed dramatically during the war. The Rosies, Wendys, Sallys, and WOWs had to keep their long hair out of their faces and machinery so "Victory Rolls" became popular. The hair was pulled back on the sides and rolled then secured. Banana curls, bangs, and curl bundles were also practical as well as fashionable. Some women simply cut their hair in a "bob" style

PIN-UP VICTORY ROLLS

and secured it with a scarf or cap. Many
Hollywood starlets wore the Victory Roll style as a
gesture of patriotic support for the boys overseas
and the home front factory war production women.

Red lips and styled hair also sent a message that
represented the dual role women were called upon
to take for the war effort. Even though they were
women doing the jobs of men, they could still be
feminine and fashionable.

There were thousands and thousands of
children in the army of soldiers-without-uniforms
learning what patriotism was all about while doing
their part for the war effort. Every school morning
began with the Pledge of Allegiance followed by a

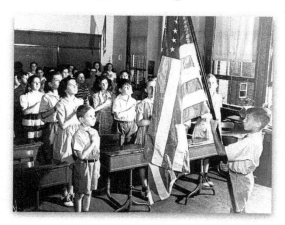

prayer for the safety of servicemen and women
fighting abroad. Geography lessons included
locating the areas of major battles discussed in the
recent news.

Government brochures were distributed to millions of school-aged children encouraging them to collect and turn in items that would be used to help the war efforts. Cartoon characters at the Saturday movie theaters were shown collecting tires, metals, and paper. The children then watched as their items became ammunition, tanks, planes, and ships.

Any Saturday, from early in the morning to late in the evening, children could be found roaming neighborhoods, junkyards, and scrap heaps dragging wagons piled high with treasures they had found to nearby drop-off areas. Tin cans, pots and pans, old kitchen utensils, old garden tools, metal bed frames, old metal toys, old bicycles, old tires, old clothing, rags…anything they could carry or load onto their wagons and deliver to the war-time collection piles, was rewarded with a free movie ticket, a comic book, a ticket for an ice cream, or a war stamp for their savings book; each war stamp was worth ten to twenty-five cents.

When the savings book was full, it could be turned in to purchase a $25 war bond.

(Author's note: While researching, I found several references questioning the real need for scrap drives during WWII. Economists said the scrap drives had almost no impact on war production output while historians say they greatly increased American pride and patriotism. Some believe the drives were established simply as a propaganda move by the government; all the material collected was simply stockpiled, not used, nor recycled. At the time, recycling was not the prime government concern, winning the war and limiting resources was. Recycling methods for many items had not been perfected, nor did the government want to spend the time or manpower to do so.

Newspapers were a good example of an item being collected but not being recycled. Any recycling of newspapers done was usually reuse by volunteers as packing material to send packages to the troops.

Aluminum pots and pans could not be used for building aircraft as the government led folks to believe; only virgin aluminum could be used - the aluminum pots and pans had additional alloys making them non-virginal. Six million pounds of aluminum pots and pans collected in the scrap drives were recycled, after the war, into new aluminum pots, pans, and tableware.

Eight-hundred-eighty thousand pounds of silk and nylon stockings were collected within one four month scrap drive. This was just a tiny fraction of what was needed for making parachutes and glider tow ropes.

The metal drives were the most lucrative and most useful for actual war production. Iron and steel was easily melted down and used for munitions. One metal drive alone collected five million tons of steel in three weeks.

Although the huge quantities of rubber items collected were not used by the military, some of it was recycled into consumer products - women's undergarments, perhaps?)

Children also gathered milkweed pods, filled

burlap bags with them, and turned them in to their schools or collection bins. The white fuzzy milkweed floss

was used by the Navy for flotation devices (life vests) after extensive testing found it to be six times more buoyant than the cork filler being used at that time. About one pound of floss in a life vest could keep a 150 pound man floating in

Milkweed floss

water for more than forty hours. The Navy called for 200,000 pounds of the fuzzy weed for production in 1942, then quickly increased the need by an additional 100,000 pounds.

The first milkweed processing factory in the world was located near Lake Michigan where vast fields of the weed grew nearby. When the weed was at the appropriate stage for picking, hundreds of school children, teachers and parents swarmed the fields during school hours and picked bags and bags full, then sent them off for processing. Since the demand for milkweed floss was high across the nation, children were most often rewarded with the most coveted prize for each bag turned in - a twenty-five cent war stamp to add to their savings bond booklet.

Fat cans were also a highly sought after item by the government. The cans were easily collected and turned in by children from their families. A fat can was a tin can or

large glass jar that leftover waste fat or lard was

poured into and saved until the container was full. It had to be free of water or juices and strained to remove impurities. The children (or housewives) turned the full can(s) in at a variety of collection areas, most often at the local butcher or meat market. A full, one pound container of fat waste turned in by a child (or adult) garnered the reward of a special red ration stamp for a good cut of meat to take home to the family (the coveted red stamp was also an incentive for the housewife to be sure to drain any fat into the fat can while cooking).

The fat was sent to processing plants and rendered for military use into glycerin, an ingredient in drugs and explosives - nitroglycerin. One tablespoon of kitchen grease provided the fire power for four bullets while one pound made enough dynamite to blow up a bridge. The Navy also used lard to grease their big battleship guns.

The Pearl Harbor attack spread public fear across mainland America. Although it was a bit unrealistic to believe the Japanese might attack the

mainland, civil defense units quickly formed. **Civil Defense** is a system of defensive measures designed to protect civilians and property from enemy attack. By the end of January 1942, the U.S. Office of Civil Defense (OCD) had established 8,478 local Defense Councils. Citizens that did not qualify for military service volunteered by the thousands to serve as civil defense workers. In Chicago, the local council was overwhelmed with twenty-three thousand volunteers at one time!

Volunteers were sent to work immediately building bomb shelters, patrolling the borders, establishing air raid warning systems, distributing information with survival tips, etc.

The OCD published a booklet titled *What to Do in an Air Raid* and had civil defense volunteers distribute over fifty-seven million copies. The booklet gave instructions on how to respond to air raid sirens at home or in the city. Citizens were to educate themselves as to where the closest air raid shelters were located and the fastest way to get to them.

Air raid sirens were also used to signal blackouts, especially in coastal areas. The German U-boats (submarines) were sitting off the Eastern coasts using the cities night lights as a guide to harbors with exiting ships. As the ships pulled out to sea, the U-boats would attack and sink them.

The sirens sounded at sunset, thereby alerting citizens to turn off their outdoor lights, pull down their dark shades or blackout curtains, and stay indoors. All pedestrians were to be off the streets after the siren sounded. Travel by car at night was strictly limited; night driving required the use of head-lights. Civil defense volunteers made sure no lights were visible, especially in coastal towns and cities.

Women firefighters during World War II.

Auxiliary firemen and police were needed to replace those who had been drafted or volunteered for military service. Women with little training filled many of these positions and quickly grasped the concepts of firefighting or law enforcement duties. Civil defense volunteers also worked as nurses' aides, rescue squads, road repair crew, utility workers, messengers, drivers, etc.

Coastal civil defense volunteers established the

Aircraft Warning Service to watch for enemy aircraft approaching the mainland. Spotters, or Skywatchers, were to report all suspicious aircraft to nearby headquarters which then relayed the information to the Army's Filter Centers. The spotters watched the skies from small little huts or cabins perched atop a hill with an unobstructed view. The tiny work area had binoculars, a telephone and a poster or notebook with pictures of Japanese and German aircraft for easy identification.

Volunteers took their job as spotters seriously and often worked in shifts to cover the twenty-four hour days. Nearly one and a half million volunteers served as AWS spotters. Enemy aircraft was never spotted, but the public appeared less fearful of an attack knowing the spotters were on the job.

Coastal ports were another fearful source of entry. The Coast Guard patrolled the coastline waters, but CD volunteers guarded port facilities, warehouses and piers. Many of the Auxiliary volunteers, with their own boats, patrolled the shorelines and small inlets the Coast Guard could not get close enough to. Volunteers painted CGR (Coast Guard Reserves) on the  sides of their boats to distinguish their craft from other private boats. Over two thousand women handled the port security paperwork and patrolled in their own boats when and where needed.

Actor Humphrey Bogart utilized his yacht off the Los Angeles coast as a CD volunteer, while Arthur Fiedler, conductor of the Boston Pops Orchestra, patrolled the Boston Harbor with his yacht.

CD volunteers also taught classes on emergency preparedness, first aid and how to survive air raids (the most popular class). Many volunteers assisted the Red Cross at blood donation centers or war bond drives.

(Author's note: Although the Civil Defense volunteers were ever watchful on both coasts, two incidents occurred in Oregon and one occurred in Washington State, unbeknownst to Americans at that time. The first occurred September 9, 1942 when a small Japanese floatplane had been transported across the Pacific in a watertight compartment attached to a submarine. The sub surfaced off the Oregon coast and launched the plane. It then flew inland close to the town of Brookings and dropped incendiary bombs over the dense forest near there. Their plan was to start devastating, massive forest fires to distract the American people from bombing Japanese cities. Apparently, the Japanese had no concept of how large the U.S. was. The plan failed due to the heavy rains that had deluged the area prior to the attack. A second attempt three weeks later also failed for the same reason.

The Japanese news reported to their people that the bombing efforts had been successful - great fires had overtaken the United States and ten thousand people had been killed.

The second attack also occurred in Oregon. In May, 1945 a Japanese balloon bomb landed in a forested area about two hundred miles inland but did not explode when it hit the ground. On May 5, 1945, a local minister and his young pregnant wife took five children from their church on a trip to the mountains for a day of hiking, fishing, and a picnic. The children, ranging in age from eleven to thirteen, and the minister's wife hiked ahead to the picnic area while the minister drove the car loaded with supplies up to meet them. When he arrived, he heard the children excitedly calling to him that they had found a balloon. Moments later he heard a large explosion. He ran to the explosion site and found the children and his wife had died instantly from the blast.

On May 10, 1945, another balloon bomb struck power lines at Hanford, Washington's nuclear plant causing a massive power failure to one of the top secret nuclear reactors. Ironically, that reactor was in the process of producing the plutonium for the bomb to be dropped on Nagasaki a few months later.

The governmental Office of Censorship withheld the news of the first two balloon bomb incidents for one month, then allowed the release of minimal information to alert citizens of the

*dangers if more balloons were located. No
information was released to the public about the
Hanford incident until nearly forty years later.*

*In 1950 Weyerhaeuser Corporation, owner of
the forest land, erected a monument at the site of
the Oregon balloon bomb explosion. A bronze
plaque set in native stone lists the names of those
killed at the site and commemorates the "only
place on the American continent where death
resulted from enemy action during World War II."
The site, known as The Mitchell Monument, is
listed on the National Register of Historic Places.)*

The **Junior Service Corps**
accepted youth under fifteen
years of age to assist with scrap
drives, handing out information,
or helping with CD community
projects.

CD volunteers wore insignias on
their helmets and armbands to identify their
specialty; the symbol was a white triangle inside a
blue circle.

By July, 1943 there were over twelve million
registered civil defense volunteers, the majority of
them women.

The **Civil Air Patrol** (CAP), formed shortly
after the bombing of Pearl Harbor, was a major
part of America's civil defense. Made up of
civilian volunteers and pilots, the organization was

formed to provide a number of duties to aid the war effort on the home front. Sixteen-hundred civilian airports across America were kept open and operational during the war years due to the efforts of CAP volunteers. Other airports, or bases-of-operation, were

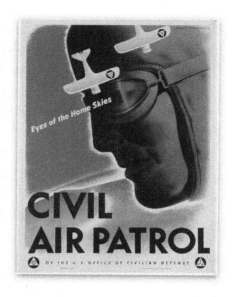

established along the East and West Coasts; East Coast bases were for sub-hunter operations, while West Coast bases watched for Japanese aircraft and balloon bomb attacks.

All CAP aircraft were owned and flown by civilians which offered a variety of aircraft types.

Coastal bases had an amphibious aircraft in case a water rescue was needed. Pilots were usually older men or women with high hours of accumulated flight time. By volunteering as a CAP pilot, many younger men were exempt from

the draft. In October, 1942 the group began a
training program that recruited and trained youth
as young as fifteen to assist with operations as well
as flight training. Young men anxious to enter the
military as fighter or bomber pilots received their
initial flight training from their local CAP unit then
joined the service with their pilot license in hand.
Flight instructors for those young men were most
often women.

German U-boats had been spotted along the
Eastern coastal waters targeting troop carriers and
cargo ships. By September 1942, 204 vessels had
been sunk by U-boats. The CAP Coastal Patrol
was finally authorized to carry bombs and depth
charges to ward off the attacks. From March, 1942
through August, 1943 the Coastal Patrol reported
sightings of 173 U-boats, attacked 57 of them, hit
10 and sank two. They flew 86,865 missions and
logged over 244,600 flight hours. The Patrol
rescued 363 survivors of U-boat attacks, reported
91 ships in distress, 17 floating mines and flew
5,684 convoy missions for the Navy.

The CAP volunteers also towed targets for the
military's gunnery practice during daylight hours
and tracking practice for crews using searchlights
and radar equipment at night. A total of 20,593
towing and tracking missions were flown.

Search and rescue missions were common for
the CAP and well received by the military. When a
military aircraft being ferried from one base to
another went down within the U.S., the CAP was

notified. Pilots and volunteers were local and knew the terrain providing a quicker response. Because their aircraft could fly lower and slower than the military aircraft, the volunteers were usually successful in locating the crash site then directed ground and rescue crews to it. Over 24,000 flight hours were logged for search and rescue missions.

The Red Cross and similar agencies utilized the CAP pilots for mercy missions often flying blood and medical supplies from one place to another when speed was of the essence (instead of utilizing trains or trucks).

When Texas ranchers reported losing thousands of cattle to wolf packs, thus limiting the supply of beef to the military and tightening rationing even more, the CAP was called to assist. Pilots with an armed spotter flew over the problem areas and "thinned" the wolf population - problem solved.

The government compensated the CAP pilots for their efforts by paying them $8 each day they flew. The government checks were always little and late which caused frustration, anxiety and in some cases, financial distress. Pilots were volunteering their time but were paying for their own fuel and the maintenance of their aircraft which was not cheap. One frustrated coastal pilot calculated that after six months and 40,000 miles of overwater flying, he cleared a government check of $10. Many pilots began limiting their volunteer time or dropping out altogether due to the expense of fuel and maintenance of their aircraft. Others felt it was their patriotic duty to continue helping with the war effort, but they usually put themselves in financial distress doing so. Altogether, eighty thousand volunteer CAP pilots and personnel spent over $1 million of their own money assisting the home front Civil Defense war efforts.

The American Women's Voluntary Services (AWVS) was the largest American women's service organization during WWII. Formed in 1940, its purpose was to provide women volunteers who would, in turn, help

the nation prepare for war then assist with support services during the war. The AWVS often sent their trained volunteers to work with the Civilian Defense volunteers, the Red Cross, and other volunteer groups. All the volunteer groups worked together to get the war jobs done. The group had 18,000 members when it first formed then grew to 325,000 as the war years progressed. All nationalities were welcomed especially African American, Chinese American, and Hispanic American. *Life* magazine called them the volunteer group "that made the most noise."

Many of the members were retired teachers and volunteered to teach the ins-and-outs of the rationing program, nutrition, cooking, and more. Nearly all of the women sold war bonds, participated in bond drives, or helped at scrap drive collection centers.

Retired nurses or women with medical backgrounds taught first aid, newborn care, child care, or volunteered to work in newly established day care centers. Other women drove city buses, taxi cabs, delivery trucks, messenger vehicles,

ambulances or fire trucks. Those with secretarial skills were in high demand for their typing skills. Switchboard operators were also needed. Volunteer jobs often became paid positions. Thousands of women volunteered to work in the canteens or collected and packed items to be sent to soldiers overseas. Young female high school graduates with an interest in aviation or aviation related fields, submitted their volunteer experience to hopefully gain favor and access toward entering the women's military units.

The AWVS organization disbanded when the war ended.

By the end of the war nearly every American man, woman, and child, not in the military, had served the nation as a volunteer of some sort in one group or another. They were indeed an army of home front soldiers-without-uniforms, soldiers-without-guns.

Chapter 20

Bonds, Mail, and Stars

War Bonds have been mentioned throughout the previous chapters, but exactly what were War

Bonds and what did they do? How were American women involved?

First called Defense Bonds in May, 1941 then changed to War Bonds or Victory Bonds in December, 1941 after war was declared, the bonds were basically a loan to the government from it's citizens to help pay for war needs.

Aircraft, ships, tanks, ammunition, guns, even the soldier's uniforms had to be paid for by the government, but war needs were not a line item in the budget at that time. At first a five percent Victory Tax was levied on citizens in the early stages of the war, but that only covered about 45% of the expenses. The Victory Tax was not enough to meet the growing financial burdens for the thousands of bombers and ships rapidly being built; therefore, the government turned to issuing bonds.

The Series E Bonds were sold at 75% of face value with maturity over ten years. The lowest

bond denomination was $25 which sold for $18.75 and would be worth the $25 face value in ten years. Other amounts were available up to a face value of $10,000. War stamps valued at ten or twenty-five cents each could be purchased or earned, placed in a special Bond booklet, then redeemed for a $25 bond when full; these booklets were especially popular with children. The government's objective was to make the purchase of bonds affordable and available to everyone. A surge in War Bond sales during the war years always seemed to occur during Christmas as folks gave them as gifts to children, family, and friends.

The advertising blitz to purchase War Bonds produced the greatest volume of ads in U.S. history. Thousands of posters and advertisements blanketed the U.S. encouraging Americans to help support the war effort. Many played on the patriotism of Americans while others pulled and tugged at heartstrings to "bring our boys home sooner with good equipment" - the good equipment coming from the purchase of War Bonds. Comic book superheroes, Disney characters and Bugs Bunny also

encouraged children to participate in purchasing bonds, thereby, helping them to understand they were also a part of the war efforts.

Bond rallies were extremely popular due in part to the participation of Hollywood stars, popular singers, musicians, and entertainers (Refer to Chapters 15 and 16 for reminders of their successes).

Women were instrumental in selling and purchasing War Bonds. Since so many women

were now working in factories and other jobs, many had payroll deductions taken towards the purchase of War Bonds. Other women participated in volunteer efforts with a variety of groups to raise money for bonds. Bake sales, handmade clothing items, and home canned preserves were often donated by women for the sales.

Eight huge War Bond Drives were held from 1942 to 1945. During these drives, advertising pushes increased ten fold via posters, radio, newspaper, and magazine ads. Competitions were held between towns and cities with volunteers

going door-to-door urging their neighbors to buy
bonds. School children held competitions between
their schools to see which one could raise the most
money for bond purchases. With each of the larger
War Bond Drives the government hoped to raise an

additional $9 - to $15 billion in sales. Their goals
were easily surpassed at each of the eight drives.

World War II cost the United States $300
billion. By the end of the war, eighty-five million
Americans, one half the population, had purchased
nearly $186 billion worth of War Bonds. This
averaged around $2,000 per person as well as
represented untold amounts of patriotism and
personal sacrifices.

The last proceeds from the Victory War Bond
campaign were deposited into the U.S. Treasury on
January 3, 1946. The famed Series E Bond was
withdrawn on June 30, 1980 and replaced by the
EE Savings Bond, the "Patriot Bond."

Soldiers were far from home, often for the first
time, fighting in horrific conditions and fearing for

their lives. **Mail Call** was the highlight of the day, and the biggest morale booster for all who were serving. A letter from home reminded them who and what they were fighting for and kept them going. Letters were tucked into pockets and carried with them to be read over and over again.

On the home front, posters and magazine ads

encouraged Americans to write letters to their soldiers letting them know how much they cared. Women wrote to their husbands, sons, brothers and "to any soldier" which generated millions of letters daily. Letters for soldiers overseas were sent by airplane which was more expensive for the sender, or by ship which could take over a month or more for delivery. Those valuable letters weighed thousands of tons and took up valuable cargo space for food, fuel, and supplies needed for the troops. The mail bags were often set aside in favor of sending supplies which delayed the mail delivery by weeks, sometimes months.

Eastman Kodak developed a simple photographic system that would speed delivery, eliminate the need for mail bags in cargo space, and bring encouragement to the soldiers waiting to hear from home. The new system was called **V-Mail**, short for **Victory Mail**.

The process was simple: the letter writer would purchase a V-Mail writing kit from the local five-

and-dime store; write her letter on a one-sided, small sized piece of paper which had a box on the top for the soldier's address, then send it to the military postal system. All letters and other communi-cations passed through censors before moving on to the next step. The mailroom photo-graphed the page onto 16-mm black and white camera film reels (micro-film). The reels were then sent overseas to the appropriate centers where the thumbnail-sized negatives were

Soldier holding V-mail film reel over the
corresponding number of letters on the reel.

enlarged, printed and sent for delivery. Thirty-
seven mail bags containing 150,000 letters
weighing 2,575 pounds were reduced to a single
bag containing the same number of letters, or
more, weighing just 45 pounds. The entire process
was reversed when soldiers wrote letters to their
loved ones back home.

The governmental Office of Censorship was
responsible for censoring all communications
coming into and going out of the U.S. By 1943,
censor stations across the U.S. employed 14,462
certified censors, of which the majority were
women. In censoring communications, the women
were trained to look for any negativity from home
front letter writers - fearing the enemy might
obtain the mail and find a sense of negativity,
hopelessness, etc. coming from home, they would
use it against the soldiers in propaganda. No
sexually explicit or graphic, sexual language was

allowed. No foreign languages were allowed - many families were immigrants and spoke their native tongue among family members - censors were not able to translate so the letters would not move forward (in most cases the letters were returned to the sender with an explanation as to why they were censored).

When the censor received a letter for review, she would skim through it quickly looking for wording that was inappropriate. The censored section would be cut out with scissors, a sharp knife or, in most cases, marked out with heavy black ink. The letter would then be stamped "Passed By Censor No. ____" then sent on to be photographed and V-Mailed.

Likewise, soldiers' letters home were also censored before being V-Mail processed. No

mention of their location, the number of troops involved, where the units were headed next, how many were killed or injured, was allowed; all would be censored, returned to the soldier, or destroyed. Once again, the fear was the enemy using the infor- mation against them to plan attacks. Locations could only be discussed if the battle was successful and occurred a month or two prior to writing the letter.

Posters across America reminded everyone that "Loose Lips Sink Ships" or "Idle Gossip Sinks Ships." In case there were enemy spies working in the factories, women could not discuss what the letters from their soldiers related regarding activities or non-censored locations. The slogan reminders were also stamped on the outside of the V-Mail envelopes.

Letters from home usually contained family information, births, deaths, illness or the latest volunteer activities. If the letter writer worked in a war factory and discussed anything about production, it would be censored. Soldiers could describe their R & R locations but not where they were to return to when their time was up. For the most part, censors agreed the letters were a bit boring to them but valuable to the recipients. The letters contained the thoughts and feelings of Americans on the home front and battle fronts as they both faced life and death war struggles on a daily basis. They may not have been historically significant, but they certainly gave insight to future generations as to what their ancestors experienced.

During the war over 1.5 billion V-Mail letters were processed.

The **Service Flag** or **Sons of Service Flag** was first used in World War I then carried over to WWII. The flags became more popular in WWII as a visual communication of a family's

commitment to the war effort. The flag, or banner, was white with a thick red border prominently displayed in the front window of families with members serving in the military. A blue star for each family member serving was attached to the white field on the banner. If a family member was killed while serving, a gold star was placed over the blue star - the gold star was smaller than the blue star thus creating a blue border around the gold star.

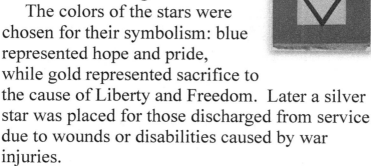

The colors of the stars were chosen for their symbolism: blue represented hope and pride, while gold represented sacrifice to the cause of Liberty and Freedom. Later a silver star was placed for those discharged from service due to wounds or disabilities caused by war injuries.

The flags used by families were usually no larger than one foot long and hung vertically in a display window. Many businesses, organizations and factories had much larger flags made to display the appropriate colored star for their members or employees serving in the war. Those flags might easily have had over fifty blue and/or gold stars.

The Service Flags became a powerful symbol of the patriotic duty and personal sacrifices American families were making to aid in the war efforts. A visitor walking down any street, in any town across America could easily spot a Service Flag hanging in the window of nearly every other home.

Blue Star Mothers of America was an organization formed in 1942 to provide support for mothers who had sons or daughters serving in the war. The groups of mothers across the country had service goals in mind when they first organized. They gathered articles for care packages and shipped them to military members serving overseas, encouraged regular V-Mail communications, assisted mothers facing hardships due to the male family members serving, offered help and support to each other with a shoulder to cry on when bad news was received. The ultimate goal was to bring their sons home and make sure they received the benefits they were entitled to. Remember, many of these men serving were just young teens, not even in their twenties. When they returned home, many needed rehabilitation from wounds or psychological traumas they suffered during their service.

Blue Star Mothers were very active visiting wounded soldiers as they returned to the States. The military hospitals may have been far from the soldiers' homes with transportation for their visiting families problematic. The moms felt if it was their son, they would want another mom to be there for support.

There were close to 30,000 Blue Star Mothers in the organization during WWII.

American Gold Star Mothers was also formed shortly after WWI and carried over into WWII. Any American woman who had lost a son or daughter in service to the U.S. was welcomed into this organization. Gold Star Mothers were/are an active group, a Veterans Service Organization, but are non-political. The mothers work together to honor their sons and daughters through service to veterans and patriotic events. Only mothers who have lost a child can know the pain each endures. Gold Star Mother's Day is observed in the U.S. on the last Sunday in September.

Blue Star and Gold Star Mothers groups are still active today, but Service Flags are not often seen.

Chapter 21

We Regret to Inform You...

"Mommy, when is daddy coming home?...
Mommy, what does war mean?...Mommy, where
did Uncle Bobby and Grandpa go?...Why?...
Mommy, why do we have to eat this stuff?...
Mommy, my shoes are falling apart and my pants
are too small...Mommy, why do we have to go
live with Grandma?...Mommy, are you going to
make a plane today at your work?" Why, why,
why. Home front wives and mothers listened to
the "whys" day in and day out for four years.
They lived with daily fear and loneliness as they
were placed in a world unfamiliar and unsecured to
them. Small sacrifices often led to hardships never
before experienced which then became constant
worries. Children sensed the anxiety and often
experienced the same worries and fear, not
understanding war or what all it entailed.

Government posters, magazine articles and
newspapers constantly admonished women to
"buck up," meet the challenges, get the job done,
be patriotic so we can bring your husbands, sons,
fathers, and the boy next door home from war
duties. Apparently, anxiety and fear were
unpatriotic. One article went so far as to say,

"Don't mope! Standing up to heartache and loneliness is your contribution to righting a topsy-turvy world."

Mothers, wives, sisters, and girlfriends waited anxiously everyday for the mailman in hopes of a letter from their military loved ones - a small note from a world away helped alleviate a bit of the anxiety and assure the home front loved ones they were still alive. Days and months would go by without any word or five letters might arrive on the same day. It was okay to watch for the mailman, but no one ever wanted to see the "death messenger."

Shortly after the war began and casualties had to be reported to anxious families, a military vehicle carrying a military chaplain and an aide would pull up to the family home to deliver the death notification telegram or letter. As military manpower on the home front became scarce, and casualties increased, the delivery of notification telegrams changed.

Operator receiving a telegram from a teletype machine.

In the backrooms of hundreds of drug stores, general stores, or in actual Western Union offices across America, the teletypewriter (teletype machine) would tick-tick-tick to life and spew ticker-tape into a basket or onto the floor. The first line told the attendant where the telegram was coming from; the next line, the recipient's address; next, the message. The attendant cut the ticker-tape into pieces, pasted them onto the Western Union form, placed the form into an envelope, then notified the delivery person that it was ready for delivery.

Western Union hired boys, too young to join the service or not draft eligible,  for telegram delivery. The delivery boys rode their bicycles through city neighborhoods or out into the rural areas, carrying the Western Union pouch, which contained the telegrams, over their shoulder. When the bike messengers were spotted in a neighborhood, all eyes were on him until he passed their homes. If he stopped, parked his bike, opened his pouch, confirmed the address, went to the door and knocked, the neighborhood went silent with prayers. The neighborhood wives then gathered at the recipient's home to help in any way they could. It was never good news.

The messenger boys had no idea what was in the telegrams they delivered, but they quickly figured it out. The messengers were only obligated to deliver the message and ride on to the next delivery - the recipient was left alone in her grief not knowing how to proceed.

The Blue Star in the window was sadly changed to a Gold Star.

Depending on the circumstances, the telegrams from the military were <u>fill in the blanks</u> and read as follows:

" The Secretary of War/Secretary of the Navy regrets to inform you that your <u>(loved one)</u> has been <u>(killed in action/captured by the enemy/ declared missing in action/presumed dead after missing in action for twelve months)</u>. If further details or other information are received you will be promptly notified. A confirmation letter follows."

The same type of letter would be sent from the Secretary of War for Army soldiers listing a non-specific location of his/her death, i.e. Germany or Italy, etc.

The confirmation letter was usually another telegram with a bit more information:

"The Navy Department deeply regrets to inform you that your husband/son_____ was killed in action in the performance of his duty and in the service of his country. The Department extends to you its sincerest sympathy in your great loss.

On account of existing conditions the body if recovered cannot be returned at present. If further details are received you will be informed. To prevent possible aid to our enemies please do not divulge the name of his ship or station.
Rear Admiral _____ Chief of Naval Personnel"

Occasionally a follow-up telegram for those previously notified their loved one had been captured, would read:

"We are pleased to inform you that _____ has been found alive in a prisoner-of-war camp located in _____."

Unfortunately, many POWs were tortured, killed, and their bodies never found which consequently left families bereaved and without closure.

For the thousands of families notified their loved one was missing in action, the wait was unbearable. Although the military sent them regular telegrams informing them the search was ongoing, in harsh, realistic terms - it was not. Because there were just too many casualties and wounded to care for, missing soldiers were a lower priority. The telegrams were an easy way for the military to avoid constant demands by the families to find their loved ones. After a year of waiting for official word from the military that their soldier had been declared dead, the families still needed word of what happened and a body to grieve over.

When the war was officially over, repatriation of remains continued to be a low priority versus getting the live and wounded home first. Nearly 60-plus years later, many families are still waiting for official word as to what happened to their loved ones.

During WWII, when a soldier was killed in action, the unit chaplain or a fellow soldier collected any personal items on the body, removed one of the deceased's dog tags, placed it in the mouth between his teeth and closed his mouth. The body was sent to a disposition area and prepared for transport back to the U.S. The other dog tag was sent to the nearest headquarters with a killed in action (KIA) report. The report was then sent back to the U.S. military offices in Washington, D.C. where identification and notification information was confirmed then sent on to the proper military service branch. At that point, a telegram was sent to the family notifying them of the death. Within a few days after the telegram is sent, an official letter of acknowledgement from the service branch is sent.

Thousands of women worked in those military offices and performed the disheartening job of identification and notification, then prepared the telegrams and letters - they typed information every day, all day. Many of those women felt if they did not have to personally present the letters to the families, they could continue with the job.

Another letter sent to the grieving family, notified them of any medals or awards due their loved one. The disposition of the remains was also discussed in this particular letter. If the soldier was awarded a medal, a plot at Arlington National Cemetery might be offered, otherwise the family was to notify the military where they wished to have the body interred. All servicemen were offered a military funeral, but the final decision of location was up to the families.

WWII was the deadliest military conflict in history. Approximately 50 million people died worldwide as well as 6 million Jews. Over 16 million Americans served. Over 400,000 Americans were killed, 670,846 were wounded, 18,745 were taken as prisoners of war, and over 73,000 are still missing to this day. The Army suffered the largest losses with 318,274 killed, Navy lost 62,614, Marines 24,511 and Coast Guard 1,917. The Army losses included 15,530 pilots, crew members, and ground personnel killed or lost within the United States due to aircraft accidents. Downed aircraft in the U.S. due to accidents numbered 7,100, many of which were training or ferrying (moving aircraft from one base to another) flights with inexperienced pilots and crew. Several of the downed aircraft within the U.S., along with their pilots and crew, have not been found to this day. The Army declared them dead after searches for remains were unsuccessful (after twelve months time).

The death of all the beloved military family members was a profound tragedy and the ultimate hardship faced by their home front families. It must be remembered that women not only worked in factories, organized various drives, volunteered, etc. but they were also the glue that held their families together during the agonizing loss of their loved ones. Lives were changed forever.

(Author's note: The military no longer sends notifications via telegram. After WWII it was determined the notifications were cold and impersonal (thanks to First Lady Eleanor Roosevelt) leaving the family member(s) dazed and confused, not knowing what to do or how to proceed. Now each military branch has CNOs - Casualty Notification Officers and CAOs - Casualty Assistant Officers. These Officers are specially trained for this specific duty and consider it an honor to serve in this capacity.

Prior to deployment, the soldier completes legal paperwork that includes who is to be notified first in case of his/her death as well as any personal preference for funeral arrangements and interment. When a military death occurs, all available information about the circumstances of death are gathered as quickly as possible then the CNOs/CAOs are notified and assigned to the surviving family. A personal, face-to-face notification is made in accordance to the soldier's pre-deployment paperwork. News media is not allowed to release the name of the military service person killed until this notification has been made. The Officers begin the process of making funeral arrangements or memorial services per the survivors wishes and in accordance to the paperwork completed by the service person.

In addition, a Casualty Assistance Call Package is given to the survivors containing beneficiary forms, benefit forms, claim forms, etc. The Officers assist the survivors in completing the forms and filing for the appropriate benefits available to them.

The Officer assigned to the surviving family makes him/herself available as long as it takes to resolve all issues - this could be days, weeks, or months. When the family feels no further help is needed, the Officer is released of his/her duties to them.

As of May 9, 2014 military statistics show 73,624 WWII soldiers are still missing. The Joint POW/MIA Accounting Command (JPAC) within the Department of Defense has been tasked with investigating leads of American military personnel killed in action or declared missing and never returned to American soil. Its mission is "to account for Americans listed as POW/MIA from all past wars and conflicts."

Operations are divided into four areas:

Analysis and Investigation, Recovery, Identification, and Closure. JPAC has eighteen recovery teams traveling world wide to accomplish their mission. Each team may have ten to fourteen members including a forensic anthropologist, forensic photographer, linguist, medic, communications technician and an explosive ordnance disposal technician. Depending on the search location, mountaineering specialists or divers may also be on the teams.

When remains and artifacts are located, they are quickly sent to JPAC's Central Identification Laboratory at Joint Base Pearl Harbor-Hickam in Hawaii. The remains are carefully analyzed to determine sex, race, age at death, stature, pathological conditions of the bones, trauma caused at or near the time of death. Personal effects or any military equipment found with or near the remains are also carefully analyzed to provide clues to the identity of the individual. DNA is collected from the remains; however, if there are no surviving family members, it is difficult to obtain a match or near match of the victim. From the time remains are received to completion of the identification process the average time spent can be up to eleven years.

When the case is complete, the information is sent to the appropriate branch of service's Mortuary Affairs office. Personnel then notify the next-of-kin and arrangements are made for a full military burial.

World War II Families for the Return of the Missing (WWRM) is an active support group formed to assist families in finding answers about their MIA service members. The group helps with research, genealogy and assistance with government agencies in obtaining information concerning their loved one. The group encourages families to donate DNA to the database files to aid in identification if/when remains are located.)

Gold Star Mothers Memorial located in the
Putnam Co. Veterans Memorial Park in
Carmel, New York.

Chapter 22

It's Over!

Radio and newspapers announced Victory in Europe Day, V-E Day, May 8, 1945, when Germany unconditionally surrendered to Allied forces. Hitler committed suicide April 30, 1945 during the vicious Battle of Berlin. His successor, Karl Donitz, authorized the surrender.

There is some speculation that Hitler committed suicide over fear of being captured, tortured and killed as Italy's Mussolini had been a few weeks earlier. Mussolini's successor also surrendered Italy to Allied forces.

But the war wasn't over yet. Japan vowed to fight to the bitter end. The bitter end came close for them on August 6, 1945 when the atomic

403

bomb, "Little Boy," was dropped over Hiroshima causing death and destruction to thousands. That atomic bomb was the first use of a nuclear weapon in warfare. Emperor Hirohito still refused to surrender. On August 9, a second nuclear weapon, "Fat Man," was dropped on Nagasaki also causing massive death and destruction. Hirohito finally surrendered August 14, 1945 and reluctantly urged his people and military to accept the surrender and begin rebuilding.

V-J Day, Victory over Japan, was announced to

Americans by President Harry Truman on the same day (President Roosevelt died suddenly of a massive stroke April 12, 1945):

This is the day we have been waiting for since Pearl Harbor. This is the day when Fascism finally dies, as we knew it would.

Finally, after three years, eight months, and seven days since the December 7, 1941 attack on Pearl Harbor, it was really over! Joyous Americans spilled out into the streets whooping, hollering, dancing,

404

celebrating, and letting go of the pent up anxieties, fears, sorrows, and anger they had experienced from the very beginning.

A formal signing ceremony aboard the USS Missouri in Tokyo Bay on September 2, 1945 was broadcast live worldwide via radio. The ceremony lasted twenty-three minutes as each of the following representatives signed the agreement: first to sign were Japanese officials on behalf of Emperor Hirohito; next, General Douglas MacArthur, Supreme Commander for the Allied Powers, on behalf of the Allied Powers; next, Admiral Chester Nimitz on behalf of the United States; then representatives for China, the United Kingdom, Soviet Union, Australia, Canada, France, the Netherlands and New Zealand.

President Truman officially proclaimed the end of WWII hostilities on December 31, 1946 Our military troops had slowly been coming home from the European theaters after V-E Day. Prisoner-of-war camps were being liberated, as well as the German concentration camps where the catastrophic devastation of death by the hand of Germany was revealed to the world. Pacific theater troops continued to battle skirmishes on isolated islands held by Japanese soldiers who refused to surrender or had no official word from their superiors to "stand down."

Home front families were overjoyed with the news! Their loved ones would finally be coming home. As the days seemed to drag on after the

announcements, old anxieties began to creep back over the wives and mothers as they wondered when, where and in what condition their husbands and sons would appear.

Demobilization of over five million men and military equipment would take twelve to eighteen months. Thousands of soldiers would serve out their remaining time as occupation forces in Germany and Japan. Unfortunately, thousands of families continued to wait and pray for the safe return of their men who had been reported captured as POWs, missing in action, or lost at sea - more than 73,000 families never knew what happened to their loved ones.

Telegrams overwhelmed Western Union and V-Mail letters overwhelmed the postal workers as military loved ones advised their families they were finally on their way home.

Government posters, newspapers and radio began preparing home front families for the return of their military members with "When-He-Comes-Home" articles. Shell shock and combat fatigue were terms to become familiar with, recognize and expect. Women were advised not to ask too many questions about the wartime experiences as that might cause a negative reaction from the returning soldier.

On June 22, 1944, just before the war ended, President Roosevelt signed into law the Servicemen's Readjustment Act which later became known as the G.I. Bill. The purpose of the law was to give returning soldiers benefits and opportunities to aid in their return to civilian life. Benefits were available to every veteran who served on active duty for at least ninety days during the war (not necessarily in combat) and was honorably discharged. Assistance with finding employment was available, unemployment pay of $20 per week for up to 52 weeks and low-interest loans for the purchase of a home, a farm, or to start a business were also available.

The one opportunity the majority of veterans took advantage of was the education and training benefit. Cash payments for tuition and living expenses were granted to those who wanted to further or complete their education in either a college or a vocational/trade school. Schools were paid up to $500 per year for tuition, books, fees, and other training costs as well as a small living allowance for as long as the student was in school. Nearly 2,232,000 veterans attended college or trade school with the help of the G.I. Bill.

The nation was definitely prepared for the return of it's military men and women with the assistance of the G.I. Bill.

Wives, mothers, children and other family members made their way to the East Coast to greet the troop carriers as they arrived from European shores. It may have been difficult to spot a certain soldier in the mass confusion of some 13,000 disembarking from the ships, but women have eagle-eye vision when it comes to finding their loved ones. West Coast ports returned troops from the Pacific with thousands of family members lining the docks anxious to embrace their battle weary loved ones.

As the joyful celebrations, parades, and home-town proclamations quieted, many military men and women began experiencing difficulties with transition. Transition from high-stress combat situations to the peaceful home front situations was strenuous and tenuous for thousands of returnees. The soldiers were young, naive, fresh, and confident teen boys and girls when they left for war, now some returned as battle weary, nervous, bitter men and women survivors. They just wanted to return to the domestic normalcy they had left, but that domestic normalcy was gone - everything had changed. Wives and mothers were working full-time jobs outside the home; there were shortages of everything, rationing, families deep in debt, or the opposite - some were wealthy after working in war production factories. Even so, it was not what the soldiers expected to come home to.

Many of the soldiers returned with missing limbs, visible wounds and physical impairments. But the signature injury of war suffered by a large percentage of returning soldiers was "shell shock" or "combat fatigue" - these were mental wounds, not visible and a reaction to the trauma of battle. Horrific scenes of death, dying and destruction spattered with pangs of guilt about being the one to escape death when their combat buddies had been blown to bits in front of them, ran as a continuous loop of tape through their minds.

Before the war ended, the Army discharged nearly ten thousand soldiers a month for psychiatric reasons, most suffering from combat fatigue. Loud or unexpected noises startled them and threw them into a panic attack or nervous fits. Sleep was impossible due to frequent interruptions by hallucinations, flashbacks, nightmares, and feelings of helplessness. Sleep became so illusive the desperate turned to alcohol as a numbing agent. Alcohol created a whole new set of problems for both the soldier on or off the battlefield and his family when he arrived home. American women definitely had their hands full.

On the other hand, many of the returning soldiers had no significant readjustment or transition problems. By applying the self-confidence and "can-do" attitude gained from their military training, they were able to push up their sleeves and get to the work of turning a new page in their lives. Alarmed by the "When-He-Comes-Home" propaganda, the new civilian veterans admonished the amateur psychiatrists to stop telling folks "how to handle these changed men and women." The veterans complained about the patronizing, over-sympathetic, kid glove treatment many were receiving and scoffed at the notion they did not want to talk about their wartime experiences. Some looked upon their experiences as the most important life event to have happened to them or that talking about the experiences would be a catharsis of sorts - an affirmation of what they had been through.

Wives and mothers experienced a combat fatigue of their own as husbands and sons returned from the war. The women's world was turned upside down again as war production facilities began closing, thereby terminating the women's employment. Loss of their jobs led to loss of income which led to family financial hardships. At first the government couldn't get enough women to work, now they were kicking them to the curb as fast as they could with nary a thank you for keeping the country running smoothly; very disconcerting to many.

Re-establishing the prewar home environment was not easy for women when their men returned. Many experienced a loss of independence especially if they lost a lucrative paying job; the sense of financial security evaporated which left them enveloped in the smoke of worry. Young children who had not seen their fathers for two or three years had no clue who these strangers were invading their homes. Older children who vaguely remembered their fathers, brothers or uncles seemed to resent their presence as interfering with their established routines.

Disabled soldiers' family members also faced difficult challenges. If the soldier was hospitalized in a Veterans' hospital far from their home and family, the family might uproot and move closer to the facility. If the moving costs were prohibitive for the family, the wife or mother may have lobbied the government to transfer her soldier to a facility closer to home; red tape and paperwork took months and months for approval and the move. Medical facilities were overwhelmed, especially Veterans' hospitals - there weren't enough of them to treat the thousands and thousands of veterans needing care.

Soldiers suffering battle fatigue or shell shock symptoms at home were at the mercy of their families when they experienced nightmares, hallucinations, behavior changes, severe headaches, crying spells, and drunkenness (usually after self-medication with alcohol). Alcoholism was an increasing problem after the war for both the soldiers and the women trying to cope with post war family issues.

Divorce rates initially soared when the war ended, then leveled off within a couple of years. Marriage rates soared followed by birth rates.

The returning veterans also had a huge impact on American economy which had been dependent on supporting war production. With shipyard, aircraft and munitions factories closing, unemployment rates rapidly rose which caused general fear of another economic Depression. It would take time for factories to shift back to pre-war production of goods such as automobiles, appliances, etc. In the meantime, jobs were scarce for everyone however, the jobs that were available were most often given to former employees or veterans returning from the war. The Selective Training and Services Act of 1940 had a provision that guaranteed returning veterans one year of employment at their old jobs, if those jobs were available, and if they so desired.

Although the All American Girls Professional Baseball League continued their games (until 1954), interest dwindled as the soldiers returned and fans wanted a return to baseball as it had been before the war. However, professional baseball players also found it difficult to return to their former teams/positions. Professional baseball developed their own set of rules for returning veterans which did not come close to the 1940 Federal law. Returning players were required to notify their clubs within 90 days from military discharge if they wanted to resume their pre-service team position. They were entitled to a trial period of 15 days of regular-season play or 30 days of spring training at which time the club could terminate the contract at its discretion. The player was to receive two weeks pay before being sold, traded, farmed out to another team or outright released from his contract.

When **Al Niemiec** was discharged from the Navy in 1946 he notified his former baseball club, the Seattle Rainiers, that he wanted to return and reclaim his previous position. Like many other returning veterans, Al had a family to support and wanted  to return to his former job, one that he knew well. The club signed him to a lucrative one year contract which included a substantial pay raise, played him in eleven games, cut him, then terminated the contract. At the age of 35, the club maintained he was too old to play his position effectively. Niemiec filed a precedent-setting lawsuit against the Rainiers and Major League Baseball and won. Hundreds of returning major and minor league baseball players, who were also cut by their teams when they returned from military service, received payments as a result of Niemiec's suit.

Although the lawsuit only affected a small group of returning servicemen, it also affected their families who were dependent on the income they had been promised. The Judge admonished the League for not bearing any of the burden in being fair to American service men, especially those involved with the beloved American sport of baseball.

The worries and fears of an impending downtrodden economy were unfounded. Veterans took advantage of the G.I. Bill returning to college or vocational schools. A housing boom seemed to manifest overnight. Automobiles began rolling off assembly lines as Americans waited impatiently for a new car they could now afford to purchase. Farmers invested in new, modern, tractors, and the new labor saving combine, both of which increased farm production, which then increased food availability. Clothing and shoes were snapped up by consumers as quickly as they were displayed in department stores, after rationing of all goods ended in 1946.

The American women during WWII became the backbone in the formation of the "Greatest Generation" - they were moving forward again and gaining even greater power and speed.

Chapter 23

We Did It!

At the height of the war, over 19,170,000 women comprised the American labor force while 16,000,000 men had gone off to war. Women outnumbered men three to one in factories across America. Of those women, one in ten were married with husbands or sons serving in the military. As the war began winding down in the European and Pacific theaters, polls indicated that up to 85% of single women workers and 68% of married women wanted to keep their jobs when the war ended. Although the vast majority of those jobs were war industry jobs, women realized war products would no longer be needed; therefore, they would no longer be needed. But the women still wanted to work and earn a paycheck.

WWII war production set astounding records: over 300,000 airplanes, 86,000 tanks, 49,000 jeeps, 91,000 military vehicles, 44 billion rounds of ammunition, 47 million tons of artillery ammunition, millions of hand guns and other small weapons, 2,710 Liberty ships, 531 Victory ships, 952 destroyers, 151 aircraft carriers, 126 submarines, over 81 cruisers, 64,000 landing craft, and 9 new battleships thanks to the Rosies, the

Rosie WOWs and the Wendy's. *Time* magazine called this "a miracle of wartime production." The women simply called it "a job well done" in a job opportunity never before available to them. They were proud to have done their patriotic duty.

Millions of women also worked outside the home in male dominated jobs to keep the home front running smoothly. They worked as transit workers, railroad workers, police and fire officers, taxi drivers, bank managers, supermarket employees, barbers, mechanics, lumberjacks, painters, and more. These women also took pride in their jobs and contributions to the war effort.

When the war ended in 1945 the first jobs to disappear for women workers were obviously the war production jobs. By 1946 four million women had lost those lucrative paying jobs. Many of those four million women were not happy about being ousted; work was still a necessity to support their families. At the Ford Motor Plant in Highland Park, Michigan, two hundred women staged a protest at the plant's entrance. They marched peacefully carrying signs that read, "How Come No Work For Women?"- "Stop Discrimination Because of Sex" - "Equal Pay For Equal Work."

One young woman wrote a letter to President Truman stating she had been a faithful three-and-a-half year employee at the Grumman Aircraft Engineering Corporation as a lathe hand, a classified skilled laborer. She was now a widow as a result of the war and had a young son to support by herself. Why was she no longer wanted just because she was a woman? She certainly sacrificed more than enough for the war effort and yet...

For the thousands and thousands of soldiers returning home disabled and unable to work or return to their previous jobs, the role of principal breadwinner, again, fell to the woman of the house. This was another stressful time for the women since the factory jobs with high pay were disappearing rapidly as well as the service jobs.

Single women found only low paying jobs as sales clerks, telephone operators, waitresses, and receptionists. Married women were discriminated against when applying for even the lowliest of service jobs. They pulled their children from day care centers and went home. Day care centers affiliated with war industry factories quickly closed leaving those workers also jobless.

Governmental propaganda posters began appearing everywhere telling women to return to their homes and tend to their families. One poster read, "Hooray! Rosie the Riveter can finally go home and be Rosie the Housewife again!" Other propaganda advertising strongly encouraged women to "seek husbands, settle down and have babies." There were also posters encouraging all types of employers to hire veterans, not women.

Teachers, nurses and typists were still in high demand across the nation; those positions were quickly filled by both single and married women with experience. Because of the demand, many women returned to college or vocational schools to finish the education they had put on hold in order to work in the war factories. Now they had the financial resources to finish what they had started before the war.

Women began thinking more about career jobs instead of service jobs. They had more confidence in themselves and their abilities. Besides teaching and nursing, other occupations were slowly opening doors to women in science, medicine, research, and engineering.

As the military women returned after the war they also had tough decisions to make regarding their futures. The majority of Army Nurse Corps members continued their service in the Veteran's hospitals across the country. Others joined the pathway to marriage, children, and homemaking.

The women veterans encountered discriminatory roadblocks in their attempts to obtain veteran benefits they were rightfully due under the G.I. Bill. The government would not recognize the women as military veterans. Eventually, after major political wrangling, 64,728 service women attended college with the help of the G.I. Bill.

Health benefits for women veterans were so extremely difficult to obtain that most women gave up trying. Instead, they pursued the care they needed on their own (or neglected care altogether) and paid with their own meager finances.

The WASP, as mentioned in a previous chapter, were disbanded in 1944 before the war officially ended. Ladies that loved to fly and who had accumulated thousands of hours of flight time did not give up flying. Although highly discriminated against and accused of trying to take positions away from returning servicemen, the women were frequently hired to teach men to fly. The odd thing was, the G.I. Bill paid for the men's lessons from the highly skilled and experienced (former WASP) pilots. With their new pilot's license in hand, it was the men who were hired with very few hours (not the women with thousands of hours) to fly commercial airlines or the mail. Didn't seem to make much sense to the women.

Most of the returning WASP became members of the Ninety-Nines, an ever increasing group of women pilots originally formed in 1929, with Amelia Earhart as the club's first president. Throughout the WWII years, women pilots who were not WASP joined the CAP volunteering to fly missions as earlier described. After the war most of these women remained in aviation profess-ionally and continued their membership in the Ninety-Nines.

The original purpose of the organization was to "coordinate the interests and efforts of women in aviation." As the organization grew, the purpose broadened to include "any movement which will be of help to them in aero-nautical research,

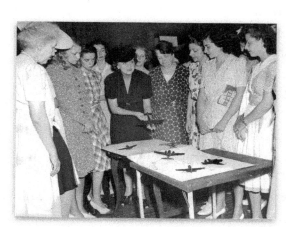

air racing events, acquisition of aerial experience, maintenance of an economic status in the aviation industry, administering through the air in times of emergency arising from fire, famine, flood, and war, or any other interest that will be for their benefit and/or that of aviation in general."

Women learning about aviation from a member of the Ninety-Nines.

These aviation experienced women not only continued to teach men to fly, they were also hired by aircraft manufacturing plants as aeronautical engineers for their aviation expertise, air traffic controllers at airport control towers, or they flew charter flights, barnstormed across the country, flew company aircraft for various businesses, or became aviation writers, aerial photographers, and artists.

A series of All-Woman Air Shows were held in Florida from 1947 to 1950, to demonstrate aviation developments and newer aircraft to the crowds. It was an opportunity to demonstrate their skills as well as educate the crowd about the importance of aviation in the future.

The Ninety-Nines also shared their love of all things aviation related with our country's youth. Air Rangers was an aviation program established by the women for Senior Boy and Girl Scouts to learn about aviation, take an actual airplane flight for the first time, attend air camps, and the ultimate goal of earning an Aviation Merit Badge. Many of these scouts pursued aviation careers as a result of their experiences with the Ninety-Nines.

The women working in war production factories also faced insurmountable roadblocks with red tape battles for the care they needed as a result of injuries and disabilities suffered on the job. Besides the social discrimination and gender harassment they faced on a daily basis, thousands of women suffered physical pain and injuries from long, strenuous hours and poor working conditions. Over 210,000 women were permanently disabled and/or disfigured as a result of the work they did, while 37,000 lost their lives (most deaths occurred in munitions plant accidents and explosions). The workers and/or their families received little, if any, compensation or medical insurance benefits.

As the soldiers gradually returned home with various physical and mental disabilities, they also had adjustments to make. If the woman of the household was now a full-time breadwinner while the soldier recovered, went back to school, or could not find a job, he had to pitch in with the housework, care of the children, shopping, cooking, laundry… This was a startling revelation and an awakening for thousands of men - managing a home, housework and childcare was actually WORK! There was just no paycheck at the end of the week. Naturally, this did not go over very well for many families. This role reversal of a man doing "woman's work" while the woman was the family breadwinner struck a low blow to the male ego adding to the post-war depression many men were suffering. These difficulties greatly added to the causes of the high divorce rate during the first couple of years after the war ended.

Thousands of women were actually glad to get back home after their factories closed. It had been an eye-opening experience working outside the home during the war years. The old social stereotypes about women had been shattered. The women learned independence and what it felt like to have a couple of dollars in their pocket. They also learned to think for themselves, expand their horizons, work as a team member, and show men they were just as capable of handling a tough job as they were.

Some of the women retreated to their homes and did not want to talk about their wartime work experiences. It was just too sad for them to remember the good times coming to an end or re-hash the bad times. They were happy raising their children, growing their gardens, keeping a happy household, volunteering... And that was okay too.

Whether the women found other jobs in the workforce or went home to the variety of jobs there, what they accomplished as a whole during WWII changed the way women were viewed from then on. Yes, indeed, America's secret weapon in winning the war was not the atomic bomb, it was the American women, although both have gone down in history as explosively changing the world forever!

Afterword

American women throughout history have always worked. Women of all races and nationalities came together to build America as we know it today. From the early women pioneers to the scientists of today, women have always been a guiding force in shaping America and its culture.

A historical turning point for all women came December 7, 1941 with the bombing of Pearl Harbor. Women across America were called upon by the government to fill the home front shoes of our men battling enemies overseas and in the Pacific. The stereotypical classification of all women fell by the wayside as all classes worked side by side to keep the home front running smoothly and war production at its peak.

The war brought women an independence they had never known and a freedom from the established societal roles they were expected to fulfill. Many had never received a paycheck, had a bank account, had a checking account, credit cards; all these were new experiences. Before the war, women were not allowed to open store charge accounts, only the man of the house could. Women rarely wrote out a check; it was the man of the house who took care of the finances. With the man of the house gone off to war, women no longer had to ask them for money to run the household. The women were making their own money, opening their own bank accounts, establishing their own credit, writing checks to pay the bills, learning how to budget, and saving money.

Everyday brought a new change, a new challenge, and everyday the women withstood those challenges. Discrimination and resentment were sometimes difficult to handle, but the circumstances of the day (war) taught women to stand on their on two feet and fight for what was right for themselves and their families.

The war also opened many doors of opportunity for women. Jobs and volunteerism enabled women to meet other people outside of their homes, learn about different cultures, races and the great big world outside of their towns and cities. Education in other fields besides nursing and teaching slowly became available.

Be sure to ask your elder family members what they did during WWII. The men will talk about the battles, the fighting, the horrors, the wounds, the fear. Watch closely as they talk about their experiences. Their eyes may mist as they stare at the sky, they will stand a bit taller and salute the flag as it passes by, or drop their head in sorrow as they remember the loss of fellow soldiers.

The women will talk about the ships or planes they built or the factories they worked in, or how they harvested the wheat all by themselves, drove the big grain truck, their bountiful Victory Gardens, their prize winning canned peaches or pickles at the county fair, how many war bonds they sold or purchased, the dreaded ration books, the cooking challenges... the women will simply smile in remembrance and pride. The women's contributions to the war effort have been quietly forgotten by history, but strongly remain in their hearts.

The men will say they served for their country and its freedom. The women will say they served for their families. WWII shaped that generation of women just as combat had shaped the men; both changed forever. Be sure to thank them, both men and women, for their service.

After talking to your mothers, fathers, grand-mothers, great grandmothers, uncles, aunts, and others, you might be surprised at what you hear and what you learn from them. Don't wait too long to ask! Our WWII generation is fading away at a rate of 1,000 a day.

Acknowledgements

The amount of research for this book was incredible, interesting, educational, and just plain fun! I hope the reader has a better understanding of what occurred during the most horrific war in American history and how important women's roles were in bringing it to an end. It doesn't matter how old/young you are, WWII had a direct impact on who you are, what you do, and how you do it today.

This book barely scratches the surface of the volumes of information available about this time period. I just wanted to touch on a few important points and people as well as peak the reader's interest for further self-studies.

I must first thank my husband for giving me the idea for this book and sending me on a research frenzy. An especially big thank you to my editor, Julie Cline, for her patience, time and effort and to Marty Bicek for his computer skills where mine are lacking. I am thankful to my many friends and acquaintances who took the time to share their experiences, as well as the experiences of their mothers and grandmothers, by contributing to the book. Special thanks also to SFC Rudy Parreno, Jr., U.S. Army and to Gold Star Mother Betsy

Acknowledgements

Reed Schultz, founder of the Captain Joseph House Foundation, for their help in my understanding of the current roles of military Casualty Assistant and Notification Officers.

Bibliography
Articles

Bazer, Gerald & Culbertson, Steven. "When FDR said "Play Ball." *Prologue*. 2002.

Beecher M.D., Henry K. "Morphine Overdosage and Poisoning." *U.S. Army Medical Department, Office of Medical History*. June 18, 2009.

Briner, Lisa. "Walt Disney Goes To War." *U.S. Army History Institute*. April 7, 2009.

Burger, Terry. "Chocolate! The Wars Secret Weapon." *America in WWII*. February, 2007.

Colman, Penny. "Keeping America Running: Women in World War II." *On Patrol*. Spring, 2012.

Crane, Kristine. "Manhattan Project opened door for future women scientists." *Symmetry Magazine*. April 17, 2009.

Defiglio, Pam. "Delivering the Bad News." *Insight Magazine*. May, 2010.

Delanna, Bella. "The Changing Roles of Women in World War II. *Knoji*. December 2, 2010.

Doucet, Lyse. "The Women Reporters Determined to Cover World War II." *BBC News Magazine*. June 4, 2014.

Finn, Robin. "Pauline Betz Addie, a Dominant Tennis Champion, Dies at 91." *The New York Times*. June 2, 2011.

Gargas, Jane. "Being WWII nurse took courage, skill, Yakima woman says." *Yakima Herald-Republic*. September 14, 2014.

Bibliography

Gilmore, Gerry L. "Women Journalists Came of Age Covering World War II." *American Forces Press Service.* February 13, 2001.

Gumbrecht, Jamie. "Rediscovering WWIIs Female 'Computers.'" *CNN.* February 8, 2011.

Hardy, Jeff. "A dream of wings." *Mobile Alabama Register - Washington Bureau.*

Herzenberg, Caroline. "Women Scientists of the Manhattan Project." *AP Central.*

Jenkins, Mark. "Gal Reporters: Breaking Barriers in World War II." *National Geographic News.* December 10, 2003.

Lineberry, Cate. "Last Survivor of a Dramatic World War II Rescue." *National Geographic.* May 23, 2013.

Litoff, Judy Barrett, & Smith, David C. "The Women's Land Army During World War II." *Prologue.* Winter 1993. Vol. 25, no.4.

MacKenzie, Bill. "Caring for Rosie the Riveter's Children." *Young Children.* November, 2011.

Madison, James. "Wearing Lipstick to War - An American Woman in World War II England and France." *Prologue.* Fall 2007. Vol. 39, No. 3.

Majors, Dan. "Christmas 1941: With world at war, Churchill joins FDR for Washington Yule." *Pittsburgh Post Gazette.* December 25, 2011.

May, Elaine Tyler. "Ambivalent Dreams: Women and the Home After World War II." *Journal of Women's History.* Vol. 13, No. 3, Autumn, 2001.

Miller, Stephan. "Jean Ruth Hay, 87, Morning Radio Host of 'Reveille with Beverly' During World War II." *Sun.* September 27, 2004.

Mola, Roger. "The Army Back Home." *Air & Space Smithsonian.* May, 2015.

Morein, Alyssa Shirley. "Prudence Penny's Wartime Wisdom." *White River Journal.* April, 2004.

Norman, Floyd. "Remembering the other Retta: Disney Feature Animation's Retta Davidson." *Jim Hill Media.* November 5, 2006.

Obermeyer, Jeff. "Disposable Heroes: Returning World War II Veteran Al Niemiec Takes on Organized Baseball." *Baseball Research Journal.* Summer, 2010.

Pace, LaCoya. "World War II's Influence on Nursing." *War nursing.com.* April 16, 2012.

Perkins, Gwen. "Not Just Nurses: American Women at War." *Washington State Historical Society.* 2007-2009.

Perkins, Gwen. "Women's Roles: Who Was Rosie the Riveter?" *Washington State Historical Society.* 2007-2009.

Schudel, Matt. "Dorothy "Dottie" Kamenshek dead; women's professional baseball player." *Washington Post.* May 22, 2010.

Taylor, Judith. "Odyssey to freedom: Remembering a daring escape from behind enemy lines." *Air Force Medical Service.* November 8, 2013.

"The Angels of Bataan." *Soldiers Magazine.* March 30, 2012.

Urwin, Cathy. "No Liquor, But Damned Good Anyway." *America in WWII Magazine.* August, 2006.

Van Ells, Mark D. "Haunted." *America in WWII Magazine.* August, 2005.

"Variety for the Servicemen: The Jubilee Show and the Paradox of Radicalizing Radio During World War I." *American Quarterly.* December, 2004.

"Voices of the Veterans." *Air & Space Smithsonian.* May, 2015.

Wellerstein, Alex. "How many people worked on the Manhattan Project?" *The Nuclear Secrecy Blog.* November 1, 2013.

Wells, Jordan. "War Time Rationing During WWII." *The American Survivor.* Vol.1 - No.2 September/October.

Wolff, Tom. "American Music Goes to War." The Gilder Lehrman Institute of American History.

Wykes, Gerald. "A weed goes to war, and Michigan provides the ammunition." *Michigan History Magazine.* February 4, 2014.

Books

Bard, Mitchell. *The Complete Idiots Guide to World War II.* Penguin Group, 2010.

Brokaw, Tom. *The Greatest Generation.* New York: Random House, 1998.

Brown, Kate. *Plutopia.* Oxford University Press, 2013.

Busby, Anna Urda. *Wherever You Need Me.* Pacific Historic Parks, 2007.

Butler, Matilda & Bonnett, Kendra. *Rosie's Daughters.* Knowledge Access Publishing, 2007.

Carl, Ann B. *A WASP Among Eagles.* Smithsonian Books, 1999.

Bibliography

Donovan, Robert. *The Buck Stops Here - The Words of Harry S. Truman.* Barnes & Noble Books, 1984.

Duffy, James P. *Lindbergh vs Roosevelt.* MJF Books, 2010.

Goodwin, Doris Kearns. *No Ordinary Time: Franklin & Eleanor Roosevelt: The Home Front in World War II.* Simon & Schuster; Reissue edition November 5, 2013.

Hagen, Claudia. *The Night A Fortress Fell To Fairfield.* Marquette, 2009.

Hagen, Claudia. *Hanford's Secret Clouds of Despair.* Marquette, 2013.

Hartman, Susan M. *The Home Front and Beyond:American Women in the 1940s.* Twayne Publishers, 1982.

Hayes, Joanne Lamb. *Grandma's Wartime Kitchen.* St. Martin's Press, 2000.

Howes, Ruth & Herzenberg, Caroline. *Their Day in the Sun - Women of the Manhattan Project.* Temple University Press, 2003.

Hval, Cindy. *War Bonds.* Pennsylvania: Casemate Publishers, 2015.

Johnston, S. Paul. *Wings After War.* Duell, Sloan & Pearce, 1944.

Kelly, Cynthia. *The Manhattan Project.* Black dog & Leventhal Publishers, 2007.

Kiernan, Denise. *The Girls of Atomic City.* Touchstone, 2013.

Langley, Andrew. *Hiroshima and Nagasaki.* Compass Point Books, 2006.

Lineberry, Cate. *The Secret Rescue.* Little Brown and Company, 2013.

Lomax, Judy. *Women of the Air.* Dodd, Mead & Company, 1986.

Lord, Walter. *Day of Infamy.* Holt paperbacks, 1957.

Nesbit, Tarashea. *The Wives of Los Alamos.* Bloomsbury, 2014.

Norman, Elizabeth M. *We Band of Angels.* Pocket Books, 1999.

Reid, Constance Bowman. *Slacks & Calluses.* Smithsonian Books, 1999.

Sanders, Jim. *Saving Lives, Saving Memories.* IF Books, 2009.

Sorel, Nancy Caldwell. *The Women Who Wrote the War.* Arcade Publishing, 2011.

Ward, Geoffrey & Burns, Ken. *The War - An Intimate History 1941-1945.* Borzoi Book, 2007.

Yellin, Emily. *Our Mothers' War.* New York: Free Press, 2004.

Websites/Webpages

"Tuskegee Air Women!" January 1, 2012. January 6, 2015. http:www.yesshedidyeswecan.wordpress.com/2012/01/26/tuskegee-air-women.

Stoltzfus, Emilie. "Child Care: The Federal Role During World War II." March 2, 2015. http://www.congressionalresearch.com/RS20615/document.php.

"Shipyard Day Care Centers of World War II: The Kaiser Experiment." February 11, 2015. http://www.wwiishipyarddaycare.tripod.com/intro.htm.

"The History of the Service Flag." March 1, 2015.
http://www.usflag.org/history/serviceflag.html.

Sundin, Sarah. "Make It Do - Clothing Restrictions in World War II." March 28, 2011. February 3, 2015.
http://sarahsundin.com/make-it-do-clothing-restrictions-in-world-war-ii/.

Sundin, Sarah. "World War II War Bonds." December 3, 2012. February 22, 2015.
http: www.sarahsundin.com/world-war-ii-war-bonds/.

Sundin, Sarah. "Make It Do - Tire Rationing in World War II." January 17, 2011. March 24, 2015.
http:www.sarahsundin.com/make-it-do-tire-rationing-in-world-war-ii/.

Todd, Robert M. "Turning Junk Into Victory: WWII Recycling and the Kids." May 31, 2012. April 12, 2014.
http://voices.yahoo.com/turning-junk-into-victory-wwii-recycling-kids-11398766.html.

Avey, Tori. "Who Was Betty Crocker?" February 15, 2013. December 27, 2013.
http://www.pbs.org/food/the-history-kitchen/who-was-betty-crocker/.

Peterik, Adam. "Women's Baseball During World War II." April, 1995. January 13, 2015.
http://www.lib.niu.ded/1995/ihy950452.html.

Lewis, Jone Johnson. "Women and World War II: Women Celebrities and the War." July 16, 2014.
http://womenshistory.about.com/od/warwwii/a/celebrities.htm.

Lewis, Jone Johnson. "World War II Homefront: Women at Home." July 16, 2014.
http://womenshistory.about.com/od/warwwii/a/women_at_home.htm.

"Carole Landis." November, 2012. January 7, 2015.
http://carolelandisofficial.blogspot.com/
2012/11/world-war-2.html.

"How many US soldiers were MIA in World War II and
remain unaccounted for?" July 11, 2014.
http://wiki.answers.com/QHow_many_US_
soldiers_were_MIA_in_World_War_2_and_
remain_unaccounted for.

"How many US soldiers were killed in World War II?"
July1, 2014.
http://wiki.answers.com/Q/How_many_US_
soldiers_were_killed_in_World_War_2.

"How many women served in WWII?" July 11, 2014.
http://answers.yahoo.com/question/index;-ylt=
AwrTccCBG8BThVMA…wNzcg Rwb3MDNAR
jb2xvA2dyMQR2dGlKAw—?qid=201103
18073914AAceouv.

"How many US soldiers served in World War II?"
July 14, 2014.
http://wikianswers.com/Q/How_many_
soldiers_served_in_world_war_2.

"Franklin D. Roosevelt's Infamy Speech."
December 7, 1941. May 19, 2014.
http://www.law.ou.edu/hist/infamy.shtml.

"Soldier without uniform." 1943. December 27, 2013.
http://www.ameshistory.org/exhibits/
events/sears_roebuck_ration3.jpg.

"Pay of the WW2 Enlisted Man."
May, 1945. July 14, 2014.
http://www.hardscrabblefarm.com/
ww2/payscale.htm.

Bibliography

Tillitt, Malvern. "Army-Navy Pay Tops Most Civilians'
    Unmarried Private's Income Equivalent
    to $3,600 salary." April 24, 1944. July 14, 2014.
    http://www.usmm.org/barrons.html.

"The American Family in World War II."
    December 12, 2013.
    http://www.u-s-history.com/pages/h1692.html.

"War Production." September, 2007. July 16, 2014.
    http://www.pbs.org/thewar/at_home_
    war_production.htm.

"The United States Homefront During World War II: The
    Economy. July 14, 2014.
    http://www.teachamericanhist...org/file/
    homefront_wwll.pdf.

Briggs, Lucia. "Women's Education and the War." 1943.
    May 13, 2014.
    http://content.wisconsinhistory.org/cdm/ref/
    collection/tp/id/46321.

"American Women in World War II."
    December 4, 2013.
    http://www.history.com/topics/american-
    women-in-world-war-ii.

Stremlow, Mary V. Colonel, USMCR(Ret.). "The First
    WRs." July 22, 2014.
    http://www.nps.gov/history/history/online_books/
    npswapa/estContent/usmc/pcn-190-003129-00/
    sec3.htm.

"Marine Corps Women's Reserve." July 22, 2014.
    http://chnm.gmu.edu/courses/rr/so1/cw/
    students/leeann/historyandcollections/history/
    Immrewwiimar.html.

Bibliography

"WASP: Women in the World War II US Army Air Force."
July 24, 2014.
http://ww2db.com/other.php?other_id=25.

"Partner in Winning the War: American Women in World
War II - Aviators." July 6, 2014.
http://www.nwhm.org/online-exhibits/partners/9.htm.

"WAVES." July 20, 2014.
http://www.u-s-history.com/pages/h1708.html.

"Dorothy C. Stratton." July 22, 2014.
http://www.uscg.mil/history/people/DSS
trattonBio.asp.

Lagan, Christopher. "History: The Women's Reserve,
America's Backbone." April 4, 2010.
July 20, 2014.
http://coastguard.dodlive.mil/2010/04/history-
the-womens-reserve-americas-backbone/.

"SPARS During World War II." 2005. July 22, 2014.
http://www.history.navy.mil/photos/prs-tpic/
females/ww2.

"Women in the Military - WWII." July 19, 2014.
http://libguides.mnhs.org/wwii_women.

"Women and World War II: Women and the Military."
July 16, 2014.
http://womenshistory.about.com/od/warwwii/a/
military.htm.

"Developments in weaponry, communication, aviation, and
medicine during WWII." July 29, 2014.
http://www.dsusd.k12.ca.us/users/scottish/develop
ments%20in%20weapon%20communicationr.htm.

"Partners in winning the war: American women in World
War II: Health Care." July 14, 2014.
http://www.nwhm.org/online-exhibit/partners/16.htm.

Bibliography

"American Military Nurses in World War II: Recruitment and Training." July 18, 2014.

    https://sites.google.com/site/americanmilitarynursesinwwii/recruitment-and-training.

"Remembering the Nurses of World War II." July 30, 2014.

    http://www.guns.com/2013/05/27/remembering-the-nurses-of-world-war-ii-video/.

"American Nurse POWs Rescued from Santo Tomas Internment Camp, 1945." August 8, 2014.

    http://militarymedic.com/angels-of-bataan-and-corregidor/.

"The Angels of Bataan." July 9, 2012. August 8, 2014.

    http://theambitiousones.wordpress.com/2012/07/09/the-angels-of-bataan-2010-expository-speech/.

"World War II Ordinance Plants." August 1, 2014.

    http://www.encyclopediaofarkansas.net/encyclopedia/entry-detail.aspx?entryID=373.

"Building Bombs and Planes. Farming in the 1940s." July 2, 2014.

    http://www.livinghistoryfarm.org/farminginthe40s/life_10.html.

"Rosie the Riveter. Women in Transportation." March 8, 2012. April 16, 2014.

    http://www.fhwa.dot.gov/wit/rosie.htm.

"The Boeing Airplane Co…Bombers and Camouflage." April 16, 2014.

    http://www.boeing.com/boeing/history/narrative/no25boe.page?

"The Boeing Airplane Co…Superfortress Goes to War." April 16, 2014.

    http://www.boeing.com/boeing/history/narrative/no25boe.page?

Lombardi, Michael. "'Rosie' A Pioneer for Women."
April 16, 2014.
http://www.boeing.com/news/frontiers/archive/
2002/may/i_history.html.

"Living Stories Spot #3: Texas Women and World War II.
Ona B. Reed." August 17-20, 2010.
August 14, 2014.
http://www.baylor.edu/livingstories/index.php?
id=76626.

Blakemore, Kim Taylor. "So Fab: Wendy the Welder."
August 23, 2013. July 31, 2014.
http://www.kimtaylorblakemore.com/2013/08/23/
so-fab-wendy-the-welder/.

"The Pop History Dig: WWII & Kaiser Shipyards -
Rosie the Riveter 1941-1945." April, 16, 2014.
http://www.pophistorydig.com/?tag=wwii-
kaiser-shipyards.

"Top Secret Rosies: The Female 'Computers' of WWII."
2010. October 30, 2014.
http://www.imdb.com/title/tt1587359/.

"Rachel Louise Carson." November 10, 2014.
http://www.fws.gov/refuges/history/bio/
carson.html.

"Manhattan District - WAC Detachment."
November 13, 2014.
http://history.army.mil/html/
documents/women/wac-manhattan/index.html.

"Historical Vignette 046 - Women Played Key Roles
in the Manhattan Project." November 13, 2014.
http://www.usace.army.mil/about/history/historical
vignettes/womenminorities/046womenmanhattan
project.aspx.

"Women and the Bomb." 2014. November 15, 2014.
http://www.atomicheritage.org/history/
women-and-bomb.

Lists of women of the Manhattan Project.
November 15, 2014.
http://www.hydeparkhistory.org.

"The Great Plains During World War II - Agriculture."
2008. December 12, 2013.
http://plainshumanities.unl.edu/homefront/
agriculture.htm.

"Rural Life in the 1940s. Farming in the 1940s."
December 16, 2013.
http://www.livinghistoryfarm.org/farminginthe
40s/life_01.html.

"Women's Land Army." November 19, 2014.
http://www.brittannica.com/print/topic/647121.

"Women's Land Army." November 19, 2014.
http://www.oregonencyclopedia.org/articles/
women_s_land_army/#.vgz1plf6B4M.

"Questions and Answers on the Women's Land Army
of the U.S. Crop Corps." November 19, 2014.
http://plainshumanities.unl.edu/homefront/
homefront.docs.0013.

"Into the Sugar Beet Fields: Japanese American Laborers."
November 20, 2014.
http://arcweb.sos.state.or.us/pages/exhibits/ww2/
threat/abor.htm.

"The Army Nurse Corps in World War II."
December 11, 2014.
http://www.history.army.mil/books/wwii/
72-14-72-14.HTM.

Bibliography

Fay, Elma Ernst, U.S.R.C. (Ret.). "A Brief History of Red Cross clubmobiles in WWII." November 23, 2014.
http://www.clubmobile.org/history.html.

"A Brief History of the American Red Cross." November 23, 2014.
http://www.redcross.org/about-us/history.

"WWII Services to the Armed Forces." December 5, 2014.
http://www.redcross.org/about-us/history/redcross-american-history/wwii/SAF.

"Red Cross Retrospective - The Gray Lady Service." December 5, 2014.
http://www.redcross.org/new/article/red-cross-retrospective-the-gray-lady-service.

"Partners in winning the war: American women in World War II - Red Cross." November 23, 2014.
https://www.nwhm.org/online-exhibits/partners/17.htm.

"The Red Cross and World War II." November 23, 2014.
http://www.historylearningsite.com.uk/Red_Cross_and_world_war_two.htm.

"World War II and the American Red Cross." November 23, 2014.
http://mentalfloss.com/article/29219/11-women-warriors-world-war-ii.

"Women Warriors of World War II - Reba Whittle: POW Nurse." December 15, 2014.
http://womenshistory.about.com/od/warwii/a/women_work.htm.

"World War II." December 13, 2014.
http://www.gwu.edu/~erpapers/maps/ww2.html#uk.

Bibliography

Lewis, Jone Johnson. "Women and World War II - Women at Work - Women in Offices." July 16, 2014.
http://womenshistory.about.com/od/warwwii/a women_work.htm.

Eleanor Roosevelt's radio address, December 7, 1941. December 14, 2014.
http://www.fdrlibrary.marist.edu/daybyday/ resource/december-7-1941-2/

"FDR reacts to news of Pearl harbor bombing. December 7, 1941." December 14, 2014.
http://www/history.com/this-day-in-history/ fdr-reacts-to-news-of-pearl-harbor-bombing.

"Eleanor Roosevelt and the Tuskegee Airmen." December 15, 2014.
http://fdrlibrary.marist.edu/aboutfdr/tuskegee.html.

"The Tuskegee Airmen." December 15, 2014.
http://www.gwu.edu/~erpapers/teachinger/ glossary/tuskegee-airmen.cfm.

"Question: What is "My Day" and why is it important?" December 13, 2014.
http://www.gwu.edu/~erpapers/teachinger/ q-and-a/q24.cfm.

"Eleanor Roosevelt." December 13, 2014.
https://roosevelt.ucsd.edu/about/about-eleanor.html.

"Eleanor Roosevelt - Facts Accomplishments Life." December 13, 2014.
http://www.historynet.com/eleanor-roosevelt.

"Quotations by Eleanor Roosevelt." December 13, 2014.
http://www.gwu.edu/~erpapers/abouteleanor/er-quotes.

"Question: What did Eleanor Roosevelt do during
     World War II?" December 13, 2014.
         http://www.gwu.edu/~erpapers/teachinger/
         q-and-a/q21.cfm.

"Eleanor Roosevelt." December 4, 2013.
         http://www.history.com/topics/eleanor-roosevelt.\

"In their words - Radio Programs." April 12, 2014.
         http://www.intheirwords.org/
         the_home_front_experience/radio-programs.

"In their words - Pop Culture." April 12, 2014.
         http://www.intheirwords.org/
         the_home_front_experience/pop_culture.

"This is no joke: this is war: A live radio broadcast of the
     attack on Pearl Harbor." December 18, 2014.
         http://historymatters.gmu.edu/d/5167/

"Women on Armed Forces Radio Service (AFRS)."
     December 13, 2014.
         http://memory.loc.gov/ammem/awhhtml/
         awrs9/owi.html.

"U.S. Office of War Information (OWI) Collection."
     December 24, 2014.
         http://memory.loc.gov/ammem/awhhtml/
         awrs9/owi.html.

"World War II. (Recorded Sound Section)."
     December 24, 2014.
         http://memory.loc.gov/ammem/awhhtml/
         awrs9/wwii.html.

National Archives and Records Administration.
     December 27, 2014.
         http://www.archives.gov/exhibits/american_
         originals/eleanor.html.

"Eleanor Roosevelt and Marian Anderson."
December 27, 2014.
http://www.fdrlibrary.marist/edu/aboutfdr/
anderson.html.

"The Women Who Fought to Report WWII:
Dickey Chapelle." January 13, 2015.
http://nojobforawoman.com/reporters/dickey-chapelle/

"Women Come To The Front - Dorothy Lange."
January 13, 2015.
http://www.loc.gov/exhibits/wcf/wcf0013.html.

"World War II on the Radio."
January 7, 2015.
http://www.otrcat.com/wwii-on-the-radio.html.

"F.M.P.U. (First Motion Picture Unit)."
January 1, 2015.
http://genordell.com/stores/lanter/FMPU.htm.

Culler, Mary Beth. "Look Closer: Women in the Disney Ink
and Paint Department." April 6, 2012.
January 2, 2015.
http://www.waltdisney.org/storyboard/look-
closer-women-disney-ink-and-paint-department.

"Wartime Entertainment in WWII: Betty Grable."
December 13, 2014.
http://www.mtholyoke.edu/~knigh20c/
classweb/grable.html.

"Thanks for the Memories! Hollywood's Role in
World War II." July 2, 2014.
http://academic-mu.edu/meissnerd/hollywood.html.

"Pop culture Goes to War in the 1940s."
December 18, 2014.
http://www.livinghistoryfarm.org/
farminginthe40s/life_07.html.

Roberts, James. "Baseball Goes To War:
    The National Pastime in World War II." 2012.
    January 16, 2015.
        http://www.americanveteranscenter.org/
        wwiichronicles/wwii-chronicles...UE-XXXIX/.

"President Franklin Roosevelt Green Light Letter -
    Baseball Can Be Played During The War."
    January 15, 1942. January 13, 2015.
        http://www.baseball-almanac.com/prz_lfr.shtml.

Lesks, Jeneane. "All-American Girls Professional
    Baseball League." January 16, 2015.
        http://www.aagpbl.org/index.cfm/pages/
        league/12/league-history.

"The College During World War II - Sarah Lawrence
    College Archives: War Board Scrap Book."
    July 17, 2014.
        http://archives.sic.edu/wwii/background.htm.

"The American Homefront." January 13, 2014.
        http://www.ushistory.org/us/51b.asp.

Lutz, Alexandra. "The U.S. During WWII:
    The Home Front." July 17, 2014.
        http://education-portal.com/academy/lesson/the-
        united-states-during-wwii-the-home-
        front..html#lesson.

Prial, Frank. "Kate Smith, All-American Singer,
    Dies at 79." June 18, 1986.
    February 18, 2015.
        http://www.nytimes.com/learning/general/
        onthisday/bday/0501.html.

"The Great Plains During World War II - Rationing."
    April 12, 2014.
        http://plainshumanities.unl.edu/homefront/
        rationing/section=homefront.

Bibliography

Home Life Series: Activities, Bicycle, Bread, Car, FDR,
Garden, Meat, Oranges, Paper, Radio, Stars,
V-mail, War bonds, Window, Woman.
January 13, 2014.
http://teacher.scholastic.com/activities/
wwii/ahf/life_.htm.

"Oregon Responds to World War II: Making Do With Less:
Shortages and Conservation."
July 5, 2014.
http://arcweb.sos.state.or.us/pages/exhibits/ww2/
services/conserve.htm.

"In their words: Scrap Drives." April 12, 2014.
http://www.intheirwords.org/the-
home_front_experience/the_war_effort/
scrap_drives.

"The Great Plains During World War II - Women."
April 12, 2014.
http://plainshumanities.unl.edu/homefront/
women?section=homefront.

Reinhardt, Claudia & Ganzel, Bill. "Rural Life in the
1940's." July 2, 2014.
http://www.livinghistoryfarm.org/farminginthe
40slife_01.html.

"Civil Defense - American Home Front in World War II."
2005. February, 22, 2015.
http://www.encyclopedia.com/topic/civil_defense.aspx.

"Dim-outs Yield New Regulations and Enforcement."
July 5, 2014.
http://arcweb.sos.state.or.us/pages/exhibits/ww2/
protect/dimout.htm.

American Gold Star Mothers, Inc. March 4, 2015.
http://www.goldstarmoms.com/.

Bibliography

"1940s Life During World War II - Lisa's Nostalgia Cafe."
    April 11, 2011.
    http://nostalgiacafe.proboards.com/thread/190/1940s-
    life-word-war-ii.

"WWII Letters: Letter Censorship During WWII."
    February 25, 2015.
    http://wwiiletters.blogspot.com/2009/03/
    letter-censorship-during-wii.html.

Graves, Donna. "Women at War - World War II in the San
    Francisco Bay Area - the many roles
    of Bay Area women during World War II."
    April 16, 2014.
    http://www.nps.gov/nr/travel/wwiibayarea/
    womenatwar.HTM.

"With Mother at the Factory...Oregon's Child Care
    Challenges." July 5, 2014.
    http://arcweb.sos.state.or.us/pages/exhibits/
    ww2/services/child.htm.

Cushing, Lincoln. "Eleanor Roosevelt visits the Kaiser
    shipyards and hospital." March 4, 2015.
    http://kaiserpermanentehistory.org/tag/child-
    care-centers-in-world-war-ii/.

Parks, Alyssa. "Childcare During World War II." 2006.
    March 2, 2015.
    http://www.forgeofinnovation.org/springfield_
    armory_1892-1945/themes/people/women/
    world_war_ii/child/index.html.

Rosie the Riveter - World War II Home Front National
    Park. March 6, 2015.
    http://www.nps.gov/nr/travel/wwiibayarea/ros.htm.

"The War at Home: Family." September, 2007.
    July 16, 2014.
    http://www.pbs.org/thewar/at_home_family.htm.

Bibliography

"Pacolet and World War II." April 3, 2014.
http://pacoletmemories.com/worldwar.html.

Casualty Assistance Officer. March 9, 2015.
http://www.military.com/benefits/
survivor-benefits/casualty-assistance-officer.html.

"Vets Use G.I. Bill for College after World War II."
March 11, 2015.
http://www.livinghistoryfarm.org/farming
inthe40s/life_20.html.

"U.S. Soldiers After World War II."
March 8, 2015.
http://www.nevelguide.com/reportessay/
history/american-history/us-soldiers-
after-world-war-ii.

"A New Set of Challenges: Welcoming Home the
Veterans." March 12, 2015.
http://arcweb.sos.state.or.us/pages/exhibits/
ww2/after/return.htm.

The Niney-Nines from 1929 to 1959.
2008. March 19, 2015.
http://www.ninety-nines.org/index.cfm/thirty-
years.htm.

"Gender in World War II: Home Front."
March13, 2015.
http://www.shmoop.com/wwii-home-front/gender.html.

"How War Changed the Role of Women in the U.S."
February 3, 2009. March 11, 2015.
http://www.yale.edu/ynhti/curriculum/units/
2002/3/02.03.09.x.html.

"American Women in World War II - On the Home Front
and Beyond." March14, 2015.
http://www.nationalww2museum.org.

Bibliography

"Rubber in WWII at a glance." March 24, 2015.
http://www.national/ww2museum.org/learn/
education/for-students/ww2-history/at-a-glance/
rubber.html.

Adams, Cecil. "Were WWII scrap drives just a ploy to
boost morale?" May, 2002. April 12,2014.
http://www.straightdope.com/columns/read/
2395/were-wwii-scrap-drives-just-a-ploy-to-
boost-morale.

"The Woman Who Invented Duct Tape." June, 2012.
March 24, 2015.
http://www.kilmerhouse.com/2012/06/the-
woman-who-invented-duct-tape.

"Hedy Lamar and a Secret Communications System."
July 16, 2014.
http://www.amightygirl.com/hedy-lamarr.

Chen, C. Peter. "Nancy Harkness Love."
August 8, 2014.
http://ww2db.com/person_bio.php?person_id=507.

"WWII POW: 'Red Cross Saved My Life.'"
October 14, 2013. November 23, 2014.
http://www.redcross.org/news/article/wwii-pow-
red-cross-saved-my-life.

"Take a closer look at V-Mail." March 24, 2015.
http://ww.nationalww2museum.org/
learn/education/ror-students/ww2-history/take-a-
closer-look/v-mail.html.

"Mary Doyle Keefe, Model for Norman Rockwell's
Rosie the Riveter, dies at 92." April 22, 2015.
http://www.theguardian.com/artand design/
2015/apr/22/mary-doyle-keefe-rosie-the-
riveter-norman-rockwell-dies.

"Florene Miller Watson, Women's Auxiliary Ferrying
　　　Squadron, Women's Airforce Service Pilot."
　　　May 4, 2015.
　　　http://www.brightok.net/~gsimmons/florene.htm.

Obermeyer, Jeff. "Disposable Heroes: Returning World
　　　War II Veteran Al Niemiec Takes on Organized
　　　Baseball." July 12, 2015.
　　　http://sabr.org/research/disposable-heroes-
　　　returning-world-war-ii-veteran-al-niemiec-takes-
　　　organized-baseball.

Wikipedia

Aircraft Warning Service. December 4, 2013.

Alice Allison Dunnigan. January 13, 2015.

Alice Marble. December 30, 2014.

All-American Girls Professional Baseball League.
December 13, 2014.
American Music During World War II. December 26, 2014.

American Red Cross Clubmobile Service.
November 25, 2014.

American Theatre Wing. January 13, 2015.

American Women's Voluntary Services. February 24, 2015.

Al Niemiec. March 12, 2015.

Angels of Bataan. August 8, 2014.

Babe Didrikson Zaharias. January 13, 2015.

Badger Army Ammunition Plant. January 10, 2015.

Bataan Death March. August 9, 2014.

Bibliography

Betty Crocker. December 27, 2013.

Blue Star Mothers Club. March 1, 2015.

Civil Defense. February 21, 2015.

Command Performance (Radio). January 7, 2015.

Dickey Chapelle. January 27, 2015.

Dorothy Lange. February 9, 2015.

Eleanor Roosevelt. May 19, 2014.

Elizabeth Mahon. January 16, 2015.

Entertainment Industry During World War II. December 13, 2014.

First Motion Picture Unit. October 30, 2014.

Florence van Straten. November 9, 2014.

Franklin D. Roosevelt. May 19, 2014.

Geneva Convention. November 23, 2014.

G.I. Bill. March 11, 2015.

G.I. Jive. December 23, 2014.

Gold Star Mothers Club. March 4, 2015.

Hazel Sewell. January 2, 2015.

Helen Kirkpatrick. January 20, 2015.

Henry J. Kaiser. April 16, 2014.

History of the Civil Air Patrol. February 21, 2015.

Hollywood Canteen. December 28, 2014.

International Sweethearts of Rhythm. December 21, 2014.

Bibliography

Jacqueline Cochran. July 22, 2014.

Janet Harmon Waterford Bragg. January 6, 2015.

Joint POW/MIA Accounting Command. March 15, 2015.

June Peppas. January 22, 2015.

Kate Smith. February 18, 2015.

Lee Miller. January 27, 2015.

Margaret Bourke-White. January 24, 2015.

Marian Anderson. December 21, 2014.

Mail Call (Radio Program). January 7, 2015.

Martha Gellhorn. January 27, 2015.

Mary Blair. January 2, 2015.

Mitchell Recreation Area. February 24, 2015.

National Service Act. July 14, 2014.

Nuremberg Trials. February 8, 2015.

Pearl Harbor Speech. July 12, 2014.

Pepper Paire. January 16, 2015.

Rationing. December 27, 2013.

Rationing in the United States. February 11, 2015.

Reba Z. Whittle. April 21, 2015.

Reba Whittle. December 7, 2014.

Red Cross Parcel. November 23, 2014.

Retta Davidson. January 1, 2015.

Retta Scott. January 1, 2015.

Bibliography

Richmond Shipyards. July 31, 2014.

Role of Music in World War II. December 26, 2014.

Rosie the Riveter. December 4, 2013.

Rosie the Riveter World War II Home Front
National Historical Park. April 16, 2014.

Series E Bond. February 24, 2015.

Service Flag. February 25, 2015.

Shelley Smith Mydans. February 6, 2015.

Spam (food). February 9, 2014.

SPARS. July 22, 2014.

Telegram Style. February 6, 2015.

The Andrews Sisters. December 27, 2014.

Thelma Eisen. January 16, 2015.

United States Army Nurse Corps. July 18, 2014.

United States Home Front During World War II.
December 4, 2013.

United States Office of War Information. April 11, 2014.

United Service Organization. April 11, 2014.

Victory Garden. December 4, 2013.

V-Mail. February 24, 2015.

War Production Board. July 16, 2014.

WAVES. December 4, 2013.

Willa Beatrice Brown. January 6, 2015.

Woman's Land Army of America. December 4, 2013.

Women Airforce Service Pilots. July 20, 2014.

Women's Army Corps. December 4, 2013.

Women in Science. August 2, 2014.

Women's Roles in the World Wars. December 4, 2013.

World War II and American Animation. January 1, 2015.

About the Author

American Women During World War II is the fourth non-fiction book by author Claudia Hagen. *The Night A Fortress Fell To Fairfield, The Mystic High Adventures of Fannie Flame & Crew,* and *Hanford's Secret Clouds of Despair* were her first published works along with her first children's book, *Our Grandma Flies A Hot Air Balloon* followed by *Keely The Rescued Kitty.*
After thirty-six years as a critical care nurse and twelve years as a commercially rated hot air balloon pilot, she is now retired and living in California's Central Valley.

Learn more about her and her books at:
www.claudiahagen.com

CPSIA information can be obtained
at www.ICGtesting.com
Printed in the USA
BVHW040421240420
578358BV00009B/559

9 781516 844128